I0013604

BlackBerry 6
Made Simple
For the
Bold and Curve

For the BlackBerry
Bold and Curve
Smartphones
running BlackBerry 6
operating system.

Martin Trautschold
Gary Mazo

MadeSimple™
LEARNING

BlackBerry 6 Made Simple for the Bold and Curve

Copyright © 2011 by Martin Trautschold and Gary Mazo

All rights reserved. No part of this work may be reproduced or transmitted in any form or by any means, electronic or mechanical, including photocopying, recording, or by any information storage or retrieval system, without the prior written permission of the copyright owner and the publisher.

ISBN-13: 978-1460945797

ISBN-10: 1460945794

Printed and bound in the United States of America 9 8 7 6 5 4 3 2 1

Trademarked names, logos, and images may appear in this book. Rather than use a trademark symbol with every occurrence of a trademarked name, logo, or image we use the names, logos, and images only in an editorial fashion and to the benefit of the trademark owner, with no intention of infringement of the trademark.

The use in this publication of trade names, trademarks, service marks, and similar terms, even if they are not identified as such, is not to be taken as an expression of opinion as to whether or not they are subject to proprietary rights.

CEO: Martin Trautschold
VP: Gary Mazo

Distributed to the book trade worldwide by Made Simple Learning 25 Forest View Way, Ormond Beach, FL 32174, USA. +1-386-506-8224 – www.madesimplelearning.com.

For information on translations, please e-mail info@madesimplelearning.com, or visit www.madesimplelearning.com.

The information in this book is distributed on an "as is" basis, without warranty. Although every precaution has been taken in the preparation of this work, neither the author(s) nor Made Simple Learning shall have any liability to any person or entity with respect to any loss or damage caused or alleged to be caused directly or indirectly by the information contained in this work.

From Martin and Gary:

This book is dedicated to our families—to our wives, Julie and Gloria, and to our kids, Sophie, Olivia and Cece, and Ari, Dan, Sara, Billy, Elise and Jonah.

Without their love, support, and understanding, we could never take on projects like this one.

More from Made Simple Learning

The Made Simple team have co-authored a number of books and created video tutorials. Find our books and videos at www.madesimplelearning.com, www.amazon.com *and fine booksellers around the world.*

Books

BlackBerry PlayBook Made Simple (coming soon)

iPad 2 Made Simple (coming soon)

BlackBerry Bold 9000 *Made Simple*

BlackBerry Bold 9700 *Made Simple* (First Edition)

BlackBerry Bold *Made Simple* (Second Edition for 9700 Series running OS 5)

BlackBerry Curve 8350i *Made Simple*

BlackBerry Curve 8500 *Made Simple* (First Edition for 8500 Series running OS 5)

BlackBerry Curve *Made Simple (Second Edition for 8500, 9300 Series OS 5)*

BlackBerry Curve 8900 *Made Simple*

BlackBerry Storm 9500 *Made Simple*

BlackBerry Storm 2 *Made Simple*

BlackBerry Torch 9800 *Made Simple*

BlackBerry Tour 9600 *Made Simple*

BlackBerry Pearl 'Flip' 8200 *Made Simple*

BlackBerry Pearl *Made Simple* for 8100 Series BlackBerry smartphones

BlackBerry 8800 & 8300 Curve *Made Simple*

BlackBerry *Made Simple* for Full Keyboard BlackBerry smartphones (87xx, 77xx, 75xx, 72xx, 6xxx Series)

BlackBerry *Made Simple* for 7100 Series BlackBerry smartphones (7100, 7130, 71xx Series)

CrackBerry: True Tales of BlackBerry Use and Abuse (with Kevin Michaluk)

DROIDS *Made Simple* (with Marziah Karch)

iPad *Made Simple*

iPhone 3G *Made Simple (For iOS 3 devices)*

iPhone 4 *Made Simple (For iOS 4 devices)*

iPod touch *Made Simple (First Edition for iOS 3 devices)*

iPod touch *Made Simple (Second Edition for iOS 4 devices)*

BlackBerry Video Tutorials

Short video tutorials that help you or your entire organization learn how to be more productive with your BlackBerry.

These can be viewed on your computer (Windows or Mac) or on your BlackBerry.

Corporate users can deploy the videos on their Intranet (e.g. Web Server, Learning Management System, or SharePoint server) or choose to have them hosted by Made Simple Learning.

We offer a full library of 3-minute video training tutorials for all popular BlackBerry models with new videos issued frequently to keep up with the latest devices.

Individuals:

Visit www.madesimplelearning.com to get started.

Corporate Training:

Contact info@madesimplelearning.com to get started.

iPhone 4 and iPad / iPad 2 Video Tutorials

We are also in the process of producing a set of video tutorials designed to help people learn how to get the most out of their iPhones and iPads. These will be coming later in 2011. Stay tuned!

Contents at a Glance

Contents

Chapter 8: Phone and Voice Dialing 226

Chapter 9: Email Like a Pro 254

Chapter 12: Text and MMS Messaging 306

Chapter 13: BlackBerry Messenger, PIN Messaging and More 315

Chapter 14: Social Networking 331

Chapter 18: Fun with Videos 390

Chapter 19: Web Browser 397

Chapter 20: BlackBerry App World 413

About the Authors

Martin Trautschold is the founder and CEO of Made Simple Learning, a leading provider of Apple iPad, iPhone, iPod touch, BlackBerry, Android, and Palm webOS books and video tutorials. He has been a successful entrepreneur in the mobile device training and software business since 2001. With Made Simple Learning, he helped to train thousands of Smartphone users with short, to-the-point video tutorials. Martin has now co-authored over twenty "Made Simple" guide books. He also co-founded, ran for 3 years, and then sold a mobile device software company. Prior to this, Martin spent 15 years in technology and business consulting in the US and Japan. He holds an engineering degree from Princeton University and an MBA from the Kellogg School at Northwestern University. Martin and his wife, Julia, have three daughters. He enjoys rowing with the Halifax Rowing Association in Daytona Beach, Florida and cycling with friends. Martin can be reached at martin@madesimplelearning.com.

Gary Mazo is Vice President of Made Simple Learning. Gary joined Made Simple Learning in 2007 and has co-authored the last nineteen books in the Made Simple series. Along with Martin, and Kevin Michaluk from CrackBerry.com, Gary co-wrote *CrackBerry: True Tales of BlackBerry Use and Abuse*—a book about BlackBerry addiction and how to get a grip on one's BlackBerry use. Gary also teaches writing, philosophy, technical writing, and more at the University of Phoenix. He holds a BA in anthropology from Brandeis University. Gary earned his M.A.H.L (Masters in Hebrew Letters) as well as ordination as Rabbi from the Hebrew Union College-Jewish Institute of Religion in Cincinnati, Ohio. He has served congregations in Dayton, Ohio, Cherry Hill, New Jersey and Cape Cod, Massachusetts. When not writing or teaching, Gary enjoys cycling and playing the piano. Gary is married to Gloria Schwartz Mazo; they have six children. Gary can be reached at: gary@madesimplelearning.com.

Acknowledgments

A book like this takes quite a bit of time to successfully complete. We would like to thank our spouses and families for allowing us to have the time needed to complete this project.

Special thanks to Wireless Wizard and their Port Orange, Florida store for allowing us to take pictures of several BlackBerry devices for this book.

We would like to thank our Made Simple Learning customers for supporting our endeavors and keeping us on our toes with great questions and suggestions.

Part 1:

Quick Start Guide

In your hands is the iconic BlackBerry with the new, modern operating system – BlackBerry 6. You have the power of the famous BlackBerry keyboard and Email experience and a brand new operating system. This Quick Start Guide will help get you and your new BlackBerry up and running in a hurry. You'll learn all about the keyboard, buttons, and ports, and how to get around your BlackBerry quickly and confidently. Our **App Reference** tables will introduce you to the apps on your BlackBerry and serve as a quick way to find out how to accomplish a task.

Getting Around Quickly

This Quick Start is meant to be just that—a tool that can help you jump right in and find information in this book—and learn the basics of how to get around and enjoy your BlackBerry right away.

We start with the nuts and bolts in the "Learning Your Way Around" section— what all the keys, buttons, switches, and symbols mean and do on your BlackBerry. You will learn how to get inside the back of your BlackBerry to remove and replace the battery, SIM card, and media card. You'll also learn how to use the **Green Phone** key, **Red Phone** key, **Menu** key, **Trackpad**, and **Escape** key.

In "Using Universal Search or Application Shortcuts" we show you how to switch between the search or shortcut hot keys when you start typing from your Home screen – both features can be very useful. Play with both options and get a feel for which is more useful to you.

In the "Copying, Pasting, and Multitasking" section, we cover the very useful copy-and-paste function and how to jump between apps on your BlackBerry.

You'll want to know how to type on your BlackBerry, so in the "Mastering Your Keyboard" section, we include some useful tips and tricks for the BlackBerry keyboard.

In "Working with the Wireless Network," we help you understand how the letters, numbers, and symbols at the top of your BlackBerry screen tell you that you can make phone calls, send SMS text messages, send and receive email, or browse the Web. We also show you how to handle your BlackBerry on an airplane, when you might need to turn off the radios.

In "App Reference Tables," we've organized the app icons into general categories so you can quickly browse the icons and jump to a section in the book to learn more about the app a particular icon represents. Here are the tables:

- Getting Set Up
- Staying in Touch
- Staying Organized
- Being Productive
- Being Entertained
- Networking Socially

- Personalizing Your BlackBerry
- Adding and Removing Apps

Learning Your Way Around

To help you get comfortable with your BlackBerry, we start with the basics—what the keys, buttons, ports, and symbols do, and how to open up the back cover to get at your battery, media, and SIM card (on all GSM and World Edition phones.) Then we move into how you start apps and navigate the menus.

Overview of Your BlackBerry

Figures 1 and 2 show many of the things you can do with the buttons and ports on your BlackBerry. Go ahead and try out a few things to see what happens. Your phone multitasks (that is it can do multiple tasks at once). Try pressing the **Menu** key for 2 seconds, press and hold the **Green Phone** key (to dial from the address book), press the side **Convenience** keys, click on an icon, and then press the **Escape** key to see what happens. Have some fun getting acquainted with your device.

Battery Strength

Keyboard Lock
Press to lock or unlock.

 # Unopened Messages

Repeat Notification Light

Mute or Play/Pause Key

Wireless Signal Strength
1-5 Bars / OFF / X

Active Profile
How Phone, Email, Calendar, Task Alarms, and more notify you - Ring, Vibrate, or Mute

Wireless Data Network
1XEV, 3G ⊞ (high speed)
1X, EDGE (low speed)
GPRS (lowest speed)
GSM, 1x (Voice & SMS only)

Headphone Jack

Micro USB Port
Connect to computer or charger

Wi-Fi Indicator

Home Screen Wallpaper
Press **Menu** key > **Options** >
Set Wallpaper, or change in Pictures or Camera.

Volume Up & Down Keys

Left Convenience Key
May start Voice Dialing
(Set in Options > Convenience Keys)

Escape / Back
Press to backup or exit

Menu Key
Click to see all icons or full menus

Red Phone / Power ("End")
Tap to power on, press and hold to power off, end phone call, multitask by jumping to Home screen

Green Phone Key ("Send")
Start phone call, see call logs, dial any underlined number.

Right Convenience Key
May start Camera
(Set in Options > Convenience Keys)

ALT Key
Press for #'s and symbols shown on top of each key.

Backspace/Delete
Erase letters to left of cursor or press with ALT key to delete characters to right of cursor

* Media Card (MicroSD)
Inside back battery cover near top of phone.

ENTER
Press to select items, jump to link in Web Browser, or new line when typing.

SHIFT Key
Press for uppercase letters or tap once to begin selecting test for copy/paste.

Space Key
In email address field, will give you "@" and "." also jumps to next item in drop-down list.

SHIFT
Press for uppercase letters

Symbol Key
Press to see special symbols

Speakerphone/Currency
On a call: Speakerphone On/Off
Otherwise: Types currency symbol

Figure 1. Keys, buttons, and, ports on the BlackBerry Bold

Battery Strength

Keyboard Lock
Press to lock or unlock.

 # Unopened Messages

Repeat Notification Light

Mute or Play/Pause Key

Wireless Signal Strength
1-5 Bars / OFF / X

Active Profile
How Phone, Email, Calendar, Task Alarms, and more notify you - Ring, Vibrate, or Mute

Wireless Data Network
1XEV, 3G (high speed)
1X, EDGE (low speed)
GPRS (lowest speed)
GSM, 1x (Voice & SMS only)

Headphone Jack

Micro USB Port
Connect to computer or charger

Wi-Fi Indicator

Home Screen Wallpaper
Press Menu key > Options > Set Wallpaper, or change in Pictures or Camera.

Volume Up & Down Keys

Left Convenience Key
May start Voice Dialing
(Set in Options > Convenience Keys)

Escape / Back
Press to backup or exit

Right Convenience Key
May start Camera (Set in Options > Convenience Keys)

Menu Key
Click to see all icons or full menus

Red Phone / Power ("End")
Tap to power on, press and hold to power off, end phone call, multitask by jumping to Home screen

Green Phone Key ("Send")
Start phone call, see call logs, dial any underlined number.

Trackpad
Glide & click

Backspace/Delete
Erase letters to left of cursor or press with ALT key to delete characters to right of cursor

ALT Key
Press for #'s and symbols shown on top of each key.

ENTER
Press to select items, jump to link in Web Browser, or new line when typing.

***Media Card (MicroSD)**
Inside back battery cover near top of phone.

SHIFT Key
Press for uppercase letters or tap once to begin selecting test for copy/paste.

Space Key
In email address field, will give you "@" and "." also jumps to next item in drop-down list.

SHIFT
Press for uppercase letters

Symbol Key
Press to see special symbols

Speakerphone/Currency
On a call: Speakerphone On/Off
Otherwise: Types currency symbol

Figure 2. Keys, buttons, and, ports on the BlackBerry Curve

Inside Your BlackBerry

You have to get inside your BlackBerry to access your battery, SIM card slot, (on GSM and World Edition BlackBerrys) and media card slot. The following instructions and Figures 3 and 4 show you how. Since the Bold and Curve are slightly different on the inside, we have split this up into two sections.

TIP: To remove the back cover, on the Bold, press with two thumbs and slide the back down and off the BlackBerry. On the Curve, lift up at the notch at the bottom and pull off.

BlackBerry Bold Devices

On your Bold, refer to Figure 3 for the following steps.

To insert a memory card (MicroSD format), you do not need to remove the battery.

1. On the Bold 9650, slide the media card into the slot from the left until it clicks into place.

2. On the Bold 9780 or 9700, slide the media card up into the slot at the top of the device, just above the battery until it clicks into place.

3. To remove the memory card, reverse the procedure.

Figure 3. Inside your BlackBerry Bold— the battery, media card, and SIM card slots

To insert or remove a SIM card, do the following:

- On the Bold 9780 and 9700, remove the battery, and then place the SIM card on the left edge with the notch in the upper-left corner. Slide it completely into the SIM card slot (see Figure 3).

- On the Bold 9650, remove the battery and slide the SIM card completely into the slot that us just under the left side of the battery compartment.

Note: Only GSM phones and World Edition phones from some CDMA carriers will have a SIM card.

BlackBerry Curve Devices

On your Curve, refer to Figure 4 for the following steps.

To insert a memory card (MicroSD format), you do not need to remove the battery.

1. Hold the media card so that the notch is in the lower left corner. Slide the media card into the slot from the left until it clicks into place.

2. To remove the memory card, reverse the procedure.

Curve 3G 9300

Curve 3G 9330

Camera /
Video Camera

Media Card Slot
MicroSD Format.
Insert with metal
contacts down.
(You do not need
to remove the
battery.)

Battery Slot
Place battery in
from bottom so
contacts line up
with these metal
contacts. Push
into place at top.

SIM Card Slot
Slide card into slot from top
so it fits completely in slot.

Photos courtesy BlackBerry.com

Figure 4. Inside your BlackBerry Curve— the battery, media card, and SIM card slots

To insert or remove a SIM card (only for GSM or World Edition phones), do the following:

▪ Remove the battery, and then place the SIM card on the left edge with the notch in the upper-left corner. Slide it completely into the SIM card slot (see Figure 4).

The Top Edge of Your Phone

The top edge of your phone has some useful keys for muting the ringer or yourself on a call as well as controlling media playback. The Bold and Curve are slightly different in their top keys.

Lock and Mute Keys on the Bold

The Bold has two keys on the top edge: the **Lock** key on the left and the **Mute/Play/Pause** key on the right (see Figure 5).

▪ Press the **Lock** key once to lock or unlock the keyboard. It's great to use when you want to put your BlackBerry into your pocket or purse and don't want it to accidentally dial someone.

▪ Press the **Mute/Play/Pause** key to mute the phone ringer, mute yourself on a phone call or play/pause media (e.g. music, video, podcast)

Figure 5. *BlackBerry Bold Top — the Lock and Mute/Play/Pause keys.*

CAUTION: The **Lock** key will <u>not</u> password lock your BlackBerry. If you want to require a password be entered to unlock your device, you first need to enable it and then use the **Password Lock** icon. To learn how, see the "Password Security" section of Chapter 1: "Getting Started."

Media Keys on the Curve

The Curve has three keys on the top edge: the **Previous Track** key on the left, the **Mute/Play/Pause** key in the middle and the **Next Track** key on the right (see Figure 6).

- Press the **Lock** key once to lock or unlock the keyboard. It's great to use when you want to put your BlackBerry into your pocket or purse and don't want it to accidentally dial someone.

- Press the **Mute/Play/Pause** key to mute the phone ringer, mute yourself on a phone call or play/pause media (e.g. music, video, podcast)

Previous Track
Previous track (song, video, podcast, etc.)

Mute/Play/Pause
Pause/Play
Music/Video
or Mute Ringer/Call

Next Track
Next track on media.

Curve:
Top Edge

Figure 6. BlackBerry Curve Top — the Previous Track, Mute/Play/Pause and Next Track keys.

The Keys Around the Trackpad

The most important keys on your phone are centered around the Trackpad on the front of your device: The **Green Phone** key ("Send"), the **Menu** key (BlackBerry logo key), the **Trackpad**, the **Escape** ("Back") key and the **Red Phone** key (also Power key).

The Green Phone Key

Start up your phone by pressing this **Green Phone** key from any location.

> **TIP:** Call Any Underlined Phone Number. Pressing the Green Phone key when you see any underlined phone number (e.g., 313-555-1212 in an email signature, web site, note, etc.) will

start a call to that number. You can learn about your phone in
Chapter 8: "Phone and Voice Dialing."

The Menu Key (BlackBerry Button)

The **Menu** key—that key with the BlackBerry logo—is the
doorway to all the possibilities of your device. In every
application, pressing this key brings up a menu with all of the
options for the app. From the basic home screen, pressing this
key brings up all the other icons.

TIP: Pressing and holding the **Menu** key will allow you to Multitask. See below for
details.

While viewing a contact, pressing the **Menu** key allows you to call, email, SMS,
or communicate in other ways with that particular contact. Try pressing it in
every program you open to see the myriad of possibilities.

Multitask or Switch Applications with the Menu key

You can multitask using the **Menu** key. Press and hold it to bring up the
multitasking pop-up window, which will allow you to multitask by taking the
following steps.

1. Press and hold the **Menu**
   key to see the pop-up
   window of running apps.

2. Roll up or down to the
   app you want to start and
   click it.

3. Click the **Home** app if you
   don't see the icon you
   want to start. Then click
   the icon you want to start
   from the home screen.

4. Repeat the procedure to
   return to the app you
   started in.

The Trackpad

The **Trackpad** allows you to move around the screen and select items by clicking it or pressing it in. It can be quite helpful when you need to carefully move the cursor or click on something small on the screen such as a list of small text items (BlackBerry Help screens or web pages).

TIP: You can fine-tune the sensitivity of the **Trackpad** by going into your Options icon and searching for the word Trackpad, then click **Trackpad Sensitivity**.

The Escape/Back Key

This key does just what its name suggests—it goes back to where you were before. It also prompts you to save, delete, or discard things you might be working on. If you do something wrong or find yourself wanting to get back to where you were a second ago, just press this key.

The Red Phone Key

This is equivalent to the "end" key that you may be familiar with from your old phone. You can end your calls, ignore calls, and perform other familiar actions with the **Red Phone** key.

You can also multitask using the **Red Phone** key. Just press it (when not on a call) and you'll jump right to the **Home** screen.

TIP: Knowing when your information is saved

When you use the **Red Phone** key or press and hold the **Menu** key to jump out of an app everything you were doing in the app you are leaving is saved. For example, if you are in the middle of typing an email message and need to check your **Calendar**. Using the **Red Phone** key or pressing and holding the **Menu** key to jump to the **Calendar** will leave your email message exactly as it was. This allows you to jump back to the **Messages** app and finish your email.

Seeing the Five Home Screens

The **Home** screen is actually grouped into five areas: **All**, **Favorites**, **Media**, **Downloads** and **Frequent**. You see each area by gliding left or right on the **Trackpad**. Once you swipe right from **Frequent** you will end up back in the **All** section. **All** has all your icons, you can assign icons to **Favorites** by long-pressing them, **Media** has all your music, videos, pictures and related items, **Downloads** are new apps you download and **Frequent** are those apps you use most often (see Figure 7).

Figure 7. The Five Home Screens: *All, Favorites, Media, Downloads* and *Frequent.*

The Quick Status Bar

If you click on the screen just under the time as shown in Figure 8, you can see a quick summary of the latest happenings in your world. You see recent **Messages** (email, instant, and related), upcoming **Calendar** events, missed **Phone** calls, **BlackBerry Messenger** alerts, **Social Feeds**, **Twitter** updates and more.

Figure 8. Click on to see a Quick Summary of all Status Messages.

Managing Connections and Airplane Mode

Roll the **Trackpad** up and click on the very top bar which includes the battery, the time and the status icons to bring up the **Manage Connections** app. This allows you to go into **Airplane Mode** by turning all your connections off, or selectively turn on or off your **Mobile Network (cell)**, **Wi-Fi**, or **Bluetooth** connections. You can also setup all these connections from this screen (see Figure 9). Click on **Turn All Connections Off** to go into **Airplane mode**.

Figure 9. Click on the Top Bar to see your Manage Connections app.

Starting and Exiting an App

Click on any icon to start the app. For example in Figure 10, we click on the **Calendar** icon to start the **Calendar** app. Then to exit to the **Home** screen, we pressed the **Escape** key. If we wanted to leave the **Calendar** running in the background, we could instead press the **Red Phone** key to jump to the **Home** screen.

Figure 10. How to start and exit apps.

Opening Folders

You will notice some icons look like folders. You can use these folders to organize sets of icons into logical groups. There will be a few folders already on your BlackBerry such as **Applications**, **Media** and **Instant Messaging**, but you can create more folders, as shown in Chapter 7: "Personalize Your BlackBerry." Click on any folder to open it and press the **Escape** key to back out and close the folder (see Figure 11).

Click the **Applications** folder icon to open the folder.

You know you are in a folder when you see the folder name here.

Figure 11. Opening folders where you store and organize icons.

NOTE: Icon versus App --In this book we use both icon and app. We thought we should clarify here. The icon is simply the picture on the **Home** screen that starts the app. For example, you click on the **Messages** icon to start the **Messages** app.

Two Types of Menus: Full and Short

You will see two types of menus on your BlackBerry (see Figure 12). The **Short Menu** that pops up in the middle of the screen after you click and hold the **Trackpad** on an item. The **Full Menu** appears when you press the **Menu** key.

Figure 12. Short Menus and Full Menus.

Scrolling Up or Down

If you want to scroll, simply place your finger on the **Trackpad** and roll it up or down. You can glide it up or down quickly to move faster.

Scrolling Menus

You can use the same scroll movement to view more menu items off the bottom or top of the screen (see Figure 13).

Figure 13. Scrolling up or down menus and showing additional menu levels.

Showing Or Hiding Controls

Also, when listening to music or watching a video, the playback controls will disappear after a second or so. To bring them back, simply click the **Trackpad** (see Figure 14). If you wait a few seconds the controls will disappear, or you can click the **Trackpad** again to immediately hide them.

Figure 14. *Click on the screen to view video or music controls.*

Save Time with the Space Key

You can use the **Space** key to save time when you are typing email addresses, web addresses, and typing the ends of sentences. You can use the **space** key to simplify typing in an email address. For instance, typing:

susan **space** company **space** com generates susan@company.com

Similarly, to get the "dots" in a web address, typing:

www **space** google **space** com yields www.google.com

In addition, pressing the **space** key twice will enter an automatic period and make the next letter you type uppercase.

Using Universal Search or Application Shortcuts

You can access either the **Universal Search** or **Applications Shortcuts** by typing letters from your **Home** screen. We describe both features below and give you much more detail on Shortcuts of all sorts in Part IV of this book.

The Switch to Select Search or Shortcuts

By default, typing on the **Home** screen will start the **Universal Search**. To change this to **Application Shortcuts**, follow these steps:

1. Press the **Menu** key from the **Home** screen and select **Options**.

2. Change the **Launch by Typing** to **Application Shortcuts**.

3. Press the **Menu** key and **Save**.

Universal Search

Once you have enabled **Universal Search** in the **Launch by Typing** part of the options shown above, you can simply type your search while viewing the **Home** screen without having to click on the **Search** icon first.

After you type a few letters such as the name of a contact, app icon, or even a web search string, you should see these letters appear in the Search window and the icons below the search bar change as you type more letters. Click on any of the icons to select those search results.

Check out the "Universal Search" section of Chapter 6 for more details.

Application Shortcuts ("Home Screen Hot Keys")

If you select Application Shortcuts in the Launch by Typing area of the Home screen options, then you can start many of the popular icons by pressing a single letter on the keyboard.

Some of the more common shortcuts are: **B** = **Browser**, **M** = **Messages**, **L** = **Calendar**, **C** = **Contacts**, **N** = **BlackBerry Messenger**, and **D** = **MemoPad**.

Check out the "Home Screen Hot Keys" section of Part IV of this book for a complete list.

Copying, Pasting, and Multitasking

A few very useful tricks on your BlackBerry are copying, pasting, and multitasking (i.e., jumping between applications—also referred to as application switching).

You may find times when you want to cut/copy and paste text from one app into another. One example might be copying directions for a trip from an email message into a calendar event so that you have them available when you need them.

1. Use the **Trackpad** to move the cursor to the beginning of the text you want to copy.

> **Subject: Meeting**
>
> Can you meet tomorrow?
>
> 2:30 pm at the Coffee Shop at 252 Park Avenue?

2. Press either **Shift** key to start selecting text and glide the **Trackpad** to select the text you want to copy.

> **Subject: Meeting**
>
> Can you meet tomorrow?
>
> 2:30 pm at the Coffee Shop at 252 Park Avenue?

3. Press and hold the **Trackpad** to bring up the short menu and select **Copy**.

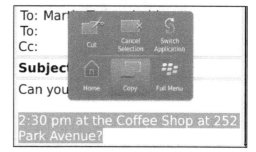

4. Press and hold the **Menu** key to bring up the Multitasking window showing apps that are running. Click the app you want or the **Home** icon, if you don't see what you want.

5. Start the app you want, in this case we want the **Calendar**.

6. Click on the time in Day view closest to the start of the event and type a subject. Roll down to **Location**, then press and hold the **Trackpad** and select **Paste**.

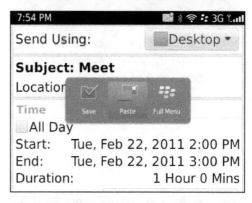

7. Now your text has been pasted into the calendar, ready for you to access when your calendar alarm rings reminding you to be at this meeting.

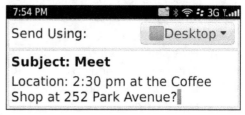

Mastering Your Keyboard

Typing on your BlackBerry is quite flexible. With the physical keyboard, you should be able to find exactly what you need at any time. Probably the easiest keyboard to use on any mobile device is the BlackBerry keyboard – it is always right there at the bottom of the BlackBerry for you to just start typing. Figure 15 shows a few special keys an how to use them on your keyboard. Chapter 6: "Typing, Word Substitution, Spelling, Search and Help" shows you more typing tips.

Q Key
Press and hold to change sound profile to **Vibrate** mode.

Q Key
Tap quickly to toggle between highlighted email addresses and names.

Martin Trautschold <->
martin@company.com

1/W Key
Press and hold to speed dial voice mail.

Other Keys
Press and hold other keys on keyboard to set up or use as Speed Dial letters.

A Key
Press and hold to **Lock** the keypad and screen.

Backspace/ Delete Key
Press ALT first for Delete.

ALT Key
Press for #'s and symbols shown on top of each key.

Enter Key

SHIFT Key
Press for uppercase letters or tap once to begin selecting test for copy/paste.

Space Key
Use for . and @ in email address, dot in web address and jump to next item.

Symbol Key
Press for special symbols

Speakerphone/Currency
On a call: Speakerphone Otherwise: Types currency symbol

Figure 15. Tips and Tricks with the keyboard.

Working with the Wireless Network

Since most of the functions on your BlackBerry work only when you are connected to the internet (**Messages**, **Browser**, **App World**, **Facebook**, etc.), you need to know when you're connected. Understanding how to read the status bar can save you time and frustration. You will also want to know how to quickly turn off your wireless radio or other radios when you get on an airplane.

Your Wireless Network Status

In Table 1, we show you how to read the status icons at the top of your BlackBerry screen so you can save time and stay connected. Check marks indicate that a connection is active and an X indicates an inactive connection. Check out Chapter 24: "Troubleshooting" for help with getting this working.

Table 1. Reading Your Wireless Network Status

In the Upper-Right Corner, If You See Letters and Symbols	Email and Web	Phone Calls & SMS Text	Speed of Data Connection
3G , 1XEV (**3G with logo**)	✓ = Active	✓	High

EDGE, GPRS, 1X	✓	✓	**Medium, Slow**
📶 (with any letters shown)	✓	✓	**High**
Lower case letters (edge, gprs, 1x) or uppercase GSM, 3G (without logo)	✗ = Inactive	✓	**None**
OFF / x	✗	✗	**None**

Wireless Network Signal Strength

The following list shows the various wireless signal strength icons that will appear (signal strength varies between one and five bars):

Strong signal:		4-5 bars is a strong signal – fast downloads, web browsing and email should, good voice quality
Weak signal:		1-2 bars is a weak signal – all data functions will be slower and possibly voice calls may be broken up.
No signal:		Your radio is on, but no wireless signal is available.
Radio off:		Your radio is turned off. From your **Home** screen, click on the top status bar where your time is shown and select **Turn All Connections On**.

App Reference Tables

This section groups the apps on your BlackBerry, as well as other apps you can download, into handy reference tables. Each table gives you a brief description of the app and tells where to find more information in this book.

Getting Set Up

In Table 2 are some apps and quick links to help you get your email, Bluetooth, contacts, calendar, and more loaded onto your device. You can even boost the memory by adding a memory card, which is important to install if you'd like to have more pictures, videos, and music on your BlackBerry.

NOTE: On your BlackBerry, most icons do not show their name directly below the icon unless you have just performed a **Universal Search**. For clarity, we do show many of the icons with names below them in these tables as well as other places in this book.

Table 2. Getting Set Up

To Do This	Use This	Where to Learn More
Set up email, Bluetooh, date/time, fonts, Wi-Fi, and personalize.	**Setup App**	Chapter 1: Getting Started Chapter 7: Personalize
Set up or change your internet email, change email signatures	**Setup App > Email Accounts**	Chapter 1: Getting Started.
Connect to Bluetooth devices	**Setup App > Bluetooth**	Chapter 1: Getting Started.
Connect to Wi-Fi networks	**Setup App > Wi-Fi**	Chapter 1: Getting Started.
Set up Social Networks (Facebook, Twitter, more)	**Setup App > Social Networking**	Chapter 1: Getting Started.
Share addresses, calendar, tasks, and notes with your computer	**BlackBerry Desktop Software (for Windows or Apple Mac)**	Windows: Chapter 2. Mac: Chapter 4.
Add memory to store your music, videos, and pictures	**Media card** Image Courtesy SanDisk Corp.	Chapter 1: Getting Started.
Load up your music, pictures, and videos	**USB Drive Mode Desktop Software Media Sync**	USB Mode: Chapter 1. Windows: Chapter 3. Mac: Chapter 5.

Staying in Touch

Getting familiar with the apps in Table 3 will help you stay in touch with your friends and colleagues. Whether you prefer calling, emailing, texting, or using instant messaging, your BlackBerry has many options. Use the browser to stay up to date with the latest happenings on the Web.

Table 3. Staying in Touch

To Do This	Use This		Where to Learn More
Read and reply to Email		**Messages**	Chapter 9: Email.
AP News Reader – Stay Informed		**AP News**	Chapter 20: App World.
Keep up on the Latest Weather		**The Weather Channel**	Chapter 20: App World.
BlackBerry Messenger		**BlackBerry Messenger ("BBM")**	Chapter 13: BlackBerry Messenger
Send and read Text and Picture messages		**Text Messages**	Chapter 12: Text and MMS Messaging.
Get on the internet/browse the Web		**Browser**	Chapter 19: Web Browser.
Call voicemail		**The 1 key**	Chapter 8: Phone and Voice Dialing.
Start a call, dial by name, and view call logs		**Green Phone key**	Chapter 8: Phone and Voice Dialing.

Dial by voice		Voice Dialing	Chapter 8: Phone and Voice Dialing.
Turn off the radio (important when flying on an airplane)		Manage Connections	Quick Start Guide.
Maximize your battery life to talk, message, and play more		Battery Life Tips	Chapter 1: Getting Started.

Staying Organized

From organizing and finding your contacts to managing your calendar, taking written or voice notes, and calculating a tip using your built-in calculator, your BlackBerry can help you do it all. See the apps in Table 4.

Table 4. Staying Organized

To Do This	Use This		Where to Learn More
Manage your contact names and numbers		Contacts	Chapter 10: Contacts.
Manage your calendar		Calendar	Chapter 11: Calendar.
Set a wakeup alarm, or use a countdown timer or stopwatch		Clock	Chapter 22: Utilities.
Store all your important passwords		Password Keeper	Chapter 22: Utilities.

| Find lost names, email, calendar entries, and more | | **Universal Search** | Chapter 6: Typing & Search. |

Being Productive

Sometimes you need to get work done on your BlackBerry. Use the apps shown in Table 5 to get things done on your BlackBerry.

Table 5. Being Productive

To Do This	Use This		Where to Learn More
Manage your to-do list		**Tasks**	Chapter 15: Tasks and Memos.
Find Things, Get Directions, See Traffic		**Google Maps**	Chapter 21: Maps.
Take notes, store your grocery list, and more		**MemoPad**	Chapter 15: Tasks and Memos.
Leave yourself a voice note		**Voice Note Recorder**	Chapter 22: Other Applications
View and edit Microsoft Office Word, Excel, and PowerPoint		**Word to Go, Sheet to Go, Slideshow to Go**	Chapter 9: Email
Use the built-in text-based help		**Help**	Chapter 6: Typing & Search.

| Calculate your MPG (miles per gallon) or meal tips, or convert units | **Calculator** | Chapter 22: Other Applications. |

Being Entertained

Use the apps in Table 6 to have fun with your BlackBerry.

Table 6. Being Entertained

To Do This	Use This	Where to Learn More
Quickly get to all your music	**Music**	Chapter 16: Your Music Player.
Play videos	**Videos**	Chapter 18: Fun with Videos.
View your pictures	**Pictures**	Chapter 17: Snapping Pictures.
Enjoy podcasts	**Podcasts**	Chapter 22: Other Applications
Take a photo	**Camera**	Chapter 17: Snapping Pictures.
Capture video	**Video Camera**	Chapter 18: Fun with Videos.
Play a game	**Games folder**	Chapter 20: App World.

Enjoy free internet radio with your own favorite music	**Slacker**	Chapter 16: Your Music Player.
Enjoy free internet radio with your own favorite music	**Pandora**	Chapter 16: Your Music Player.

Networking Socially

Connect and stay up to date with friends, colleagues, and professional networks using the social networking tools on your BlackBerry (see Table 7).

Table 7. Networking Socially

To Do This	Use This	Where to Learn More
Connect with Facebook friends	**Facebook**	Chapter 14: Social Networking and Social Feeds.
Setup and View RSS Feeds	**Social Feeds**	Chapter 14: Social Networking and Social Feeds.
Follow people and tweet using Twitter	**Twitter**	Chapter 14: Social Networking and Social Feeds.
Connect with colleagues	**LinkedIn**	Chapter 14: Social Networking and Social Feeds.

Personalizing Your BlackBerry

Use the apps in Table 8 to personalize the look and feel of your BlackBerry.

Table 8. Personalizing Your BlackBerry

To Do This	Use This		Where to Learn More
Mute or Vibrate your Phone and other Sounds	(Normal) Sound and A...	**Sounds**	Chapter 7: Personalize.
Change your background home screen picture	12:24 Wallpaper	**Setup > Wallpaper**	Chapter 7: Personalize.
Change your font size	A Fonts	**Setup > Fonts**	Chapter 7: Personalize.
Change your programmable **Convenience** key	Convenience Key	**Setup > Convenience Key**	Chapter 7: Personalize.

Adding and Removing Apps

Use the apps shown in Table 9 to add apps to your BlackBerry.

Table 9. Adding and Removing Apps

To Do This	Use This		Where to Learn More
Add and remove apps on your BlackBerry	App World	**BlackBerry App World**	Chapter 20: App World.
Find all the apps you've downloaded	Downloads	**Downloads folder**	Chapter 20: App World.
Manage Applications		**Options > Manage Applications**	Chapter 23: Troubleshooting

Part 2:

Introduction

Welcome to your new BlackBerry. In this section we will introduce you to how the book is organized and where to find useful information. Also at the end of this section we include our "A Full Day with Your BlackBerry" section, where we give you some scenarios to describe how you can use your BlackBerry for work and play. We even show you how to find some great tips and tricks sent right to your BlackBerry as well as how to view Video Tutorials either on your computer or load up videos on your BlackBerry.

Introduction

Congratulations on Your BlackBerry!

The BlackBerry Bold and Curve are what BlackBerry purists would call the 'workhorse' devices. The screen size, the feel of the keyboard, and the size of the device – they are all just 'right.' They are lightweight and quite powerful, also, you can drop them (several times) and they still just seem to work. The only thing you cannot do is dunk them in the pool – they definitely do not do well in water!

With this guide, we hope to help you unleash the full power of these great devices.

Back in 2001 the BlackBerry name came into the marketplace. One popular story is that the keys on the very early devices looked like seeds to some of the creators. The creators looked at various seeded fruit and decided that "BlackBerry" would be a friendly and inviting name for the device.

However, the origin of the name is less important than understanding the philosophy. One thing to understand from the outset is that this is not just a phone. The BlackBerry is a handheld computer—a sophisticated messaging device that does a bunch of things at the same time—and a phone.

The BlackBerry takes most of the major needs that we have—information, communication, constant contact, media, accessibility, and more—and puts them in one device that can do just about everything.

Key Features on your BlackBerry

Your BlackBerry has many shared features with the BlackBerry family and some unique features as well. Following are some of the key features (some of which are described in greater detail in the following subsections):

- Powerful messaging abilities
- BlackBerry 6 operating system
- Built-in social networking
- BlackBerry keyboard (arguably one of the best on the market)
- Camera (Bold devices have a flash, too)
- Media player (for pictures, video, and audio)

- Video recording
- Memory Expansion with MicroSD Media Card
- 3G/Wi-Fi capability

Messaging

A BlackBerry is first and foremost a messaging device. Whether it is a quick check and reply to an email, sending a **Text Message** or chatting on **BlackBerry Messenger** or **PIN Messaging**, your BlackBerry gets you in and out of all your messaging needs quickly and efficiently.

Built-In Social Networking

Use your BlackBerry for accessing all your Social Feeds; your Facebook page, Twitter, YouTube, Flickr and virtually every IM program. Keep in touch with everyone in the ways you like most.

BlackBerry Keyboard

The BlackBerry design allows you to quickly type your messages using the keyboard which has been refined over many BlackBerry models for the past 10 years.

Expansion Memory (Media Card)

Your BlackBerry may come bundled with a 4 or 8 GB MicroSD card (which can be expanded further) that allows you to store large numbers of pictures, songs, and videos.

Always on, Always Connected

Perhaps nothing sums up what a BlackBerry can do better than the fact that it always keeps you connected. Your BlackBerry will push your email (up to ten different accounts) right into your hand—all the time, day and night. (Now, you can put limitations on that—but the reason it is sometimes called a CrackBerry is that once you experience this, you might not want to limit it at all!)

You may be used to turning your old cell phone on and off and only checking it to see if you missed a call. Your BlackBerry stays on all the time—even when it is in standby mode, it is still on. You will find yourself looking at it not only to see if you missed a call, but to see what emails have come in, who is sending you an instant message, who just posted a note on your Facebook page, what time your next appointment is, what you need to pick up at the store, and so on. In short, your life can be managed from your BlackBerry.

Things This Powerful Are Not Always Easy to Grasp—at First

Your BlackBerry is grouped into the category of things called "smartphones" by many. A BlackBerry, however, is really . . . a BlackBerry—more than a smartphone by any other name, because it does so much so well.

The pros of that are clear—in your hand is probably the most capable and most complicated technology available today.

The cons are that the BlackBerry is not always intuitive at first use. For some, this is frustrating—they want their BlackBerry to do what their old phone did—in just the same way.

Like a computer, your BlackBerry has a unique operating system (OS) called **BlackBerry 6** that is proprietary and only found on the newest BlackBerry devices.

Take your time—this is not a device to pick up for an hour and then throw down in frustration—there is a lot to learn here. Remember when you got your first Windows or Mac computer? When we did, we didn't know what a window was, let alone where to find things or how to type a letter—it took time.

With the BlackBerry—like most other things in our lives—the more we invest in learning, the more we will ultimately get out of it.

Getting the Most out of This Book

You can read this book cover to cover, but you can also peruse it in a modular fashion, by chapter or topic. Maybe you just want to check out **BlackBerry App World**, try the web browser, and get set up with your email and contacts; or you might just want to load up your music. You can do all this and more with our book.

You will soon realize that your BlackBerry is a very powerful device. There are, however, many secrets locked inside, which we help you unlock throughout this book.

Take your time—this book can help you on your way to learn how to best use, work, and have fun with your new BlackBerry. Use this book to get up to speed and learn all the best tips and tricks more quickly.

Remember that devices this powerful are not always easy to grasp—at first. You will get the most out of your BlackBerry if you can read a section and then try out what you read. For most people, reading about and then doing an activity gives us a much higher retention rate than simply reading alone. So, in order to learn and remember what you learn, we recommend the following: *read a little, try a little on your BlackBerry, and repeat!*

How This Book Is Organized

Knowing how this book is organized will help you more quickly locate things important to you. Here we show you the main organization of this book. Remember to take advantage of our abridged table of contents, detailed table of contents, and comprehensive index to help you quickly pinpoint items of interest.

Part 1: Quick Start Guide

The Quick Start Guide covers the following topics:

Learning your way around: Learn about the keys, buttons, and ports on your BlackBerry, as well as how to get inside and change the battery, SIM card, and memory card. Then learn many time-saving tips about getting around quickly, as well as how to multitask.

Using Universal Search or Application Shortcuts: Learn how to switch between the search or shortcut hot keys when you start typing from your **Home** screen – both features can be very useful.

Copying, pasting, and multitasking: We cover the very useful copy-and-paste function and how to jump between apps on your BlackBerry.

Mastering your keyboard: We explore the keyboard and provide some useful tips about how to get more out of keyboard shortcuts.

Working with the wireless network: Learn how to read the letters, numbers, and symbols at the top of your BlackBerry screen so you know when you can make phone calls, send SMS text messages, send and receive email, and browse the Web. Also learn how to handle your BlackBerry on an airplane.

App references: This section includes a series of reference tables that allow you to quickly peruse the icons or apps in particular categories. Get a thumbnail of what all the apps do on your BlackBerry and chapters to jump right to the details of how to get the most out of each app in this book.

Part 2: Introduction

Here we describe the layout of the book.

A Full Day with Your BlackBerry

Located right after this Introduction chapter, this is a list of the myriad ways you can use your BlackBerry along with cross-reference chapters. So, if you see something you want to learn, simply thumb to that chapter and learn about it— all in just a few minutes.

Part 3: You and Your BlackBerry

This is the meat of the book, organized in easy-to-understand chapters packed with loads of pictures to guide you every step of the way.

Part 4: Keyboard Shortcuts

This is where we have gathered all the best keyboard shortcuts to help you speed your day with your BlackBerry.

Quickly Locating Notes, Tips, and Cautions

If you flip through this book, you can instantly see these items based on their formatting. For example, if you wanted to find all the calendar tips, you would flip to the Calendar chapter –and quickly find them.

NOTE: Notes, tips, and cautions are all formatted like this, with a gray background, to help you see them more quickly.

Email Tips

Check out the authors' web site at www.madesimplelearning.com for a series of very useful BlackBerry tips and tricks. On this site, we have taken a selection of great tips out of this book and even added a few new ones. Click the Free Tips section and register for your tips in order to receive a tip right in your BlackBerry inbox about once a week. Learning in small chunks is a great way to master your BlackBerry.

Video Tutorials

The authors also offer video tutorials on their web site that cover much of the material presented in this book and some new things. Whenever there is a video tutorial available for the material covered in the book we add the graphic shown here.

How to get the videos? Visit www.madesimplelearning.com from your computer and click on the BlackBerry.

Some of the videos are free, for example the entire set of videos showing you how to use **Desktop Software** for Windows.

In addition, there are over 80 video tutorials that can be purchased to show you how to use your BlackBerry.

You can choose to watch on your computer or load these videos up and take with you to view on your BlackBerry, anytime, anywhere.

A Full Day With Your BlackBerry

Here we give you a brief glimpse into the possibilities of what you can do with your BlackBerry. With all the apps, there are so many things you can do.

Time	What I do with my BlackBerry...	Learn more...
6:00 AM	My BlackBerry Alarm wakes me.	Alarm Clock – Ch.23
6:10 AM	I connect my BlackBerry up to my stereo Bluetooth docking station in the bathroom to listen to my music free Pandora or Slacker Internet radio.	Play Music – Ch. 16 Bluetooth – Ch. 1
6:45 AM	At the breakfast table, I check my email to get a jump on my day before I get to the office. I also browse the New York Times and other web sites from apps I've installed.	Email - Ch. 9 App World - Ch. 20
6:55 AM	I check traffic using Google Maps and find out I need to take my alternate route to work today.	Traffic – Ch. 21
7:00 AM	I do a little social networking and check out the latest about my friends on Facebook, my colleagues on LinkedIn, and post a couple of Tweets on Twitter.	Facebook – Ch. 14 LinkedIn – Ch. 14 Twitter – Ch. 14
8:30 AM	Waiting for a meeting, I snap a picture and send a Multi-Media Message (MMS) and post the picture on Facebook.	MMS – Ch. 12 Facebook – Ch. 14
9:00 AM	I take pictures of my new client's art work with my BlackBerry to send to a prospective buyer. I select a few and email the best snapshots.	Camera - Ch. 17 Email Pictures - Ch. 9
10:00 AM	I find out I have to fly from New York to Vancouver tonight to visit a client - so I check travel web sites on my BlackBerry Browser and book my airplane and rental car.	Web Browser – Ch. 19

10:05 AM	I received an email message from my client with the location of our meeting in Vancouver. I map the address and then add this as a Favorite in Google Maps.	Email – Ch. 9 Google Maps – Ch. 21
10:10 AM	I need to find hotels around my Client's address so I just type "hotels" into Google Maps search window and quickly find all hotels in the area. I call to reserve a room right from Google Maps.	Search Business – Ch. 21
10:25 AM	I add a bookmark for Vancouver, BC, Canada on www.weather.com to my Bookmark list and see that it will be really cool and rainy. Now I know how I need to pack.	Add Bookmark –Ch. 19
11:00 AM	An alert pops up on my BlackBerry reminding me to deal with the email message I received yesterday about the meeting. (Flag for Follow-up feature) I then add the event to my Calendar.	Follow-up – Ch. 9 Calendar – Ch. 11
11:05 AM	I look up the phone number for the restaurant and call them using Google Maps to reserve a table.	Google Maps – Ch. 21
11:07 AM	I reply to the text message and say "Sure – we're all set for 1PM - see you there!"	SMS Text – Ch. 12
1:30 PM	While at lunch, I show my spouse my cool new pictures I took on the BlackBerry in the Pictures app.	Pictures – Ch. 17
2:00 PM	Since I am traveling internationally, I check out the Travel Tips to make sure I'm not surprised by a huge data or voice roaming bill when I return.	Travel Tips – Ch. 21
3:45 PM	The buyer emails me back and says she wants to buy some of the art pieces. I click on her phone number in her email signature and give her a call right away. I then conference call the artist and we seal the deal right there. I then make sure to add her to my Contacts app.	Call Number – Ch. 8 Contacts – Ch. 10
4:30 PM	Another quick check of Google Maps for traffic for the commute home and again for the trip to the airport. Armed with the latest information, I'm set.	Google Traffic – Ch. 21
5:00 PM	I turn on Pandora Internet radio and listen to my favorite custom station on the commute home. It sounds great because I stream the music through my Bluetooth car stereo system.	Pandora – Ch. 16 Bluetooth – Ch. 1

8:00 PM	Sitting at the gate in the airport, I browse BlackBerry App World for a fun game or two to play on the airplane.	App World – Ch. 20
8:50 PM	I settle into my seat and make sure to turn off my wireless radio so I can use my BlackBerry without causing trouble with the pilots. I rest assured that my time zone will update automatically when I land on the East Coast with the auto-update time zone feature.	Airplane Mode - Ch. 1 Time zone - Ch. 7
9:00 PM	Sitting back in my seat, I plug in my headset and play some of my new games. Another great day with my BlackBerry!	App World - Ch. 20

Part 3:

You and Your BlackBerry

This is the heart of *BlackBerry 6 Made Simple*. In this section, you'll find clearly labeled chapters—each explaining the key features of your BlackBerry. You'll see that most chapters focus on an individual app or a specific type of application. Many of the chapters discuss applications that come with your BlackBerry, but we also include some fun and useful apps you can download from BlackBerry App World. Sure, the BlackBerry can help you get work done, but it's for a whole lot more, too. We finish with some handy troubleshooting tips that can help if your BlackBerry isn't working quite right.

Chapter 1: Getting Started

This chapter is about setting up your BlackBerry. We cover everything from email setup (both Internet and Enterprise), connecting to Bluetooth and Wi-Fi, security tips and how to prolong your battery life.

Your BlackBerry supports a wide array of email accounts including (Google, Comcast, Yahoo, MSN, or more generic POP3/IMAP accounts as well as Microsoft Exchange and Lotus Domino corporate accounts). The various types of accounts will have different wireless sync capapbilites for contacts and calendars in addition to email. We show you all the differences and help you get each type set up in this chapter.

Sometimes email setup can cause problems; we show you how to fix some common errors and make sure you receive all your email on both your computer and your BlackBerry. While you can adjust email setup from your BlackBerry, you may also want to adjust your email settings from your computer; we cover that in this chapter.

If your BlackBerry is tied to a BES (BlackBerry Enterprise Server), we show you how to get connected or 'activated' on the server. And, RIM, BlackBerry's maker, announced a free version of the BES software. This is a fantasic value if your organization uses Microsoft Exchange and would like to take advantage of the BES features without additional software licensing and, in most cases, without additional hardware costs.

> **CAUTION:** Before you read any further, or use the **Setup** App or anything else, please take a few minutes to check out the Quick Start Guide earlier in this book, if you haven't already. It is meant to help you find lots of useful things in this book, as well as give you some great time-saving tips and tricks so you can get up and running quickly.

The Setup App

The first time you turn on your BlackBerry, you will most likely be placed in the **Setup** app. Most of the basic setup (email, instant messaging, social networking, Bluetooth and Wi-Fi) as well as personalization or customization can be accessed from **Setup**.

If you want to start the **Setup** app at any time, click on the **Setup** icon which is found in your **All** folder on your **Home** screen.

To see all of your icons, press the **Menu** key and select **Open Tray** then swipe up in the **All** folder.

You will be presented with screens similar to the ones that follow.

> **NOTE:** These Setup screens may vary based on your carrier and can be updated by RIM, BlackBerry's maker, so you might see them in a different order or see some different icons.

Scroll the **Trackpad** up and down to see all the icons grouped into the following categories: **Setup**, **Personalization** and **Help & Tutorials** (see Figure 1-1).

Figure 1-1. Setup app screens

We cover the many of the various set up options shown as icons in Figure 1-1 in this and subsequent chapters. Below is a handy list showing you where to find more information.

Email Accounts	See "Setup Internet Email" or "Setup Enterprise Email" in this chapter.

Instant Messaging	See Chapter 12: "SMS Text and MMS" and Chapter 13: "BlackBerry Messenger"
Social Networking	See Chapter 14: "Social Networking and Social Feeds"
Bluetooth	See "Connecting With Bluetooth" in this chapter.
Wi-Fi	See "Connecting With Wi-Fi" in this chapter.
Personalization	See Chapter 7: "Personalize your BlackBerry" and Chapter 8: "Phone and Voice Dialing."

The nice thing about the icon layout inside the **Setup** app is that you can choose to setup as little of or as much of your BlackBerry as you want at any single time. You are not forced into setting everything up at once. If you want to setup **Email** today, click the **Email Accounts** icon. You can come back into the **Setup** app at a later time and complete **Instant Messaging, Social Networking** or **Bluetooth** setup when you need them.

In the next sections, we assume you are already inside the **Setup** app so you can click the icon shown inside **Setup** to get started.

Setup Email Accounts

You can setup both **Internet Mail** (e.g. Gmail, Yahoo, AOL, or other) and **Enterprise Account** (e.g. your work email) accounts from this **Email Accounts** icon.

Email
Accounts (6)

> **NOTE:** You need to have an enterprise email service plan from your wireless carrier to be able to setup Enterprise Accounts, skip to the "Setup Enterprise Account" section to setup your work email account.

Setup Internet Mail Accounts

As of publishing time, you can setup a maximum of 10 Internet Mail accounts on your BlackBerry using this process. If you are not able to successfully login to your Internet mail account using the steps in this section, then please see the "Troubleshooting Email Settings" section for help. Sometimes email accounts require that you enter a few advanced settings to work correctly with your BlackBerry.

1. Click the **Email Accounts** icon inside the **Setup** app.

2. If you see an option for **Internet Mail Account**, click it.

3. If you do not have an Internet Email Setup account yet, you will be asked to create one. After you have created your account, you will see the login screen shown.

4. Enter your **User name** and **Password**, click **Remember password** so you don't need to re-type your password every time.

5. Click **Continue** to login.

6. If you see a screen similar to the one shown to the right, then you had another BlackBerry device setup previously and can simply move the email accounts to your new BlackBerry. Click **Move** and re-enter the password for each of the accounts listed. Then you are done with email setup. Only if you want to add more accounts do you need to continue below.

7. The first time you login, or when you choose to setup another email account, you will see the screen shown to the right allowing you to setup various types of email accounts.

8. Click **Yahoo!**, **Gmail**, **AOL**, or **Windows Live** to setup one of those types of accounts. If you have another type, click **Other**.

NOTE: Only click **Create New Address** if you want to create a brand new email address that is associated only with your BlackBerry. You don't click this item if you want to integrate one of your existing email accounts.

9. If you clicked **Yahoo!, Gmail, AOL, Windows Life** or **Other**, you will see a screen asking you for your **Email address** and **Password**. Click **Continue** when done.

TIP: Click the **Show Password** checkbox to see the letters typed in your password. This can be very helpful if you password contains numbers or symbols.

10. If the BlackBerry is able to successfully login to your email account you will see a screen similar to this one.

NOTE: If the BlackBerry is not able to login to your email account and you have verified your login settings, then skip to the "Troubleshooting Email Settings" section for help.

11. Click **Continue** to setup another email account or click **Return to Setup** to get back to the **Setup** app.

TIP: You can adjust your email signature and other settings by clicking the **Change Settings** button. This is the same as editing the email account which we show you in the "Edit Internet Email Accounts and Signature" section below.

12. Each email account you setup will be listed at the top of the **Email Accounts** screen as shown to the right.

13. Click on the **Set up another email account** button if you need to setup more accounts. Then repeat steps 7 – 11.

14. When you are done setting up accounts, press the **Red Phone** key to exit to your **Home** screen. You will see a new icon for each email account you just setup. Click on **Messages** to see all your accounts in one unified inbox. Email will start flowing to each account after about 20 minutes as each Activation email message shows.

> From: Activation Server
> **Email account information**
> Jan 6, 2011 1:13 PM
>
> Congratulations, you have successfully set up martin.trautschold@gmail.com with your BlackBerry(R) device. You should begin receiving new messages in approximately 20 minutes.

Hiding Extra Email Account Icons

As you set up each email account, a new icon will appear on your home screen tied to that particular account. If you like having individual icons, you can leave them alone. However, since all your email goes into your main **Messages** inbox, you can hide these icons to clean up your **Home** screen. Follow these steps to hide these extra icons:

1. Click and hold the icon you want to hide until you see the pop-up menu as shown.

2. Select **Hide**.

If you want to get the icon back, then follow the steps to shown in the "Hiding and Showing Icons" section of Chapter 7.

> **TIP:** Press the **space** key to get the @ (at) and . (dot) symbols whenever typing an email. For example, for sara@company.com, type, **Sara** *space* **company** *space* **com**.

Maintaining Your Internet Email Accounts and Signatures

You can add more accounts, delete or edit your email accounts including your signature and other settings on your Internet Email accounts from the **Email Accounts** icon.

1. Click on the **Email Accounts** icon (and click on **Internet Mail Account**, if asked) within the **Setup** app.

2. After logging into your account, you should see all your email accounts listed as shown.

3. Click on the email account you wish to adjust to see the pop-up menu shown to the right.

   ▪ Click on **Delete** to remove this account and confirm your selection on the next screen.

   ▪ Click on **Edit** to make changes to the account and follow the steps below.

   ▪ Click on **Add Email Account** to add more accounts.

4. Scroll down the page a little to the Signature section and type your new email signature.

5. To adjust your username or password for this email account, scroll down and click on Login information to enter the new information.

6. To have a blind carbon copy (BCC) of every email you send from your BlackBerry sent to another email address, enter that in the

Delivery Options section.
This might be good for record
keeping purposes.

7. If you do not want to
synchronize deleted items (or
Calendar and Contacts, if
shown) between your
BlackBerry and your main
mail account, then uncheck
the boxes in the
Synchronization Options
section.

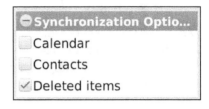

8. To force an SSL (Secure
Socket Layer) connection,
make sure the Use SSL box is
checked in the **Advanced
Options** section at the
bottom. (You may not see this
section for all account types.)

9. Click on the **Save** button at
the bottom to save all your
settings.

Setup Enterprise Accounts ("Enterprise Activation")

If you have an enterprise service plan from your carrier, and have received an
Activation Password from your email administrator, you are ready to activate or
connect your BlackBerry to the secure Enterprise Server.

NOTE: If you have not received your Activation Password, then you need to ask
your help desk or technology support department for that password before you
can complete this process.

This will allow you to securely send and receive corporate email, securely
browse the corporate intranet and receive wireless updates of your Contacts,
Calendar, Tasks and MemoPad items on your BlackBerry.

1. Click the **Email Accounts** icon inside the **Setup** app.

2. Click on the **Enterprise Account** option.

> BlackBerry email account.
>
> **Enterprise Account**
> Set up a work email account to use with your organization's BlackBerry Enterprise Server.
>
> Return to Setup

NOTE: You must see this selection screen in order to be able to activate your BlackBerry on the server. If you don't see this screen, you will need to contact your IT Help Desk to let them know that your BlackBerry may not have the correct enterprise service plan.

3. Now enter your work email address in the **Email** field and the **Activation Password** you received from your administrator. Usually, the administrator will email you the password so check your work email account on your computer. The other thing to keep in mind is that these passwords expire within 24 – 48 hours.

> provided by your system administrator in the fields below.
>
> Email: martin@company. com
>
> Activation Password:
>
> ***********
>
> Activate

NOTE: The **Activation Password** is not the same as your regular email login password.

4. If you entered the **Email** and **Activation Password** correctly, you should then see a series of status screens showing messages similar to the screen shown to the right.

> **TIP:** You can click on the **Hide** button and continue using your BlackBerry while the synchronization is taking place in the background. This process could take 30 minutes or more to complete depending on the size of your contact list, calendar items and related items.

Enterprise Activation	☀ 🔊 3G ☷ ⚇
Synchronization may take several minutes. You can hide this window; synchronization will continue.	
Hide	
Synchronizing service Desktop...	
Address Book	Initializing
Address Book Opti...	Complete

How Can I Tell If I Am Activated on the BlackBerry Server?

A simple rule of thumb is that if you can send and receive email and you have names in your BlackBerry address book (which you can access through the **Contacts** icon), then it has been successfully set up (enterprise activation is complete).

To verify that your BlackBerry is successfully configured with your server, do the following:

1. Click on your BlackBerry **Contacts** icon.

2. Look at the very top, just under **New Contact**, you should see a row called **Remote Lookup** as shown to the right. You will also see a new menu item called **Lookup**.

> **TIP:** The **Remote Lookup** or **Lookup** command allows you to search your corporation's complete address list on the server (sometimes called a "Global

Address List"). Then you can add them to your personal address book in the **Contacts** app on your BlackBerry.

Wireless Email Reconciliation

The BlackBerry allows you to turn on or off wireless reconciliation, which is the feature that synchronizes deletion of email between your regular mailbox and your BlackBerry. In other words, you can set it up so that if you delete an email on your BlackBerry, the same email message is also automatically deleted from your regular email account.

Disable or Enable Wireless Email Reconciliation

Usually, this is turned on by default and set to **Prompt** the user about deleting emails, but you can disable or adjust it.

NOTE: If you work at an organization that supplied your BlackBerry to you, this feature may be controlled centrally by your administrator and may not be adjustable.

Some wireless carriers (phone companies) do not support this feature.

1. Click the **Messages** icon.

2. Press the **Menu** key and select **Options** (or press the letter **O** to jump down to **Options**).

3. Then select **Email Reconciliation**.

4. Set Delete On to **Handheld**.

5. Uncheck the box next to **Wireless Reconcile** to disable it.

Re-Enable Reconciliation

To re-enable email reconciliation, set **Delete On to Mailbox & Handheld**, and check the box next to **Wireless Reconcile**.

On Conflicts

A conflict can occur if you work with the same email message on both your computer and your BlackBerry. Adjusting the **On Conflicts** field will give priority to either the handheld or the mailbox in case of conflict.

Purge Deleted Items

If you have turned on **Wireless Reconcile** and want to get rid of old email that you deleted from either your main email inbox or your BlackBerry, then press the **Menu** key and select **Purge Deleted Items**, and then select the email address.

Syncing Google Contacts Using Email Setup

You can choose to sync Google Contacts and Calendar using the Email Setup app, however as of publishing time, we recommend using the separate Google Sync app and not the email setup. See the Caution below.

> **CAUTION:** As of publishing time, when we had a BlackBerry on AT&T service with the enterprise service plan, we experienced that syncing contacts with the email setup shown earlier in this chapter caused all the first line of the street addressed to be erased by the sync. Therefore, we recommend you <u>do not use</u> the email setup to sync your Google Contacts and Calendar, instead use the **Google Sync** app. We describe how to setup **Google Sync** in the Contacts and Calendar chapters.

Troubleshooting Your Email Accounts

Sometimes your email accounts just don't work quite right, and unfortunately, sometimes email isn't as easy to set up as just shown. The following subsections provide a few tips for handling some of the more common errors.

Unable to Login to Email Accounts

With certain types of internet email accounts, entering the email address and password of your account does not work. In these cases, you need to enter some advanced settings screens shown below.

1. If you have attempted to login with the correct username and password, but cannot get it to work, you will be left at this screen. Click on the link **I will provide the settings**.

TIP: Make sure to check the **Show Password** box as shown so you can make sure your password is entered correctly, especially if it has numbers or characters in it.

2. Contact your email administrator to ask them for the correct **Email Server** name (usually **mail.yourdomainname. com**) and **User name** (usually your full email address) for this screen.

3. Then click on **Continue**.

4. Then, if the settings are correct, your BlackBerry should login to your email account and show you a screen similar to the one in step 9 above.

Verifying That Your Email Server Is POP3 or IMAP

Some email servers cannot be accessed by BlackBerry Internet Service, so you cannot use these types of email accounts on your BlackBerry. Contact your email service provider, tell them you are trying to access your email from a BlackBerry smartphone, and verify that the server is of a type called POP3 or IMAP.

Verifying Your Email Server Settings (Advanced Settings)

Another setup issue might be that your server uses SSL security or has a nonstandard email server name. Contact your service provider to find out about these settings. To change these settings on your BlackBerry, you need to follow the steps shown in the "Maintaining Your Internet Email Accounts and Signatures" section earlier in this chapter.

Solving a Gmail Enabled IMAP Error Message

If you receive an error message in your email inbox telling you to turn on IMAP settings in Gmail, you need to log into your Gmail account from your computer and follow these steps:

1. Click the **Settings** link (usually in the top-right corner).

2. Click the **Forwarding and POP/IMAP** tab.

3. Make sure that **IMAP Access** is set to **Enable IMAP**, as shown in Figure 1-2.

4. Then click the **Save Changes** button.

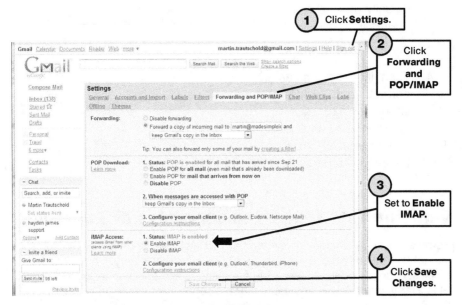

Figure 1-2. Gmail Settings – Forwarding and POP/IMAP Screen.

5. After you make this change, you will need to go back into your Email setup and validate the account.

6. Click on the invalid account and select **Validate** from the pop-up menu.

7. Type the password for your invalid email account and click **OK**.

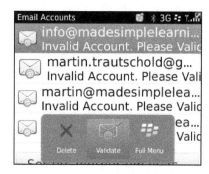

Why Is Some Email Missing from My BlackBerry?

If you download your email messages to your computer using an email program such as **Microsoft Outlook**, **Outlook Express**, or similar, and you have your Internet Email Account set up on your BlackBerry, then you need to turn on a specific setting in your computer's email program. If you do not leave a copy of your messages on the server from your computer's email, you may end up receiving all email on your computer, but only a limited set of email on your BlackBerry.

Why Does This Happen?

By default, most email programs pull down or retrieve email from the server every 1 to 5 minutes, and then erase the retrieved messages from the server. By default, the BlackBerry Internet Email service usually pulls down email every few minutes. So, if your computer has pulled down the email every minute and erased it from the server, your BlackBerry will only receive a very limited set of messages (those that haven't yet been pulled down by your computer).

How to Fix This

The answer is to set your computer's email program to keep your messages on the server. This way, the BlackBerry will always receive every email message. Here's how:

1. In your computer email program (e.g., Microsoft Outlook), find the location where you can configure or change your email accounts. For example, Tools, Configure Accounts, Account Settings, or something similar (Figure 1-3).

2. Select or change the appropriate email account.
(Sometimes you just double-click the account to edit it.)

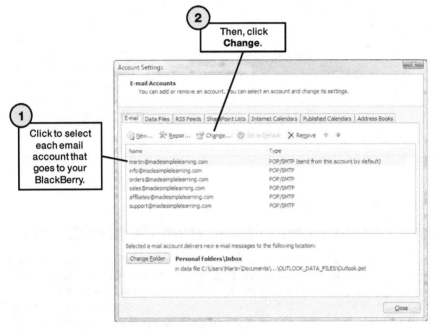

Figure 1-3. Account Settings screen in Microsoft Outlook

3. You will then usually go to an Advanced Settings area to make changes to **Leave a copy of the message on the server**. In Microsoft Outlook, click the **More Settings** tab and then the **Advanced** tab (Figure 1-4).

Figure 1-4. Internet email settings in Microsoft Outlook

4. At the bottom of the screen, under Delivery, check the **Leave a copy of the message on the server** box (see Figure 1-5).

5. Then check the **Remove from server after [X] days box**. We suggest changing the number to at least **10**. This allows you time to make sure that the message reaches both your BlackBerry and your PC, but doesn't clutter the server for too many days. If you make the number of days too high, you may end up with a "Mail Box Full" error and have your incoming email messages bounced back to the senders.

Figure 1-5. Leave a Copy of Messages On Server in Microsoft Outlook

NOTE: Remember to repeat the preceding process for every email account that you have going to both your computer and your BlackBerry.

BlackBerry Enterprise Server Express

If you work at an organization that uses a **Microsoft Exchange** or **Microsoft Windows Small Business Server**, then you can now acquire the **BES Express** software for free.

A **BES** ("**BlackBerry Enterprise Server**") is a server that typically sits behind your organization's firewall and securely connects your BlackBerry to your organization's email and data, as well as wirelessly synchronizes (shares) contacts, calendar, tasks, and memo items between your corporate computer and your BlackBerry.

Image from RIM

BES allows your organization to gain all the benefits of a BlackBerry Server with no additional software costs. This saves thousands of dollars over the old pricing model from RIM. You might want to let your IT group know about this great new deal if you use BlackBerry devices at your workplace.

You should be able to support up to 75 BlackBerry users on the same box as your email server. You can support up to 2,000 users by putting the BES Express software on a separate server.

Finding the BES Express Software

To acquire BES Express, go to www.blackberry.com and follow these steps:

1. Click the **Software** link at the top.

2. Click **BlackBerry Enterprise Server Express** under **Business Software** in the left column, and you'll see a screen similar to the one shown in (You might be able to get straight to the page by typing this link: http://us.blackberry.com/apps-software/business/server/express/.)

3. Then follow the onscreen steps to start the free download.

4. Once the software is downloaded, the administrator uses a web-based console to set up and administer all the users. The full setup instructions for **BES Express** are beyond the scope of this book, but please follow the onscreen help and tutorials found at www.blackberry.com.

Connecting with Bluetooth

Bluetooth allows your BlackBerry to communicate with devices as varied as headsets, GPS devices, and other hands-free systems with the freedom of wireless. Bluetooth is a small radio that transmits from each device. The BlackBerry gets paired, or connected, to the peripheral. Many Bluetooth devices can be used up to 30 feet away from the BlackBerry.

In this section, we will show you how to pair to a Bluetooth headset, how to connect to a Bluetooth stereo device, and how to prioritize your Bluetooth connections.

We'll start by explaining how to use Bluetooth with your Blackberry. We'll walk you through how to enable Bluetooth, to how to use it to connect to various devices, to troubleshooting some potential issues.

Bluetooth Security Tips

If you're going to use Bluetooth on your Blackberry, you need be cognizant of the security concerns around this technology. For example, here are a few security tips from a recent BlackBerry IT Newsletter. Following these will steps help you prevent hackers from getting access to your BlackBerry through Bluetooth:

- Never pair your BlackBerry when you are in a crowded public area.

- Disable the **Discoverable** setting (or use the **2 Minute** setting) after you're done pairing your BlackBerry with a device.

- Do not accept any pairing requests with unknown Bluetooth devices, and only accept connections from devices with names you recognize.

- Change the name of your BlackBerry to something other than the default value (e.g., *BlackBerry 9800*). This will help you keep hackers from easily finding your BlackBerry.

You can find this information and many other useful facts from BlackBerry's web site: www.blackberry.com.

Supported Devices

Your BlackBerry should work with most Bluetooth headsets, car kits, hands-free kits, keyboards, and GPS receivers that are compliant with Bluetooth 2.0 and earlier. At the time of writing, Bluetooth 2.1 was just entering the marketplace; you will need to check with the device manufacturer of newer devices to make sure they are compatible with your BlackBerry.

Ways to Get to Bluetooth Connections Screen

There are a couple of ways to get to Bluetooth and other wireless settings on your BlackBerry. You can get there from the **Bluetooth** icon inside the **Setup** app as shown in the left portion of Figure 1-5 or you can click on the top status bar from any **Home** screen (where the time is shown), then click on **Bluetooth Connections** (see Figure 1-6).

Figure 1-6. Two Ways to Get to the Set Up *Bluetooth Connections Screen*

Pairing with a Bluetooth Device

You can think of *pairing* as the act of establishing a wireless connection between your BlackBerry and a peripheral, whether it's a headset, global positioning device, external keyboard, or a Windows-based or Mac computer. Pairing is dependent on entering a required *passkey* that locks your BlackBerry into a secure connection with the peripheral. Use one of the methods shown in Figure 1-6 above to get to the Bluetooth settings screen.

From the **Bluetooth** settings screen, you can pair devices and manage all your Bluetooth connections.

NOTE: If you are pairing your BlackBerry with your computer, then you need to make sure that both your BlackBerry and your computer are in **Discoverable** mode. Set this in the **Bluetooth Options** screen by setting the **Discoverable** property to **Yes** or **Ask**. (The default setting is **No**, which will prevent you from pairing your BlackBerry and computer.)

1. Begin by putting your Bluetooth device (headset, computer, car stereo) in **pairing** mode, as recommended by the manufacturer. Also, have the passkey ready to enter later on in the process.

2. From the **Bluetooth** settings screen, make sure **Bluetooth** is set to **On**.

3. If you are connecting to a Bluetooth device that needs to find the BlackBerry to connect to it, set **Discoverable** to **2 Minutes**, otherwise set it to **No**. (If you are connecting a headset or keyboard that will be listening for your BlackBerry to connect, then setting **Discoverable** to **No** is fine.)

NOTE: All devices currently paired are listed at the bottom of the screen. In the image above there is a **scala-500** headset and a **VW UHV** car stereo.

4. Click on **Add New Device** to get started.

5. Then, you may be prompted to change the name of your device from the default **BlackBerry** to help avoid Bluetooth hackers. Go ahead and make the name something unusual, in this example we just used **xyz**. Click on **OK.**

6. Click **Search** to search for Bluetooth devices in pairing mode. Click **Listen** if another device is looking for your BlackBerry.

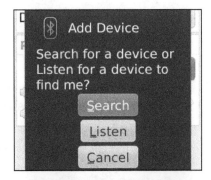

7. Then, as long as the other device you are searching for is in pairing mode and close to your BlackBerry, it should be found as shown to the right. Click on the device name that appears.

TIP: If the BlackBerry cannot find any devices, then make sure the other Bluetooth device is truly in pairing mode and try searching again.

8. You may be prompted to enter the four-digit passkey provided by the manufacturer of the Bluetooth peripheral. Enter this passkey, and then press the **Enter** key. (Many default passkeys are just *0000, 1111,* or *1234.*)

NOTE: Many newer headsets will pair automatically now without the need to enter a passkey.

9. You will then be prompted to accept the connection from the new device; do so.

> **TIP:** If you check the box next to **Don't display this again**, you will only have to do this once.

10. Now you should see your newly connected Bluetooth device shown at the bottom of the Bluetooth settings screen. In this image you can see the **scala-500** headset.

11. Repeat the above procedure to connect with any Bluetooth devices.

Answering and Making Calls with a Bluetooth Headset

Some Bluetooth headsets support an **Auto Answer** feature that will, as it sounds, automatically answer incoming calls and send them right to the headset. This is very helpful when driving or in other situations where you should not be looking at your phone to answer the call. Sometimes, you will need to push a button – usually just one – to answer your call from the headset. You have two options for answering and making calls with a headset, which are covered next.

Option 1: Answering Directly From the Headset

When a call comes into your BlackBerry, you should hear an audible beep in the headset. Just press the **Multi-function** button (usually the main button) on your headset to answer the call. See Figure 1-7. Press the **Multi-function** button again to hang up the phone call.

The **Multi-function** button. Use to answer, hang up or start **Voice Dialing**.

Slide up/down for **Volume** control. Press and hold for **power** or **paring mode**.

Figure 1-7. A Bluetooth Headset (Scala-500 model) showing the Multi-Function button.

Option #2: Transferring the Caller to the Headset

When a phone call comes into your BlackBerry, follow these steps to transfer the caller to your headset:

1. Press the **Menu** key.

2. Scroll to **Activate (***your Bluetooth headset's Device Name***)**, and the call will be sent to the selected headset.

In image to the right, the headset's **Device Name** is *Jawbone*.

You can switch back to the handset by pressing the **Menu** key and selecting **Activate Handset**.

Voice Dialing from the Headset

Pressing the Multi-function button on your Bluetooth headset will start Voice Dialing when you are not on a phone call. See Figure 1-7 above.

The Bluetooth Connections Menu Commands

There are several options available to you from the **Bluetooth Connections** menu. Learning these commands can help you to take full advantage of Bluetooth on your BlackBerry.

To get to the **Bluetooth Connections** screen, click on the top status bar of your **Home** screen to view your **Manage Connections** screen. Then scroll down and click on **Bluetooth Connections** near the bottom. (See Figure 1-6 above).

You can access the following functionality from the **Bluetooth Setup** menu:

- **Disable Bluetooth:** Gives you another way to turn off the Bluetooth radio, which can help you to save battery life if you don't need the Bluetooth active.

- **Connect / Disconnect:** (This option is only visible if you have highlighted a device in the list at the bottom of the screen before pressing the **Menu** button.) Lets you immediately connect/disconnect you to/from the highlighted Bluetooth device.

- **Add Device:** Lets you connect to a new Bluetooth peripheral.

- **Delete Device:** Removes the highlighted device from the BlackBerry.

- **Device Properties:** Lets you check whether the device is trusted or encrypted. It also lets you see whether the **Echo Control** is activated.

- **Transfer Contacts:** (This option is only visible if you have highlighted a device in the list at the bottom of the screen before pressing the **Menu** button.) Enables you to send your address book through **Bluetooth** to a PC or another Bluetooth smartphone, assuming you are paired and connected to that device.

- **MAP Options:** Shows you the Message Access Options screen where you can check or uncheck your various email accounts and SMS/MMS. If you uncheck an email account or message type, then it is not accessible via **Bluetooth** connectivity.

- **Options:** Shows the **Options** screen, which we've covered previously.

Sending and Receiving Files via Bluetooth

Once you have paired your BlackBerry with your computer, you can use Bluetooth to send and receive files. At the time of writing, these files were limited to media files (e.g, videos, music, and pictures) and address book entries; however, we suspect that you will be able to transfer more types of files in the future.

Transfer Contacts

From the **Bluetooth Connections** screen, highlight the device from which you want transfer contacts or press the **Menu** button and select **Transfer Contacts**. Follow the steps on the screen to complete the transfer.

Transfer Media Files

Sending and receiving media files through Bluetooth on your BlackBerry is a straightforward process. All you need to do is follow these simple steps:

1. Click on the icon for the type of media you wish to transfer, such as **Music**, **Ringtones**, **Pictures** or **Videos**.

2. Navigate to particular item you wish to transfer.

3. Press the **Menu** button and select Send, then select **Bluetooth.**

4. Select the device to which you want to transfer the files, usually your computer.

5. From here, you will need to follow the prompts on your computer to receive the file.

> **NOTE:** You may need to set up your computer so it can receive files through Bluetooth.

If you are receiving a file (or files) on your BlackBerry, then you need to select the **Receive via Bluetooth** option. Go to your computer and select the file or files you want to send, and then follow the commands required to **Send via Bluetooth**. You may be asked on the BlackBerry to confirm the Bluetooth transfer.

> **NOTE:** You can send (transfer) only media files that you have put onto your BlackBerry yourself. You cannot use Bluetooth to transfer the pre-loaded media files.

Troubleshooting Bluetooth

Bluetooth is still an emergent technology, and sometimes it just doesn't work as well as you might hope. If you are having difficulty, perhaps one of these suggestions will help. So in this section, we will cover common problems and possible approaches to solving them.

Problem 1: The Device Refuses Your Passkey

Sometimes a Bluetooth device just won't accept your passkey. In this case, it's possible that you have the incorrect passkey. Most Bluetooth devices use either *0000, 1111,* or *1234* for the passkey; however, but some have unique passkeys.

If you lost your product manual for the Bluetooth device, you can often find a PDF version of the manual online using a search engine such as Google or Yahoo. Typically, you'd find this PDF at the device manufacturer's site, but it can show up on other sites, too.

Problem 2: The Device Won't Pair Even with the Correct Passkey

Sometimes you have the right passkey, but you still cannot pair the device. In this case, it is possible that the device is not compatible with your BlackBerry. One thing you can try is to turn off encryption. Follow these steps to do so:

1. Get to the **Bluetooth Connections** screen as shown above.

2. Highlight the **Name** of the problem device and then press the **Menu** button to select **Device Properties**.

3. In the **Device Properties** dialog, disable encryption for that device and try to connect again.

Problem 3: You Cannot Share Your Address Book

Sometimes you might encounter problems when trying to share your address book with a Bluetooth device. Follow these steps if you encounter this issue:

1. Inside the **Bluetooth Connections** screen, press the **Menu** key and select **Options**.

2. Double-check that you have enabled the **Contacts Transfer** field. If you haven't, do so.

NOTE: Many Bluetooth headsets and car kits do not fully support address book transfers; be sure to double-check the documentation that came with your Bluetooth device.

Media Card (MicroSD Format)

Most BlackBerrys come with 256MB or 512MB (Megabytes) of flash memory for programs for things like pictures and music, but all that won't all be available to you. The operating system and installed software take up some of that room and so will all your personal information.

Since your BlackBerry is also a very capable media device, you will probably want more room to store things like music files, videos, ring tones, and pictures.

The image of the SanDisk MicroSD card and the SanDisk logo are copyrights owned by SanDisk Corporation.

That's where the MicroSD memory card comes in. Some wireless carriers are pre-installing an 4GB or 8GB memory card in the BlackBerry—if you have a smaller card or no card at all, you can expand the memory to 32GB MicroSD memory card if you need.

Installing Your Media Card

The BlackBerry actually has the MicroSD card slot inside the back cover, near the battery. Please refer to the "Inside Your BlackBerry" section of the Quick Start Guide at the beginning of this book to learn how to insert a Media Card into your device.

CAUTION: Before you remove the media card, we recommend using the **Safely Remove Media Card** from the **Storage** screen in **Options**. To get to this command, type **Storage** in the universal search, click on the **Options** icon, click on **Storage**, press the **Menu** key and select **Safely Remove Media Card**. Then you can follow the steps above to remove the card.

Verify Memory Card Installation

Once installed, it is a good idea to double-check that the card is installed correctly and the amount of free space is available.

1. Click on the **Search** icon in the upper right corner of the **Home** screen and type **Storage**.

2. Click on the **Options** icon.

3. Click on **Storage** from the results list.

4. This image shows that a media card has been inserted (see **Media Card Storage** at the bottom).

5. The total space figure at the bottom of the screen shows that a 2.0 GB card will read about 1.8 GB Total Space (1GB equals about 1,000 MB). If you see that, all is well.

Storage	
Enable Compression:	
Media Card Support:	✓
Application Storage	
Free Space:	18.4 MB
Media Card Storage	
Total Space:	1.8 GB
Free Space:	231.2 MB

Formatting or Repairing

You can format or repair the media card from this same **Storage** screen in **Options**.

Press the Menu button in the **Storage** screen.

- To format the media card, select **Format**.
- To repair the media card, select **Repair**.
- To remove the media card, select **Safely Remove Media Card**.

Transferring Content to your BlackBerry Using USB Drive Mode (for Mac and Windows)

This works regardless of whether you have a Windows or a Mac computer. We will show images for the Windows computer process, and it will be fairly similar for your Mac. This transfer method assumes you have stored your media on a MicroSD media card in your BlackBerry.

1. Connect your BlackBerry to your computer using the USB cable.

2. Select **USB Drive** from the options.

NOTE: Select **Sync Media** if you are syncing media (music, pictures, etc.) using BlackBerry Desktop Software.

3. After your BlackBerry is connected and in USB Drive mode, just open your computer's file management software.

   a. In Windows, press the **Windows** key + **E** to open **Windows Explorer**.

   b. On your Mac, start your **Finder**. Look for another hard disk or "BlackBerry (model number)" that has been added.

You may see two separate disks:—

Removable Disk (your media card) and

BLACKBERRY1 (your BlackBerry internal memory).

You will notice that all your files are stored in separate folders.

In the BlackBerry internal memory (shown as **BLACKBERRY1**), the main folder where all your information is stored is called **home** then **user.** In that folder there are separate folders depending on the type of files.

In the media card (**Removable Disk**) they are all under the main folder called **BlackBerry.** From there you will see audiobooks, camera, documents, etc. In that folder there are separate folders depending on the type of files.

In the images above, you notice that different types of media are stored in different folders.

To copy a specific type of media, navigate to the correct folder on your BlackBerry or the media card and copy or paste files into that folder.

You can also drag and drop files between these folders and folders on your computer as you normally do with other files on your computer.

For example, to copy media (pictures, videos, music) from your BlackBerry, select the files from the **BlackBerry / pictures** folder. Then draw a box around the pictures, or click one and press **Ctrl+A** or **Command+A** (Mac) to select them all.

Or hold the **Ctrl** key (Windows) or **Command** key (Mac) down and click individual pictures to select them. Once selected, right-Click on (Windows) or right-Click on the Mac.

Or press **Ctrl** and click (Mac) one of the selected pictures and select **Cut** (to move) or **Copy** (to copy).

Then click any other disk/folder—like **My Documents**—and navigate to where you want to move / copy the files. Once there, right-Click on again in the right window where all the files are listed and select **Paste**.

On your Mac, click the **Finder** icon in the lower left-hand corner of the Dock.

You will see your Devices (including both BlackBerry drives) on the top and your Places (where you can copy and paste media) on the bottom.

You can also delete all the pictures / media / songs from your BlackBerry in a similar manner. Navigate to the BlackBerry / (media type) folder, like **BlackBerry / videos**. Press the key combination shown previously on your computer keyboard to select all the files, and then press the **Delete** key on your keyboard to delete all the files.

You can also copy files from your computer to your BlackBerry using a similar method. Just go to the files you want to copy, and select them (highlight them). Then right-Click on **Copy** and paste them into the correct BlackBerry / (media type) folder.

> **Important:** Not all media (videos), pictures (images), or songs will be playable or viewable on your BlackBerry. If you use desktop software such as Desktop Software for Windows (See Chapter 3: "Windows PC Media and File Transfer") for Mac (See Chapter 5: "Apple Mac Media and File Transfer") to transfer the files, most files will be automatically converted for you.

Connecting with Wi-Fi

Wi-Fi is a wireless-connection technology that enables you to connect computers, printers, game consoles, mobile devices (like your blackberry) and more to the Internet. Today we are fortunate to live in a world where Wi-Fi is increasingly ubiquitous. Indeed, it is difficult to go anywhere and not have access to a Wi-Fi network.

In this section, we will show you how to connect your BlackBerry to available Wi-Fi networks, how to prioritize and organize your networks, and how to diagnose wireless problems.

Understanding Wi-Fi on Your BlackBerry

Like other devices that use Wi-Fi, your BlackBerry can send and receive a wireless signal to and from a wireless router. If your BlackBerry is Wi-Fi equipped, you can take advantage of high-speed Web Browsing and file downloading speeds through your home or office wireless network. You can also access millions of Wi-Fi hotspots in all sorts of places, such as coffee shops and hotels, many of which are free!

> **NOTE:** The origin of the term *Wi-Fi* is disputed. According to some, Wi-Fi stands for Wireless Fidelity (IEEE 802.11 wireless networking), whereas others say that the term refers to a wireless technology brand owned by the Wi-Fi Alliance. Regardless of the term's origins, we're immensely grateful for its increasingly widespread adoption!

The Wi-Fi Advantage

Wi-Fi is a great advantage to BlackBerry users around the globe. The advantages to using a Wi-Fi connection (as opposed to a carrier data connection such as GPRS/EDGE/3G) are many:

- Web browsing speeds are much faster.
- You are not using up data from your data plan,
- Most file downloads will be faster.
- You can get often great Wi-Fi signals when you cannot get any regular cell coverage (1XEV/EDGE/3G), such as in the bottom floors of a thick-walled building.

Setting up Wi-Fi on Your BlackBerry

Before you can take advantage of the speed and convenience of using Wi-Fi on your BlackBerry, you will need to set up and configure your wireless connection.

Similar to getting to the Bluetooth screen, there are a couple of ways to get to the **Set Up Wi-Fi** screen. You can get there from the **Wi-Fi** icon inside the **Setup** app as shown in the left portion of Figure 1-8 or you can click on the top status bar from any **Home** screen (where the time is shown), then click on **Setup Wi-Fi Network**.

Figure 1-8. Ways to Get to the Set Up *Wi-Fi Network Screen*

Visible Wi-Fi Networks

If the Wi-Fi network is broadcasting its network name (also known as the "ssid"), then you can see it on your list of available networks from the **Set Up Wi-Fi** screen. Connecting is as easy as clicking on the network name.

1. From the **Set Up Wi-Fi** screen, you will immediately see all Wi-Fi networks that are broadcasting their network names. In this image you can see two available networks: **trautschold** and **johnsonwifi**.

2. If you see the network to which you want to connect, click on it.

3. If the network has security enabled, you will be asked for the passphrase. Type it in and click Connect. Otherwise, if the network is unsecure, then you will be connected automatically.

4. Once you have been connected to the network, you will see a checkmark next to the network name as shown here.

Wi-Fi Protected Push-Button Setup

If you have a newer Wi-Fi router, it will have a special button to help you quickly connect Wi-Fi devices such as your BlackBerry. You will need to have a button

that looks like this on your router to use this method.

1. From the **Set Up Wi-Fi** screen, click the **Other ways to connect** button near the bottom.

2. Press **Wi-Fi Protected Setup** on this screen.

3. Here you have two choices: **Choice 1:** (Easier) Click **Press button on router** and press the

button on your router. Then the BlackBerry will wait for a signal from the router to connect.

4. **Choice 2:** (Harder) Click **Enter PIN into router**. Then, then if the BlackBerry finds a network you will see a screen where you press **Start**. Then you will see a screen showing a randomly generated pin number. You will need to enter that PIN into your router configuration screen (usually by typing 192.168.1.1 or similar number into your computer's web browser and

logging in).

5. When successfully connected, you will see this screen with the network name in the top row with a checkmark next to it.

Manually Connect to a Network

Sometimes, you will have to manually type in the Wi-Fi network information, this could be because the network is not broadcasting its name or it has advanced security settings. Contact the Network Administrator prior to using this option, because you will have to type in detailed information about the Wi-Fi network and its security settings in order to connect to it.

1. From the **Set Up Wi-Fi** screen, click the **Other ways to connect** button near the bottom.

2. Press **Manually Connect to Network** on this screen.

3. Type in the **SSID** (network name) and click **Next**.

4. If the network has no security, then leave **Security Type** set to the default **None** and click **Save and Connect** at the bottom.

5. If the Network has security enabled, then follow these steps.

6. Select the **Security Type** and select one from the list: **WEP, WPA/WPA2 Personal,** or **WPA/WPA2 Enterprise.**

7. After selecting the **Security Type**, more fields will appear. Type in the requested information, such as the passphrase or other information.

8. Click the **Save and Connect** button at the bottom.

9. Now the BlackBerry will try to connect to the specified network. You will see a checkmark next to the network name on the **Set Up Wi-Fi** screen.

10. If you have problems connecting, you may need to verify your information and try again.

Connecting to Free Wi-Fi Networks Requiring Web Browser Login or Agreements

Sometimes you will be able to connect to a Wi-Fi network easily as described above, but you will not have full internet access until you open your BlackBerry web browser and click a check box or enter a password.

1. Go to the Wi-Fi setup as you did above.

2. Choose a network to connect to; in this example we are connecting to the Panera Hotspot.

3. Click OK if you get a screen notifying you that there might be some legal terms or conditions to which you need to agree.

4. Agree to the terms and conditions of the hotspot in order to connect.

NOTE: In the case of this Panera Hotspot, we had to agree to a limited 30 minutes of access during peak times.

Move, Change, or Delete Saved Wi-Fi Networks

One of the nice things about Wi-Fi is that you can connect to a wireless network just about anywhere. While you may have saved your home and work networks in the steps above, there may be times you want to prioritize, change or delete networks.

Let's say you connect to your home wireless network 90% of the time. You will want to make sure that your home network is at the top of the list of networks your BlackBerry searches for.

Follow these steps to move, change or delete your saved Wi-Fi networks:

1. Access your **Wi-Fi settings**, as described previously.

2. Click the **Saved Wi-Fi Networks** button.

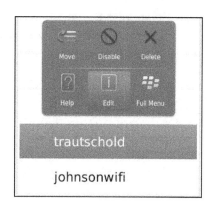

3. Press and hold the network you wish to move, change or delete until you see the pop-up menu as shown to the right.

4. Click **Edit** to change the network settings.

5. From here you may:

   a. Click on **Move** to move the network up or down the priority list (higher networks are connected first.) Then click on a new location to move the network to that location on the list.

   b. Click on **Disable** to disconnect from this network.

   c. Click on **Delete** to remove this saved network.

6. When done, press the **Escape** key and select **Save**.

Troubleshoot - Wi-Fi Diagnostics

There may be times when your Wi-Fi Connection doesn't seem to be working well. Thankfully, your BlackBerry has powerful, built-in troubleshooting programs to help you in those instances.

CAUTION: These troubleshooting tools are highly technical and should be used only by highly technical individuals or while talking to the network administrator. We have not described their detailed use because it is beyond the scope of this book.

1. Get to the **Setup Wi-Fi** screen as shown above.

2. Press the **Menu** button and select **Troubleshoot** to see the screen shown here.

3. Select **Wi-Fi Diagnostics** to see technical information about your current network.

4. Select **Site Survey** to see relative signal strengths of available Wi-Fi networks.

5. Select **DNS Lookup** to see the local name servers (used to connect you to the Internet), and

6. Select **Ping** to see how long a packet of data from your BlackBerry takes to get to a specific location on the Internet.

Using your BlackBerry as a Tethered Modem

Tethering is the process of connecting your BlackBerry to your computer and using the BlackBerry as a "modem" to access the internet. This is particularly useful if you are in an airport or a hotel with no internet connection on your notebook, and you need capabilities more robust than those provided by your BlackBerry.

Connecting Your Laptop to the Internet with Your BlackBerry

Depending on your wireless carrier (phone company) and what type of software you use, you should be able to use your BlackBerry to connect your laptop (PC or Mac) to the internet. This is variously called a *tethered modem*, *tethering*, or even an *IP modem*. You need a USB cable to connect your BlackBerry to a PC; however, sometimes you can use Bluetooth to connect to a Mac.

NOTE: Not every BlackBerry wireless carrier supports using your BlackBerry as a modem. Please check with your carrier before attempting to use this feature. Because there are so many ways to connect using your BlackBerry and the methods vary considerably, we could not include them all in this book. Please contact your carrier or the software provider for assistance with this feature.

Tethering (Usually) Costs Extra

Most (but not all) wireless carriers charge an extra fee to allow you to use your BlackBerry as a tethered modem. You may not be able to connect using your BlackBerry as a modem, however, unless you have specifically signed up for a *BlackBerry as Modem* service or a similar data plan.

Your Tethering Options

You have several options to choose from if you decide to use your BlackBerry as a tethered modem for your laptop (PC or Mac):

- **Option 1:** Purchase third-party software. We recommend **Tether**, available at http://tether.com/

- **Option 2:** Use your wireless carrier's software (contact your carrier to ask whether it has Tethering software available).

- **Option 3:** Use the **BlackBerry Desktop Software** (this is usually only an available for you if Option 2 is not.)

Securing Your BlackBerry Data

You have a lot of valuable and highly personal information on your BlackBerry; obviously, keeping it private and personal is critically important. In this section, we will cover general security principles for your BlackBerry, including how to secure your BlackBerry data. For example, we will cover how to prepare for the possibility that you lose your BlackBerry, and the steps you should take to hedge the potential downside from such an unfortunate occurrence.

We will also show you how to enable and use password security and alert you to good email and web security tips and tricks.

Consider what would happen if your BlackBerry were lost or stolen. Would you be uncomfortable if someone found and easily accessed all the information on your BlackBerry? For most of us the answer would be, "Yes!"

On many of our BlackBerry smartphones, we store vital information about our friends and colleagues, including their names, addresses, phone numbers, confidential emails, and notes. Some of our devices may even contain Social Security Numbers, passwords, and other important information in your **Contact** notes or your **MemoPad** program.

For this reason, you will want to enable or turn on the **Password Security** feature. When you turn this on, you and anyone else, will need to enter the correct password to access and use the BlackBerry. In many larger organizations, you do not have the option to turn off your password security; it is automatically turned on by your BlackBerry Enterprise Server Administrator.

Worst Case Scenarios

Fortunately, you can take several steps to make this worst-case scenario less painful, should it ever occur. For example, taking the following steps will help you minimize the potential impact of losing your BlackBerry or having it stolen:

- **Step 1**: Back up your BlackBerry to your computer, a detached hard drive, a USB memory stick, or some other device or service.

- **Step 2**: Turn on (**enable**) the BlackBerry's **Password Security**.

- **Step 3**: Fill out the **Owner Information** field; be sure to include an incentive for returning your BlackBerry.

In the next several sections, we will walk you through how to implement each of these steps.

Step 1: Back up or Sync Data

Windows and Mac users can use the data backup feature of **BlackBerry Desktop Software** described in Chapters 2 and 4.

> **CAUTION:** If you have important media or other information (e.g., personal pictures, videos, music, and so on) stored on your media card, see Chapters 3 (Windows) and 5 (Mac) to learn how to transfer or sync that media from your BlackBerry to your computer.

Step 2: Turn on Your Password

A critical step in securing your BlackBerry is to make sure you enable **Password Security**. This is really your "Plan B" to safeguard all your data, should the device get lost or stolen. Follow these steps to enable **Password Security**:

1. Click the **Search** icon in the upper right corner of your Home screen and type the word "lock." Then, click the **Options** icon (wrench).

2. Click **Password** from the Options screen.

3. Click **Enable** to turn on the checkmark next to it.

4. Click **Set Password** to create your password. You can adjust the other settings unless they are locked out by your BlackBerry administrator.

5. Press the **Escape** key and **Save** your settings.

CAUTION: If you cannot remember your password, then you will lose all the data on your BlackBerry, including email, addresses, calendar events, and tasks – everything!. Once you enter more than the set number of password attempts (the default is ten attempts), the BlackBerry will automatically *wipe,* or *erase all data.*

Step 3: Set the Lock Screen Text

We recommend including something like this in the message shown on the screen when your BlackBerry is locked: *Reward offered for safe return.* This is the text that appears on the screen if someone found your BlackBerry in a **Locked** mode.

1. Click the **Search** icon in the upper right corner of your Home screen and type the word "lock." Then, click the **Options** icon (wrench).

2. Click **Message on Lock Screen** from the **Options** screen.

3. Now type your name in the **Display Owner Name**. We recommend typing something that offers a reward in the **Display Information**. This may give the finder of your BlackBerry incentive to return it to you.

4. Press the **Escape** button and **Save**.

Now test what you've entered by locking your BlackBerry by pressing the **Password Lock** icon (scroll all the way to the bottom of your **All** folder on your **Home** screen).

CAUTION: Just pressing the **Lock** button on the top of your BlackBerry will not Lock your device to where you need to enter the password. Instead, only the screen is locked until you press the **Lock** button again.

When your BlackBerry is locked, you should now see your owner information, as shown in the figure to the right.

Email Security Tips

You should *never* send personal information or credit card information via email. Examples of other information you should never send through email include: credit card numbers, Social Security Numbers, your date of birth, your mother's maiden name, or sensitive passwords / PIN numbers (e.g., a bank account ATM card). If you have to transmit this information, it's best to call the trusted source or, if possible, visit that source in person.

Web Browsing Security Tips

Next, we'll cover some basic safety tips you should keep in mind when browsing the Web. If you are in an organization with a BlackBerry Enterprise Server, then all the browsing you do with the built-in Browser program is secured by the encryption from the Server. Your communications will be secure as long as you are browsing sites within your organization's intranet. Once you go outside the intranet to the internet, and you are not using an HTTPS connection, your web traffic is no longer secure.

Anyone who visits a site with HTTPS (Secure Socket Layer) connection will also have a secure connection from your BlackBerry to the web site, just as when you're using your computer's web browser.

Whenever you are browsing a regular HTTP web site on the internet (not your organization's secure intranet), then you need to always be aware that your connection is not secure, even if are using a BlackBerry Enterprise Server. In this case, please make sure that you do not to type or enter any confidential, financial, or personal information.

If You Lose your BlackBerry

If you work at an organization with a BlackBerry Enterprise Server or use a Hosted BlackBerry Enterprise Server and you lose your Blackberry, then you should immediately call your Help Desk and let it know what has happened. Most Help Desks can send an immediate **Wipe** command to erase all data stored on your BlackBerry device. You or the Help Desk should also contact the cell phone company to disable the BlackBerry's phone service.

If you are not at an organization that has a BlackBerry Enterprise Server, then you should immediately contact the cell phone company that supplied your BlackBerry and let it know what happened. Hopefully, a good Samaritan will find your BlackBerry and return it to you.

Turning Off Password Security

It's possible that you might want to turn off your BlackBerry's **Password Security** feature for some reason. Follow these steps to disable **Password Security**:

1. Follow the steps shown above to get to this **Password** screen inside **Options**.

2. Click **Enable** to turn off the checkmark next to it.

3. Press the **Escape** key and **Save** your settings.

4. You will have to enter your password one last time to complete the process.

NOTE: If you work at an organization with a BlackBerry Enterprise Server, you may not be allowed to turn off your password.

Battery Life Tips

As everyone knows, your BlackBerry's battery is critical to its smooth operation. But what you may not know is what happens when it gets too low, how often you should charge it, whether there are extended-life batteries available, or even what things can cause it to be drained more quickly. In this section, we will give you an overview of battery issues that relate to using your BlackBerry.

Charging your BlackBerry

Many people wonder how frequently the BlackBerry's battery should be charged. We recommend charging the battery every night. Using your phone is the fastest way to consume your battery life; so, if you talk a lot on your BlackBerry, you will definitely want to charge it every night. Another big drain on your battery is using its speaker to play music or video sound – especially at higher volumes.

TIP: Plug in your BlackBerry charger cable wherever you set your BlackBerry down every night. Then, before setting the BlackBerry down, plug it into the charging cable.

Low Battery Warnings

Also, your BlackBerry provides displays a series of increasingly critical warnings as your battery power drops below certain percentages of a full charge. The following list describes the various battery-related warnings the BlackBerry displays:

- **Low Battery Warning**: This warning is displayed if the battery drops to only 15% of its full charge. If this happens, you will hear a beep and see a warning dialog. Also, the device's **Battery Indicator** meter will usually change to red. At this point, you will want to start looking for a way to charge your BlackBerry – either by connecting it to your computer with a USB cable or through its regular power charger.

- **Very Low Battery:** When the battery gets down to 5% of its full charge, you are in a **Very Low Battery** condition. At this point, the BlackBerry will automatically turn off your wireless radio to conserve what little remaining power there is. This will prevent you from making any calls, browsing the Web, sending/receiving email or messages of any kind at all. You should try to charge the device immediately or turn it off.

- **(Almost) Dead Battery:** When the BlackBerry senses the battery is just about to run out altogether, then it will automatically shut off the BlackBerry itself. This is a preventative measure, meant to ensure your data remains safe on the device. However, we recommend getting the BlackBerry charged as quickly as possible after you are in this condition.

Places to Recharge Your BlackBerry

You can charge your BlackBerry in many on-the-go other settings, including in your car or from your computer. The next couple sections provide more information on the various places you might be able to recharge your BlackBerry.

Recharging from Power Outlet

This is the fastest and most effective way to charge your BlackBerry. Connect the USB cable to the power charger and plug it into the wall. If you're in a hurry and have access to an outlet, use this method.

Recharging in a Car

Obviously, if you're traveling, you will want to be able to recharge your BlackBerry in a car. The easiest way to do this is to purchase a car charger from a BlackBerry accessory store. To find a car charger online, type *blackberry car charger* in your favorite search engine.

> **NOTE:** If you are coming from an older BlackBerry, you will notice the newer BlackBerry devices use the new thin Micro USB charger; your older chargers may not fit this device.

The other way to charge your BlackBerry is to use what is called a *vehicle power inverter* that converts your vehicle's 12V direct current (DC) into alternating current (AC) that you can plug your BlackBerry charger into. The other option with a power inverter is to plug your laptop into it, and then connect your BlackBerry with the USB cable to the laptop (a true mobile office setup!).

Recharging from Your Computer

As outlined previously in this book, you can also recharge your BlackBerry by connecting the device to your computer with a USB cable. Your device will charge as long as your computer is plugged into a power outlet (or vehicle power inverter) and your BlackBerry is connected to your computer through the aforementioned USB cable.

Extending Your Battery Life

If you are in an area with very poor (or no) wireless coverage, you can extend your battery life by turning off your device's wireless radio through the **Manage Connections** feature. When the wireless radio is searching for the network, it consumes much more battery power.

Here are some additional tips you can follow to extend your BlackBerry's battery life:

- **Use headphones instead of the built-in speaker to listen to music or watch videos:** The built-in speaker consumes much more power than a headset does, so minimizing the use of the speaker will extend your expected battery life.

- **Use your speakerphone sparingly:** The speakerphone uses much more energy than either the regular speaker or your headset.

- **Decrease the backlight brightness or reduce the timeout:** You can control this property through your device's **Screen Display** options. (Get to this screen by typing "screen" in your **Search** icon, click on **Options** then click on **Screen Display**.)

- **If possible, set your profiles to ring and/or vibrate less often:** You might want to turn off the vibration feature for every email you receive. This will not only extend your battery life, but it may help you live a calmer and more peaceful existence. Instead, you can check your BlackBerry for new messages at regular intervals, not as every single message arrives.

- **Use data intensive applications sparingly:** Such applications make a lot of use of the radio transmit/receive feature, which uses up the battery more quickly. For example, mapping programs transmit large amounts of data to show the map moving or related satellite imagery.

- **More email and texting instead of talking on the phone:** The phone is one of the largest consumer of battery life. If possible, send an email or SMS text message instead of making a call. Lots of time, this is less intrusive for the recipient, and you may be able to get an answer when a phone call might not be possible. For example, your contact might be in a meeting and able to respond by text, even though he can't talk to you if you were to call instead.

Chapter 2:
Windows PC Setup

This chapter shows you how to install BlackBerry Desktop Software (formerly called "BlackBerry Desktop Manager") on your Windows computer. Then it shows you how to synchronize your contacts, calendar, tasks and memos, backup and restore, and more.

If you want to transfer files and media, then check out Chapter 3: "Windows PC Media and File Transfer."(You will need some of the instructions in this chapter on how to install Desktop Software if you want to use it as your method to transfer files.)

Have an Apple Mac computer? Please go to Chapter 4: "Apple Mac Setup."

Unless you work at an organization that provides you access to a BES (BlackBerry Enterprise Server), if you are a Windows user, you will need to use BlackBerry Desktop Software to do a number of things:

- Transfer or synchronize your personal information (addresses, calendar, tasks, and notes) between your computer and your BlackBerry.

- Back up and restore your BlackBerry data.

- Install or remove an application. (You can also do this right on your BlackBerry– see Chapter 20: "BlackBerry App World")

- Transfer or sync your media (songs, videos, and pictures) to your BlackBerry (see Chapter 3.)

CAUTION: Do not sync your BlackBerry with several computers .You could corrupt your BlackBerry and/or other databases, and end up with duplicates, or worse yet, deleted items.

Downloading Desktop Software for Windows

Each new version of RIM's Desktop Software program has come with more functionality and more versatility than the previous versions. So, it is always a good idea to keep up to date with the latest version of the Desktop Software.

The Disk from the BlackBerry Box

It is fairly likely that the disk that arrived with your brand new BlackBerry has a version of Desktop Software that is already out of date. This is because many times, the CD was produced more than a month ago, and in the meantime a new version has been released. So we recommend grabbing the latest version from the internet directly from www.blackberry.com, as shown below.

Checking Your Current Version

If you have already installed Desktop Software, you should check which version you currently have. The easiest was to do that is start up your Desktop Software program by clicking on the icon or doing a search from your Windows search bar.

1. Click on the Help (Question mark) icon in the upper right corner as shown.

2. Select **About BlackBerry Desktop Software**.

3. The version number of your particular version will be shown here under the name. If you don't have version **6.0.1** or higher, it is time to upgrade.

4. If you are not on the latest version, or just want to verify, then from the same **Help** menu (question mark), select **Check for Updates**.

5. Then you will see a pop-up window saying you have the latest version or there is a new one available.

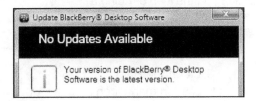

Getting the Latest Version of Desktop Software

If you have Desktop Software installed already use the Check For Updates method above. If you don't have it installed, then go to BlackBerry.com by using this link: http://us.blackberry.com/apps-software/desktop/ (link will be different if you are from a country other than the US). Otherwise, perform a web search for "BlackBerry Desktop Software download," pick the search result that looks correct, and go to the BlackBerry web site. Then follow the links to get to the download screen shown in Figure 2-1. Click the **Download** button at the bottom to get started.

TIP: We offer a free video tutorial showing you how to Update your version of BlackBerry Desktop Software on YouTube: http://www.youtube.com/watch?v=dnJpGugmyVc

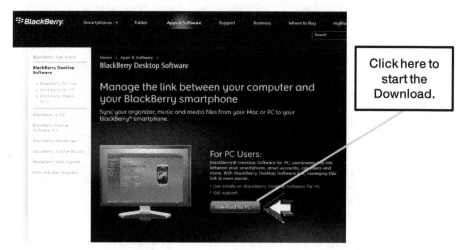

Figure 2-1. BlackBerry Desktop Software download page

Save the file to a place where you will remember it. This is a large file so it may take some time to download.

Installing BlackBerry Desktop Software

Locate and double-click the installation file that you downloaded. It will usually be in your **Downloads** folder unless you changed the default and will probably look something like Figure 2-2.

Figure 2-2. Locating the downloaded installation file on your computer

What the file looks like will depend on your view in Windows Explorer (e.g., Small Icons, Large Icons, List, or Details). The first few numbers in the file name correspond to the version of Desktop Software; in Figure 2-2 it shows **601_** for version **6.0.1**.

After you double-click the install file, then follow the directions to complete the installation.

Desktop Software Overview

One of the great things about your BlackBerry is the amount of information, entertainment, and fun that you can carry in your pocket at all times. But what would happen if you lost your BlackBerry or lost some of your information? How would you get it back? What if you wanted to put music from your computer on your BlackBerry? Fortunately, your BlackBerry comes with BlackBerry Desktop Software, which can back up information and load new applications on your BlackBerry, as well as synchronize your computer to your BlackBerry and add media to it.

TIP: We offer a free video tutorial showing you a Tour of BlackBerry Desktop Software v6.0 on YouTube: http://www.youtube.com/watch?v=uOkiJdllycg

To get started, click the **BlackBerry Desktop Software** icon on your computer, or go to **Start ➤ All Programs ➤ BlackBerry ➤ BlackBerry Desktop Software.** When it starts, you should see a screen similar to Figure 2-3.

Discovered Music Question

You will only see this pop-up window if you have already synced music from your computer library. We recommend selecting **Yes** to avoid having duplicates added to your computer media library (iTunes or Windows Media Player).

Make sure your BlackBerry is attached to your computer via the USB cable provided.

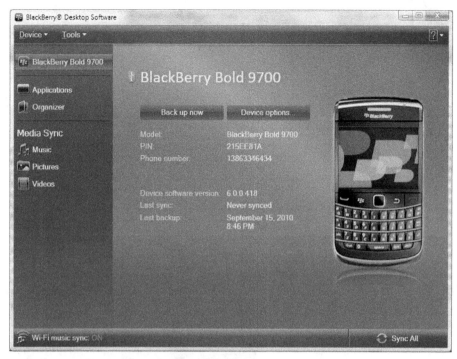

Figure 2-3. BlackBerry Desktop Software main screen

NOTE: The BlackBerry Bold 9700 is shown in this screen and several others. You will see your BlackBerry model when you connect to Desktop Software. Also, version 6.0.1 is shown in Figure 2-3; your version may be higher.

Entering Your Device Password

If you have enabled password security on your BlackBerry, you will have to enter your password on your computer right after you connect your BlackBerry to your computer.

Switch Devices (Old Phone to New BlackBerry)

TIP: We offer a free video tutorial showing you how to Switch Devices using BlackBerry Desktop Software v6.0 on YouTube: http://www.youtube.com/watch?v=sDUcgGoOPBA

If you are upgrading from another BlackBerry, Palm, or Windows Mobile device, you will want to use the Switch Devices function in Desktop Software.

1. To start the process, select **Device** > **Switch Devices** from the menu.

2. Then connect your old device to your computer with the USB cable and select it from this screen.

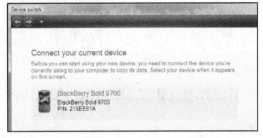

3. Then select whether or now you want both **Device Data** and **Third Party Applications**,(the default) and click **Next**.

NOTE: Some applications from your old BlackBerry may not work on the new BlackBerry.

4. Then all your data, settings and applications will be backed up from your old device.

5. Finally, you will be asked to connect your new BlackBerry to your computer to complete the process.

NOTE: You will not be able to copy any software from your Palm/Windows Mobile device to your BlackBerry. If you have a favorite application from Palm/Windows Mobile, then check out Chapter 20: "BlackBerry App World" or the software vendor's web site to see if they have a version compatible with your BlackBerry.

Synchronizing Organizer Data (Contacts, Calendar, Tasks and MemoPad)

You will probably come to rely on your BlackBerry more and more as you get comfortable using it. Think about how much information you have stored on it.

TIP: If you use Google for your contacts and calendar, you should use the Google Sync application instead of BlackBerry Desktop Software – see Chapter: 10 "Your Contact List" and Chapter 11:" Manage Your Calendar" for detailed steps.

Now ask yourself, "Is all my information safely stored in my computer or other safe place?" Then ask, "Is all my BlackBerry information synchronized or shared with the information in my computer software?" Synchronizing your BlackBerry with Desktop Software is very important. Your data will be safe and backed up or shared with the correct program on your computer—making things like your calendar, address book (contacts), and tasks more useful.

TIP: We offer a free video tutorial showing you how to Synchronize your Organizer Data using BlackBerry Desktop Software on YouTube:
http://www.youtube.com/watch?v=Q_i5eMcbsYE

Setting Up the Sync

Start up Desktop Software on your computer as shown above.

1. Connect your BlackBerry to your computer using the USB cable and make sure you see the green USB logo next to the name of your Blackberry in the main screen.

2. Click **Organizer** in the left column.

3. Click the **Configure Settings** button as shown in Figure 2-4.

Figure 2-4. BlackBerry Desktop Software – Configure Organizer Sync

4. Now you will see the main IntelliSync program window shown in Figure 2-5.

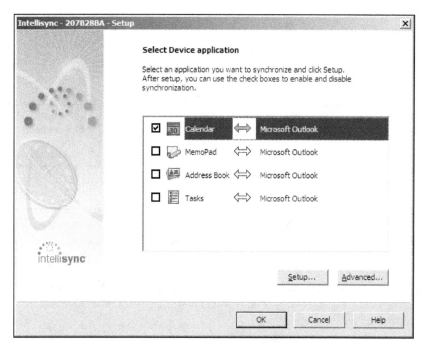

Figure 2-5. IntelliSync main setup screen in Desktop Software

5. To get started, just check the box next to the icon you want to sync (or click the name of the icon, or click the check box and then click the **Setup** button at the bottom). For example, clicking **Calendar** and **Setup** will bring you to screens with details on how to sync your computer's calendar to your BlackBerry.

6. Select your desktop application from the list in Figure 2-6 and click **Next**.

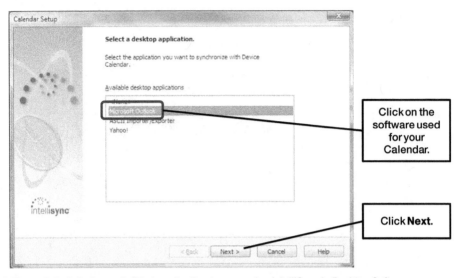

Figure 2-6. *Select your desktop application to sync using IntelliSync in Desktop Software.*

7. Now you will see options for two-way or one-way sync. Two-way sync means that any changes you make on your computer or BlackBerry will be synchronized to the other device. This is what you usually will want. Under special circumstances, you might require or want one-way sync.

8. Click **Next** to see an advanced screen with more options. This screen shows options for the calendar. The screens for the address book, tasks, and MemoPad may have different options. We recommend the settings shown to help make sure you never miss out on any data you enter on your BlackBerry if you forget to sync every day. These settings will sync calendar events up to 30 days old from your

BlackBerry and 180 days into
the future.

9. Repeat the procedure for all the applications you want
   synced. Click **Next** then click **Finish** on the next screen.
   You'll see similar screens for all four applications; with
   some minor variations (see Figure 2-7).

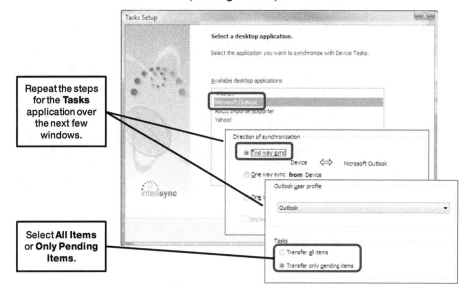

Figure 2-7. Task sync options in Desktop Software

Once the setup is complete for two-
way sync for all four applications,
your screen should look similar to the
image shown here.

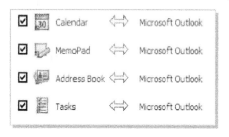

After the configuration is set, go back to the main synchronization screen and
check the **Synchronize Automatically** box if you want Desktop Software to
automatically synchronize as soon as you connect your BlackBerry to your
computer.

Finally, close out all the sync setup windows to save your changes.

Running the Sync

To get the sync started the first time, you have a few options. Desktop Software
allows you to Sync All (which includes both the Organizer and Media sync), or

sync either type of data separately (see Figure 2-8). Click the **Device** menu and select **Sync All** or **Sync by Type > Organizer**. Or you may click the **Sync All** button in the lower right corner.

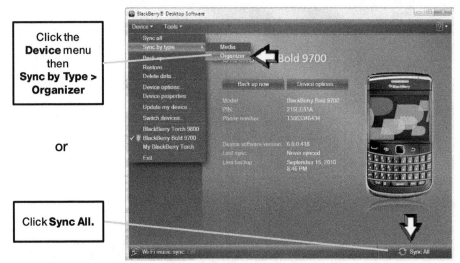

Figure 2-8. Steps to start the sync in Desktop Software

After starting the sync, you will see a small window pop up showing you status of the current sync. We show you some common messages below.

Automating the Sync

You can automatically sync your BlackBerry every time you connect it to your computer in the Device Options screen.

1. From the menu, select **Device** then **Device Options**.

2. Check the box next to **Organizer data** as shown. Click the box next to **Media files** to automatically sync those as well.

3. Click **OK**.

Accepting or Rejecting Sync Changes

During the sync, if there are additions or deletions found in either the BlackBerry or the computer application, a dialog box will appear giving you the option to accept or reject the changes. Click **Details** if you want to see more about the specific changes found.

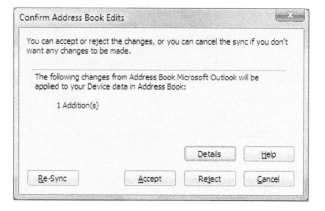

Usually, we recommend accepting the changes unless something looks strange. Finally, the synchronization process will come to an end and your data will be transferred to both your BlackBerry and your computer. If you want more details on what has changed on your BlackBerry and computer, click the **Details** button.

Troubleshooting the Organizer Sync

Sometimes you will encounter errors or warning messages when you try to sync. In this section we try help you through some of the more common issues.

Message That Default Calendar Service Has Changed

Sometimes you may see a message similar to the one shown. This could happen when you add new email accounts to your BlackBerry. Click **Cancel** on the screen shown to the right and follow the steps below to verify everything is **OK** before you sync again.

After pressing the **Cancel** button, follow these steps:

1. Click on the Search icon and type **Default**.

2. Click on the **Options** icon.

3. Click **Default Services**.

4. You will see a screen similar to the one shown. Verify that the email address under the **Calendar** item at the top is set correctly. If not, click and adjust it.

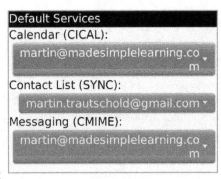

5. Press the **Menu** key and select **Save**.

6. Re-sync using Desktop Software, and if you see the same error—ignore it by clicking **OK**.

Closing and Restarting Desktop Software

Try closing down Desktop Software and restarting it; sometimes this can help with many issues you may be experiencing.

Removing and Reconnecting your BlackBerry

Sometimes a simple disconnect and reconnect can also help. Give it a try.

Getting More Help for Desktop Software Issues

Some of the Desktop Software sync issues can be particularly tricky. Before you pull out too much hair, you should go try the BlackBerry Technical Solutions Center. You should also try some of the more popular BlackBerry online discussion forums to see if others have experienced and solved similar issues.

To use the **BlackBerry Technical Solution Center** use your computer's web browser and find the site by doing a web search for it, or you can go to this web link: http://www.blackberry.com/btsc

Alternatively, you can pull up your favorite web browser search engine and try a web search for the particular issue you are facing.

The following are some of the BlackBerry forums that could be helpful with a variety of issues:

- www.crackberry.com
- www.blackberryforums.com
- www.berryreview.com
- www.blackberryrocks.com
- www.blackberrycool.com

Backup Data

TIP: We offer a free video tutorial showing you how to Add or Remove Applications using BlackBerry Desktop Software on YouTube: http://www.youtube.com/watch?v=8Fn1T5D_Vw0

In order to protect the information on your BlackBerry from being lost, damaged or stolen, we highly recommend you backup your BlackBerry on a periodic basis. You can even automate the backup in Desktop Software.

1. Start up **Desktop Software** and connect your BlackBerry to your computer.

2. Click the **Back up now** button in the middle of the screen or you click the **Device** menu and select **Backup** as shown.

3. You may be shown the **Back Up Options** screen where you can adjust the items related to the backup. If you do not see the **Backup Options** screen, (see Figure 2-9), then click the **Device Options** button in the middle of the screen and click the **Backup** tab at the top.

Skip Confirmations:

*   **Manual Backups** – check this box if you want to skip seeing a window asking you to confirm your backup options prior to a manual backup.

*   **Automatic Backups** – check this box if you want to skip seeing a window asking you to confirm your backup options prior to an automatic backup being performed.

Preferred Backup Settings (Backup Type):

*   **Full** includes all email and settings,

*   **Quick** does not include email and

*   **Custom** allows you to select individual types of data to backup.

Backup Files

*   **Save backup files to** – we recommend changing this to a location on your computer that is backed up regularly or to an external drive such as a network disk or USB thumb drive for safe keeping.

*   **Encrypt Backup Files** – for additional security you can force a password to be required to access the backup file.

4. Click the **OK** button to save your settings.

Figure 2-9. Backup Options Screen in Desktop Software

Automating the Backup Process

Backups are like chores you like to
forget – that's why there is a way
to automate them.

1. Go to the **Device** menu
    and select **Device
    Options** to see this
    screen.

2. Check the box next to
    Back up my device and
    select **Daily**, **Weekly**, **Bi-
    weekly** (every 2 weeks),
    or **Monthly**.

3. Click **OK** to save your
    settings.

Restore Data

Sometimes you may need to restore the data you have backed up to your
BlackBerry, we show you how below.

1. Start up **Desktop Software** and
    connect your BlackBerry to your
    computer.

2. Click the **Device** menu and select
    Restore as shown.

3. Click on the backup file you wish to restore. If you cannot
    see it listed, then click the **Change folder** button and move
    to the correct folder (see Figure 2-10).

4. You can choose to restore **All data and settings** (the default) or
    Select device data and settings. Choosing the second option then
    opens up a new part of the screen where you can check of individual
    data types to restore. This allows you to selectively restore only your
    Address Book, Calendar or other items.

5. Click **Restore** to start.

Figure 2-10. Restore Options Screen in Desktop Software

Delete Data

There are times when you may want to delete all the data on your BlackBerry or selectively delete just your address book (contacts), calendar, tasks or other data. In this section we show you how to accomplish this.

1. Start up **Desktop Software** and connect your BlackBerry to your computer.

2. Click the **Device** menu and select **Delete data** as shown.

3. You can choose to delete **All data** (the default) or **Selected data**. Choosing the second option then opens up a new part of the screen where you can check of individual data types to delete. This allows you to selectively delete only your Address Book, Calendar or other items (see Figure 2-11).

4. You also have check boxes allowing you to delete files from the internal media storage and to backup the data file before deleting (a good precaution). Finally, you can encrypt the backup if you choose.

5. Click **Delete** to start.

Figure 2-11. Delete Device Data Screen in Desktop Software

Working with Applications

Use **Applications** function in **Desktop Software** to add or remove software from your BlackBerry. This is also used to update your BlackBerry OS or system software. There are easier ways to load or remove software from your device—see Chapter 20: "BlackBerry App World."

TIP: We offer a free video tutorial showing you how to Add or Remove Applications using BlackBerry Desktop Software on YouTube:

http://www.youtube.com/watch?v=8Fn1T5D_Vw0

1. First, make sure your BlackBerry is connected to your computer.

2. Now click **Applications** in the left column to see the screen shown in Figure 2-12.

Figure 2-12. Applications main window in Desktop Software

3. To remove applications, click the **X** in the right column.

4. Sometimes after you download applications to your computer from the Internet, they do not automatically appear in this list. To add these files, you will need to click the Import Files button in the upper right corner and look for files that end with .ALX and .COD file extensions. Once you import these files, they will appear in the list.

5. When you're done selecting files, click the **Apply** button in the lower left corner.

Update Your Device System Software

If you do not have BlackBerry 6 on your device yet, you may be able to update your the device software using Desktop Software. You can upgrade or downgrade software using this feature.

Selected BlackBerry models can currently be updated to BlackBerry 6, we show you below how to check at BlackBerry.com to see if your device is eligible.

If you work at an organization that supplied your BlackBerry to you, your IT support team will have to enable your update, you cannot do it individually.

If you are an individual user, you can update your device yourself. It is a two step process:

Step 1: See if your device is available and download the BlackBerry 6 software for your device to your computer.

Step 2: Use Blackberry Desktop Software to update your device.

Step 1: Visit BlackBerry.com to check to see if the update is available for your device. Click the image below, or visit: http://us.blackberry.com/apps-software/blackberry6/update.jsp

Step 2: Use BlackBerry Desktop Software for Windows or Mac to install the update.

NOTE: You have the option of trying an 'over the air' update without using Desktop Software, but that process can take several hours and we have found that that process is somewhat prone to failure.

Watch our free video on YouTube showing how to update your BlackBerry using Desktop Software for Windows. The Mac process is a little different, but you should be able to get the feel for how to update using this video.

TIP: We offer a free video tutorial showing you the BlackBerry System Software update process on YouTube: http://www.youtube.com/watch?v=1cInMFp6IAY

Getting an Email when Software Updates are Available

Select **Device** then **Device Options** from the menu. Near the bottom you will see the section where you can be notified of software updates. Check the box or boxes and enter your email address. Click **OK** to save.

Notify me when software updates are available for my device

☑ Keep me subscribed to email notifications

☑ Use a different email address:
nartin@madesimplelearning.com

Checking the BlackBerry Site for System Software Updates

You can check yourself at any time for the latest software for any BlackBerry wireless carrier from this web page:
`http://us.blackberry.com/support/downloads/download_sites.jsp`

Click the carrier from your country.

Here is the link for AT&T software downloads:
`https://www.blackberry.com/Downloads/entry.do?code=577BCC914F9E55D5E4E4F82F9F00E7D4`

Here's the link for Verizon Wireless:
`http://vzw.smithmicro.com/blackberry/`

Once you get to the correct site, you need to select your BlackBerry from the drop down list and scroll down to see the available software.

Compare the version number shown in the main screen of Desktop Software to the version next to Applications shown on the web site. See Figure 2-13.

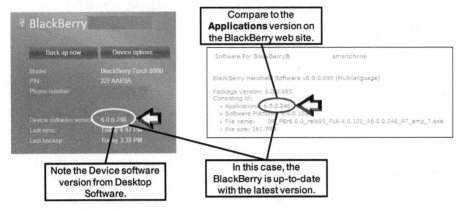

Figure 2-13. Applications main window in Desktop Software

If you see the version available on the BlackBerry web site is newer (higher), then click the download link.

After the software is downloaded, you need to install it on your computer by double-clicking on the downloaded file. You will have to close the Desktop Software in order to complete the installation.

Installing the BlackBerry System Software Update

When an update is available, you will see a new button in the main window in Desktop Software. This button will be called **Update My Device** and show you the new version that is available. Click that button and follow the steps to backup your BlackBerry and install the new system software.

> **NOTE:** This system software update can take 30 minutes or longer, so be prepared to do it when you don't need your BlackBerry for quite a while.

Chapter 3:
Windows PC Media and File Transfer

In this chapter we will help you get your important files and media from your Windows computer to your BlackBerry. Your BlackBerry is quite a capable media player on which you can enjoy music, pictures, podcasts, and videos. Like your computer, your BlackBerry can even edit Microsoft Office (Word, Excel and PowerPoint) documents.

You have a variety of choices about how to transfer documents and media and we explore all the most popular ones in this chapter. You will quickly see that some methods such as **USB Drive** transfer work well for pictures and documents (spreadsheets, word processing or presentation files), whereas you will want to use the Media Sync feature in BlackBerry Desktop Software to transfer your music playlists. Here are a few ways to transfer files and media between your BlackBerry and your computer:

- BlackBerry Desktop Software Media Sync

- USB Drive File Transfer

- Email the files to yourself as attachments *(if they are small enough)*

Verify Your Memory Card is Installed

Before you go too wild transferring all your music, videos, pictures and other documents to your BlackBerry, you want to make sure you have a Media Card installed. Since your BlackBerry has only 256 MB or 512 MB of on-board memory for programs and media files (depending on the model), you will need to make sure you have a memory card (also called a "media card") installed. It's easy to verify that you have the memory card installed and see how much free space is available. We show you how in the "Verifying the Memory Card

Installation and Free Memory" section of Chapter 1: "Getting Started." If you don't have a memory card, we show you how to install the MicroSD format card in your BlackBerry also in Chapter 1.

USB Drive File Transfer Method

The **USB Drive** transfer method allows you to directly copy or drag-and-drop any file types to your BlackBerry when it looks like another disk drive to your computer. We describe how to set up and use this method in the "Transferring Content to your BlackBerry Using USB Drive Mode" section of Chapter 1.

Sync Media with BlackBerry Desktop Software

> **NOTE:** In order to use the Media Sync, you need to install the latest version of BlackBerry Desktop Software. We show you how in Chapter 2: "Windows PC Setup."

Media Sync is a great tool that allows you to sync music, playlists, pictures and videos to your BlackBerry. You can even sync music using the Wireless Music Sync that takes place over your Wi-Fi network.

> **NOTE:** For those of you who have used BlackBerry smartphones for a while you will know that BlackBerry used to provide a separate stand alone Media Sync application but that application has now been absorbed into the Media Sync functionality within Desktop Software.

Confirm Your Media Sync Options

Before you use the Media Sync in Desktop Software, it is a good idea to make sure the Media options are set up correctly.

1. Start Desktop Software and connect your BlackBerry to your computer with the USB cable.

2. Click the **Device options** button in the main screen or select **Device** > **Device Options** from the menu (see Figure 3-1).

3. Click the **Media** tab at the top.

4. If you want to enable **Wi-Fi music sync**, check the top box.

5. Select your **Music source**. You can choose between **iTunes** and **Windows Media Player**.

6. We recommend leaving the box checked that says **Start iTunes to acquire album art**, otherwise you may not see any album art on your BlackBerry.

7. The next two buttons allow you to adjust where pictures and videos that you have taken on your BlackBerry will be stored on your computer. The defaults are the **pictures** and **videos** folders on your computer, but you might want to change it to a location that is backed up regularly.

8. You can also adjust where the synced media is stored on your BlackBerry. We recommend the media card.

9. You can use the slider at the bottom to adjust how much free space should be left over after the media sync is complete. This is space for any other files such as Microsoft Office documents, PDF files, or files you save from email attachments. Click **OK** to save your settings.

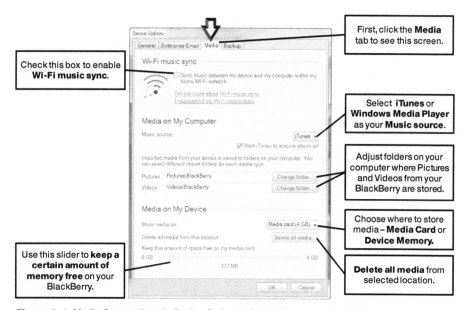

Figure 3-1. Media Sync options in Device Options of BlackBerry Desktop Software

Once you have your media options set, you are ready to sync your media.

Syncing Music

In order to set up the music, pictures and videos sync, you need to have BlackBerry Desktop Software running and your BlackBerry connected to your computer with the USB cable.

1. Click **Music** in the left column (see Figure 3-2).

2. If you want to sync all your music check the **All music** box at the top. Unless you have a smaller music library, it is fairly likely all your music will not fit on the BlackBerry. In that case use the other checkboxes to select more specifics.

3. Check boxes in the **Artists**, **Playlists** and **Genres** to sync all music from that particular artist, playlist or genre.

4. To view songs in a particular artist, playlist or genre, click on that item to highlight it and view the songs listed at the bottom of the screen.

5. If you want to find a song, click the **Search** area in the top right of the screen.

6. If you are feeling like trying something new or want to just be surprised by what is synced, click the **Random Music** button in the lower right corner. This will fill your BlackBerry with random songs from your library.

7. Click the **Sync** button in the lower right corner to start the music sync.

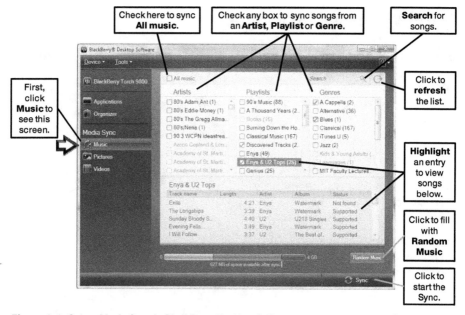

Figure 3-2. Set up Music Sync in BlackBerry Desktop Software

Some Music Cannot Be Synced

After you sync your music, you may see a pop-up message similar to this one saying certain songs could not be synced. Usually, this is because the songs are protected with DRM (Digital Rights Management) and can only be played on certain devices (e.g. iPod.) Sometimes songs are just not found.

Click the link at the bottom to view songs and determine exactly why they were not able to be synced.

Wi-Fi Wireless Music Sync

BlackBerry now offers a new feature called **Wireless** or **Wi-Fi Music Sync**. What this allows you to do is   view your computer's entire music library from your BlackBerry.

After you enable the **Wi-Fi Music Sync** as shown below, inside your **Music** app on your BlackBerry you will see that Wi-Fi Sync has been enabled.

Below are the steps to enable **Wi-Fi Music Sync**, then we show you how to use it on your BlackBerry.

Installing the Music Sync App on Your BlackBerry

Before you can sync music wirelessly, you need to use have the Wireless Music Sync app loaded on your BlackBerry. Here's how to get that done:

1. Start up **BlackBerry Desktop Software** and connect your BlackBerry with the USB cable to your computer.

2. From the **Device** menu, select **Device Options** and click the **Music** tab at the top.

3. Check the box under **Wi-Fi music sync** as shown in Figure 3-3.

Figure 3-3. Check the Wireless Music Sync in the Device Options Screen.

4. Click the **OK** button in the bottom right corner to load the app on your BlackBerry.

5. Then you will see a status window while the Wi-Fi Music Sync app is loaded on your device and your device is rebooted. This could take up to 30 minutes, but usually does not take any longer than about 10 minutes (see Figure 3-4).

Figure 3-4. Installing Wi-Fi Music Sync Status Window.

How to Enable or Disable Wi-Fi Music Sync

After you check the box and wait for the installation screen shown in Figure 3-3 and 3-4, your Wi-Fi Music sync should be enabled. If you want to check the status or disable the music sync, you need to start up the **Wi-Fi Music Sync** in the **BlackBerry Desktop Software** on your computer and follow these steps.

1. Start BlackBerry Desktop Software and connect your BlackBerry to your computer with the USB cable.

2. Select **Tools > Wi-Fi music sync** as shown.

3. On the next screen, select **Turn wireless sync on**.

TIP: This is the same screen where you will turn off wireless sync if you want to do that later.

4. Then, the app will make sure you have installed the **Wireless Music Sync** app on your BlackBerry. If it was not installed, the **Wireless Music Sync** will be installed at this time. It will then load up a list of your computer's music library on your BlackBerry including album art.

5. Finally, you will see a status message the Desktop Software screen showing that **Wi-Fi Music Sync** is **ON**.

TIP: Click this status message to turn Wi-Fi Sync off.

After this process is done, you will see a screen which gives you the requirements for Wi-Fi Music Sync to operate properly:

- Turn on Wi-Fi on your BlackBerry (See "Connecting with Wi-Fi" section of Chapter 1: "Getting Started.)

- Turn on your Wi-Fi router (This is a little strange -- Has your router ever been turned off?)

- Turn on your computer and have it connected to the Wi-Fi network.

- Click on any dimmed song or playlist on your BlackBerry to add it to your sync queue. When you come in contact with your home network, these songs are synced.

Now, you can grab any of the dimmed songs shown on your BlackBerry using Wi-Fi Music Sync.

NOTE: Some newer dual-band routers have more than one network to which you can connect. Your BlackBerry and computer must be connected to the same network for Wi-Fi Music Sync to work properly.

Using Wi-Fi Wireless Music Sync

After you setup the **Wi-Fi Music Sync**, you will notice that some songs, playlists and albums appear grayed out or dimmed in your BlackBerry **Music** app. These songs are in your computer library but not on your BlackBerry. If you click on any of these dimmed items, you can request that they be synced to your BlackBerry (see Figure 3-5).

> **TIP:** You can even request songs, artists or playlists when you are away from your home Wi-Fi network. What happens is that these requests are logged and when you return home the items are synced wirelessly and automatically behind the scenes!

The next time you come in contact with the Wi-Fi network where your computer is located (and your computer is turned on), you will receive the requested songs wirelessly via your Wi-Fi network.

| Click on any **dimmed song**. | Check to skip seeing this message again. | Click **Download** | See wireless download progress here. | When the download is complete, you can play the song. |

Figure 3-5. How Wireless Music Sync works in the Music app on your BlackBerry.

Some Songs Cannot Be Wirelessly Synced

You will notice that when you try to click on a dimmed song from your **Music** app, you will see a couple of different error messages.

Unsupported Format – this means the media is not playable on your BlackBerry or that it has been protected with Digital Rights Management (DRM).

Cannot be found – this means the song cannot be located on your main music library on your computer.

In both cases, you cannot sync these songs to your BlackBerry. Try checking to see if you can play these songs on your computer. Some of these songs may have been purchased in iTunes and are protected to only play on your Apple device.

Working with Pictures

You can transfer the pictures you snap on your BlackBerry back to your computer and sync selected pictures to your BlackBerry using media sync. Start up BlackBerry Desktop Software and connect your BlackBerry to your computer with the USB cable.

Click **Pictures** in the left column.

Working with Pictures on your Device (BlackBerry)

Click the **Device Pictures** tab at the top of the screen (see Figure 3-6).

If you want to change the default folder (Pictures/BlackBerry) location where your pictures will be imported, then click the **Change Import Folder** button.

If all the settings look fine, then click the **Import** button in the lower right corner to copy all pictures from your BlackBerry to the selected folder.

NOTE: You will see all the pictures disappear from view in the main window after they are copied, however they are not deleted from your BlackBerry. They are no longer marked as new pictures. In order to view the pictures on your BlackBerry, you need to use the pull-down menu under the **Device Pictures** tab and select **All Pictures**.

Figure 3-6. Importing Pictures taken on your Device (BlackBerry) to your Computer.

How to Delete Pictures from Your BlackBerry

You cannot delete pictures directly from within the view shown in BlackBerry Desktop Software, so you need to take an extra step.

1. You need to be able to click on one of the pictures shown on your device. If you no longer see any pictures, use the pull-down menu and select **All Device Pictures** near the top of

the screen.

2. **Right-click** on any image from the Device Pictures view and select **Show in Explorer**.

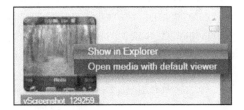

3. Now you will see all the pictures in the Microsoft Explorer program. From here, you can delete, move, copy or do whatever you want to one, several or all of the pictures.

4. Select one or more pictures using these methods:

    a. Use **Shift + Right-Click** to select several pictures in a row, or **Ctrl + Right-Click** to select individual pictures. **Ctrl + A** will select all pictures.

    b. Right click any highlighted image to **Delete**, Copy, or Cut them.

Working with Pictures on your Computer

Click the **Computer Pictures** tab at the top of the screen (see Figure 3-7).

You can do the following on this screen:

- If you want to add new folders to sync to your BlackBerry click the **Add Folder** button.

- Check or uncheck entire folders to sync.

- Check or uncheck individual pictures to sync.

When you're done selecting items, click the **Sync** button in the lower right corner to start the sync.

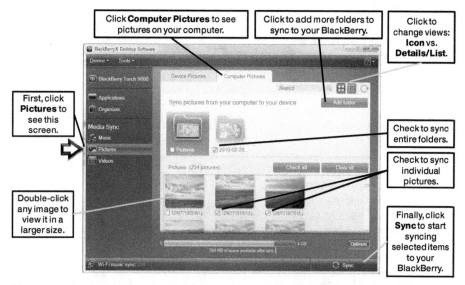

Figure 3-7. Syncing Pictures and Folders of Pictures from your Computer to your BlackBerry.

Working with Videos

You can transfer the videos you take on your BlackBerry back to your computer and sync selected videos to your BlackBerry using media sync. Start up BlackBerry Desktop Software and connect your BlackBerry to your computer with the USB cable.

Click **Videos** in the left column. The functionality for working with Videos is identical to the Pictures shown above, so once you get the feeling for working with pictures, you can use exactly the same steps to work with your videos. You can import, sync and delete in exactly the same way as with pictures.

Video Conversion and Quality

The only thing that is different with videos compared to pictures is that many of the videos need to be converted in order to play on your BlackBerry. This will happen by default if you don't change anything. However, you may want to make some adjustments to the conversion settings or turn it off altogether.

You will notice in the lower right corner of the screen when you click on the **Computer Videos** tab at the top of the screen that there is a check box and pull down menu.

The **Convert videos** check box is checked by default and we recommend leaving it checked unless you have a strong reason to uncheck it. (For example if you are certain that the videos you want to sync are already formatted and encoded to play perfectly on your BlackBerry.)

If you want to save space and are OK with a slightly grainier look and feel on your videos, then use the pull-down menu and select **Medium quality** or **Low quality**.

Troubleshooting Desktop Software

Sometimes when you are previewing a file or performing some other function, Desktop Software Manager may crash and stop responding. If this is the case, you can stop the program by following these steps:

1. On your computer, press **Ctrl + Alt + Delete**.

2. If you are given a choice, then select **Start Task Manager**.

3. From Window Task Manager (Figure 3-8), click the **Processes** tab.

4. Then scroll down and highlight the image name of **Rim.Desktop.exe**, as shown.

5. Click the **End Process** button at the bottom.

Figure 3-8. *Windows Task Manager*

6. On the screen that says **Do you want to end this process?** click **End process** to stop the program.

7. Now you can restart the program and try again.

Chapter 4:
Apple Mac Setup

This chapter shows you how to install the new BlackBerry Desktop Software on your Apple Mac computer and do the basics of synchronizing your contacts, calendar, tasks and memos, backup and restore, and more. If you want to transfer files and media with your Mac, then check out Chapter 5 "Apple Mac Media and File Transfer." (You may need some of the instructions in this chapter on how to install Desktop Software if you want to use it as your method to transfer files.)

Do you have a Microsoft Windows computer? If so please go to Chapter 3.

> **CAUTION:** If you plan on syncing with more than one computer (e.g., work, home, etc.)? Be sure to check the **with other computers (safer sync)** option on the **Device Options** screen (discussed later) if you plan on syncing your BlackBerry with multiple computers using Desktop Software. Otherwise, you could end up corrupting your BlackBerry and/or computer databases!

If you are a Google Contacts and Calendar User

Do you want a wireless, two-way automated sync and you use Google Contacts and Google Calendar? Try using **Google Sync** for your BlackBerry. This is a free application and give you a full two-way wireless sync.

BlackBerry Desktop Software for Mac

For years, Windows users have enjoyed seamless synchronization of their contacts, calendar, notes, and tasks with their PC via the BlackBerry Desktop Software. Now, the peace of mind that comes with knowing your data is fully backed up is available to the Mac user.

If you have never used BlackBerry Desktop Software, you will now be able to not only synchronize your data, but you will be able to back up, restore, sync your iTunes playlists, and more.

The Disk from the BlackBerry Box

It is fairly likely that the disk that arrived with your brand new BlackBerry has a version of Desktop Software for Mac that is already out of date. This is because many times, the CD was produced more than a month ago, and in the meantime a new version has been released. So we recommend grabbing the latest version from the internet directly from www.blackberry.com, as shown below.

Downloading and Installing Desktop Software for Mac

Desktop Software for Mac software is available for free from BlackBerry.com. The following exercise shows you how to install it:

1. Open up your web browser and go to the download page (Figure 4-1):
   http://na.blackberry.com/eng/services/desktop/mac.jsp.

2. Fill out the required information on the download page and then click **Download Now** to download the software.

Figure 4-1. Locating the download file on the BlackBerry web site

3. Once the file is downloaded, follow the steps you normally would perform to install any software on your Mac. If you have trouble or need assistance, please do a web search for "installing BlackBerry Desktop Software for Mac" to find all the latest online help.

NOTE: If you have been using another application to sync your BlackBerry to your Mac (e.g. Pocket Mac or the Missing Sync), you will receive another warning note letting you know that in order to proceed, the connection between your BlackBerry and the third-party synchronization software will need to be discontinued.

The installation process will begin. Follow the onscreen prompts as your Mac installs the new **Desktop Software** starting with the screen shown in Figure 4-2.

Figure 4-2. First BlackBerry Desktop Software installation screen

Starting Desktop Software – Device Options Screen

To locate the Desktop Software app, click the **Finder** icon and then click your **Applications** icon. The **BlackBerry Desktop Software** icon will be in your **Applications** directory.

Double-click the **BlackBerry Desktop Software** app and the Welcome/Device Options screen will appear, showing you information about your particular BlackBerry (Figure 4-3). On this screen you can adjust your device options.

Figure 4-3. BlackBerry Desktop Software for Mac Device Options screen

1. You can adjust the **Name** of your BlackBerry if you choose.

2. We recommend leaving the check box to Automatically sync when device is connected checked.

3. Next you see the **This device is synchronized** option.

   a. If you synchronize your BlackBerry with other computers, a network server, Google Sync for Calendar, or Google Contacts, select **with other computers (safer sync)**.

   b. If you are only planning on syncing your BlackBerry with this one Mac, you can choose **with this computer only (faster sync).**

4. Finally we recommend leaving the last box checked as well that has the software check for any device software updates (that is the operating system software for your BlackBerry).

5. Click **OK** when done.

Main View in Desktop Software

After you connect your BlackBerry the first time, Desktop Software will show you a picture of your BlackBerry, a clean interface displaying information along the left-hand bar, and commands along to top bar (Figure 4-4).

NOTE: This figure shows a BlackBerry 9800; your BlackBerry may look slightly different.

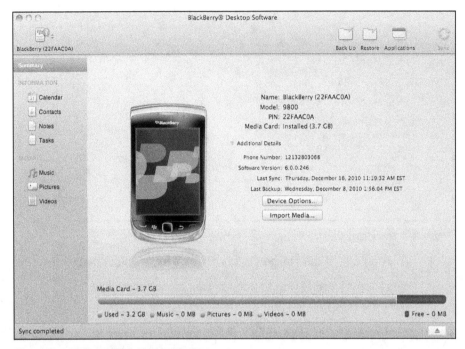

Figure 4-4. *Main screen in Desktop Software*

> **NOTE:** You see the BlackBerry 9800 Torch in this and other screen shots, you will see your own BlackBerry model (e.g. Bold or Curve) as you connect it to your Mac.

Using Desktop Software for Mac

One of the first things you will notice is the **Device Options** button next to the picture of your BlackBerry (Figure 4-4).

Clicking this brings you to the same **Device Options** screen you saw when you first started Desktop Software; see Figure 4-3).

Backup Options

From the **Device Options** screen, click **Backup** Back Up icon along the top.

Figure 4-5. Backup options in Desktop Software for Mac

If you want to create a backup each time you connect your device, just check the **Automatically back up when device is connected** box. You can then specify exactly what you wish to be backed up. (We cover the specific backup options in greater detail later in the chapter.)

Setting Up Your Sync Options

Click **OK** or **Cancel** to return to the main screen of Desktop Software (Figure 4-4), and look at the left column under where it says **INFORMATION** (Figure 4-6).

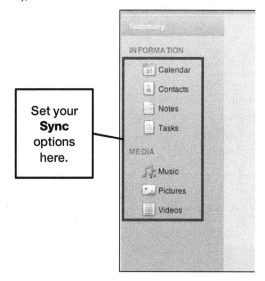

Figure 4-6. Sync options in Desktop Software for Mac

This is where you set the sync options for your calendar, contacts, notes, tasks as well as Media (Music, Pictures and Videos which we cover in Chapter 5).

1. Click any of the items below **INFORMATION**. In this case we will start with the **calendar** to be taken to the sync setup screen.

2. This screen has a similar look and feel to the calendar sync screen within iTunes, for those who are familiar with syncing an iPad, iPhone or iPod Touch and a Mac (see Figure 4-7).

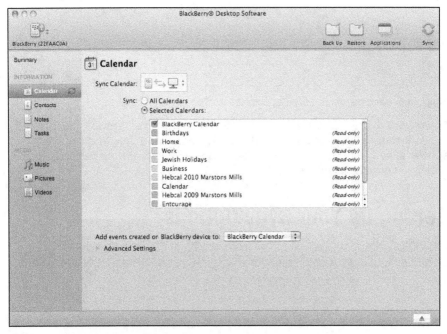

Figure 4-7. Calendar sync options screen

3. Desktop Software will notice all the calendars you have on your BlackBerry. In this example, we use Google Calendar, and have many different calendars, each set to a unique color. You see this in the list of calendars.

4. Click the box with the **Sync Calendar** option. The red X on this icon shows that the BlackBerry calendar will not be synced with the Mac calendars.

5. If you click the box and select the next item in the drop-down, the picture will change to show that now you desire a two-way sync between the Mac calendar and the BlackBerry calendar.

Sync Calendar:

6. You can also select into which calendar you want events to go that you create on your BlackBerry. The default is the Business calendar, but that can be changed to any calendar that you have set up on the device.

Add events created on BlackBerry device to: BlackBerry Calendar

Advanced Settings

Click the **Advanced Settings** tab at the bottom, and the options shown in Figure 4-8 will be revealed.

Add events created on BlackBerry device to: BlackBerry Calendar

Advanced Settings

Sync: ◉ All events
○ Only future events
○ Only events 14 days prior and 90 days after

☐ Replace all calendar events on this BlackBerry device

Figure 4-8. *Advanced sync settings in Desktop Software for Mac*

Like Desktop Software for the PC, you can specify as to whether you want to sync all events or future events only, or you can set individual parameters for synchronization.

> **TIP:** We do not recommend selecting **Only future events** unless you have a strong reason to do so. For example, say you made some notes on an event that was held yesterday in the BlackBerry calendar notes field. If you selected **Only future events**, these important notes would not be transferred to your Mac.

To replace all calendar events on the BlackBerry with events from your Mac's calendar, just click the check box at the bottom of the screen.

Syncing Contacts, Calendar, Notes, and Tasks

The procedure for setting the sync options for contacts, tasks, and notes is identical to what was just shown. The only things that change are the groups or events to choose within each category (see Figure 4-9).

Figure 4-9. Sync Contacts setup screen

On this screen, you can click next to **Sync Contacts**, as discussed previously, and choose either to not sync with the Mac or to perform a two-way sync. You can then choose to sync either all contacts or groups, or only selected groups from your address book.

Back Up and Restore

One of the great features now available to Mac users is the ability to backup and restore either you entire BlackBerry contents or just selected information on your Mac. **Back Up** and **Restore** begins with the two icons at the top of the main screen in Desktop Software.

Using Backup

The following explains how to use back up:

1. Click the **Back Up** icon 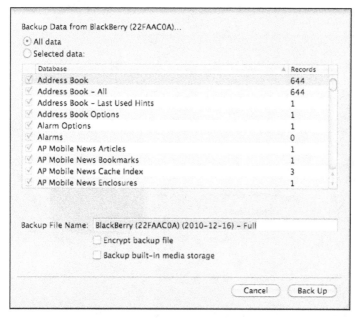 and you will be taken to the next screen where you specify exactly which information you wish to be backed up on your Mac (Figure 4-10).

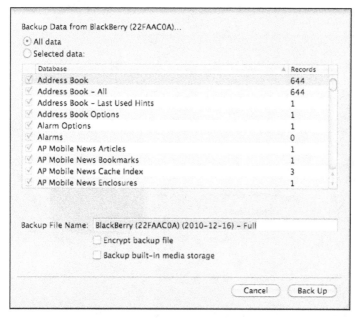

Figure 4-10. Backup screen in Desktop Software for Mac

2. Select either **All data** or **Selected data**, and then choose exactly which items you wish to back up.

3. Let's say that you are only really concerned with backing up your contacts, calendar, and notes—just check off each of those boxes and your backup will complete much faster.

4. You can specify the name of your backup for easy retrieval in the future.

5. Once you have made all your backup selections, click the **Back Up** button and the progress of the backup will be displayed in a dialog box.

Restoring from Backup

We all know that sometimes-unexplained things happen and we lose information in our BlackBerry. Maybe we try to update the OS and make a mistake, or maybe we sync with other computers and the information gets corrupted. Now Mac users have a reliable and safe way to restore data on their devices.

1. Click the **Restore** icon along the top row of the main screen in Desktop Software. You will then be taken to the restore options screen (Figure 4-11).

Restore Data to BlackBerry (22FAAC0A)...

Select the backup file to restore:

Backup File	Date
BlackBerry (22FAAC0A) (2010-12-08) - Full	12/8/10 1:56 PM
BlackBerry Bold (321490F9) (2010-10-21) - Full	10/21/10 10:05 AM
BlackBerry Bold (321490F9) (2010-06-13) - 2 - Full	6/13/10 10:43 AM
BlackBerry Bold (321490F9) (2010-06-13) - Full	6/13/10 10:40 AM
BlackBerry Bold (321490F9) (2010-06-04) - Full	6/4/10 5:02 PM
Backup before update BlackBerry Bold (321490F9) (...	5/29/10 4:05 PM

○ Restore all data
○ Restore selected data:

Database	Records
Address Book - All	643
Address Book - Last Used Hints	1
Address Book Options	1
Alarm Options	1
Alarms	0
AP Mobile News Articles	1
AP Mobile News Bookmarks	1

Dimmed entries are read-only databases and cannot be restored.

Open Another Backup File...   Cancel   Restore

Figure 4-11. Restore screen in Desktop Software for Mac

2. If you have made a backup file on your Mac (which is required so that you'll have a file you can restore), it will be shown in the top box under **Backup File**. If you have multiple backup files, they will all be listed here.

3. Select the file from which you wish to restore information (or, if you did a selective backup, selected data will be displayed in the second screen below.)

4. Click the **Restore** button and your BlackBerry will be restored just as it was when you made the backup file.

Adding and Removing Applications

For the first time, Mac users are now able to add or remove applications on their BlackBerry using the Desktop Software.

TIP: Most of the time, you will be using the BlackBerry App World app on your BlackBerry to add or remove applications. See Chapter 20: "BlackBerry App World" for more info.

1. Click the **Applications** icon (in the upper-right corner of the main screen) and you will be taken to the Install/Remove Applications screen in Desktop Software (see Figure 4-12).

Install/Remove Applications

Select a check box to add an application or clear a check box to remove it.

Install	Application	Version	Size
✓	Aces Traffic Pack Classic	1.0.2	4 MB
✓	Aces™ Cribbage Classic	1.0.1	6 MB
✓	AOL Instant Messenger	2.5.63	925 KB
✓	AP Mobile	2.5.6	612 KB
✓	AT&T AppCenter	3.0.33	893 KB
✓	AT&T Maps & AT&T Navigator	2.0.9037	7 MB
✓	ATT Code Scanner	1.0.22	1 MB
✓	BeeTagg QR Reader	3.0.6.15	792 KB
✓	Bejeweled	5.44.58	733 KB
✓	BlackBerry App World	2.0.1.12	976 KB
✓	BlackBerry Application Center	6.0.0	98 KB
✓	BlackBerry Maps	6.0.0.14	212 KB

+ Available Application Memory: 238 MB

Check for Updates   Cancel   Start

Last checked: Saturday, December 18, 2010 2:16:35 PM EST

Figure 4-12. The Install/Remove Applications window in Desktop Software for Mac

2. To check for updates to any of the applications installed including your BlackBerry operating system software, click the **Check for Updates** button in the lower-left corner.

3. Place a check mark in the box for any application that isn't checked already, and it will be installed on your device. Conversely, uncheck any box, and that application will be removed from your BlackBerry.

4. Click the **Start** button, and the selected or deselected applications will be either installed or uninstalled, depending on your selection.

TIP: For peace of mind, it is always a good idea to perform a backup both before and after you add or delete applications from the device.

Automating the Sync

In order to have your BlackBerry sync every time you connect it to your Mac, you will need change a setting in the Device Options screen.

1. Click the **Device Options** button below the picture of your BlackBerry on the main screen (Figure 4-13).

2. Then check the check box next to **Automatically sync when device is connected**.

Figure 4-13. Automate the sync in Desktop Software for Mac.

Chapter 5: Apple Mac Media and File Transfer

Your BlackBerry can be a great media player. In order to get all of your songs, videos, and other media from your Mac onto your BlackBerry, you'll need to learn some of the information in this chapter.

There are a few ways to load up media (music, videos, and pictures) and Microsoft Office documents (for use with **Documents to Go**) onto your BlackBerry:

- Use BlackBerry Desktop Software for Mac (described in this chapter).

- Use USB Drive Mode transfer (See the "USB Drive Mode Transfer" section of Chapter 1: "Getting Started" for help with this method).

- Attach a file or two to an email message you send yourself from your computer and open them on your BlackBerry (if they are under about 2 MB file size). This method will work for smaller files such as low-resolution pictures, small Microsoft Office documents, and smaller PDF files. This email attachment method will not work for music or videos because they are usually too large to email.

Setting Your Media Sync Options

Before you get set up to sync your Media, you will want to verify the options screen.

1. Start up Desktop Software for Mac as shown in the previous chapter.

2. Connect your BlackBerry to your Mac with your USB cable.

3. Click the **Device Options** button.

4. Click **Media** icon along the top of the screen (see Figure 5-1).

Device Options – BlackBerry (22FAACOA)

General Backup Media Import

Wi-Fi music sync
☑ Sync music between my device and my computer within my home Wi-Fi network

(Learn More...)

Store media files on: [Media Card – 3.7 GB ▲▼]
Adjust amount of space to reserve non-media data. Free Space will be available for media files.

Reserved: [10] %

■ Reserved – 377 MB   ● Free – 3.7 GB

Delete all media on device synchronized by BlackBerry®
Desktop Software: (Delete...)

(Cancel)   (OK)

Figure 5-1. Media Sync in Desktop Software for Mac

5. The top check box for Wi-Fi music sync will allow you to sync your music wirelessly. We cover this in detail later in this chapter.

6. Set the **Store media files on** either your **Media Card** or **Device Memory**. We recommend using the **Media Card** as your **Device Memory** is usually much more limited and you want to leave that free for emergencies.

7. We recommend increasing the **Reserved** space beyond the default 10 percent to something like 20-25 percent.

TIP: The reason you might want more **Reserved** space is to allow you to open or save items that you receive as email attachments on your BlackBerry or might decide to download while you are web browsing on your BlackBerry.

8. Click the **Delete** button next to the **Delete all music on device** statement (see Figure 5-1), and you can remove any or all the music synced to your device using Desktop Software.

9. Click **OK** to save your changes.

Why would you want to do that? Let's say you had previously synced a number of music playlists, videos and pictures you no longer want on your BlackBerry. Deleting all media with this button will be faster than changing your sync options.

You now have the option of syncing your iTunes playlists complete with album art, so you might want to start fresh and get rid of the other music on your BlackBerry.

Syncing Music

BlackBerry Desktop Software allows you to sync your iTunes playlists right onto the media card or device memory of your BlackBerry.

1. Click the **Music** icon under the **Media** line along the left-hand column of the main screen.

2. You will then be taken to the **Music Sync** screen. It provides you with some very nice options, as shown in Figure 5-2.

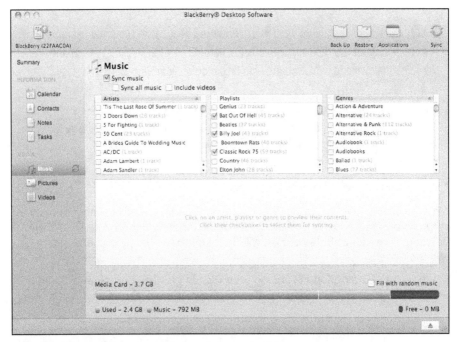

Figure 5-2. Sync Music screen in Desktop Software for Mac

As with iTunes, you can choose to sync all music and playlists or just selected playlists. New to the Mac Desktop Software is the ability to also sync specified **Artists** and/or **Genres**.

3. Just place a check mark in the **Sync Music** box at the top of the screen, and you can then select which playlists you wish to sync between your Mac and your BlackBerry.

4. Place a check mark in the **Fill with random music** box to have additional songs randomly placed on to the BlackBerry until the **Reserved** free space is met. (You set the **Reserved** space in the Media Options screen above).

5. In this example, we selected three playlists that we wanted on our BlackBerry—so we placed check marks in the appropriate boxes (see Figure 5-3).

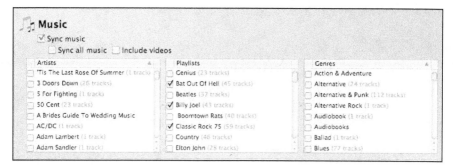

Figure 5-3. Syncing specific playlists, artists or genres in Desktop Software for Mac

Click the **Sync** icon at the top right of the screen to perform the music sync to your BlackBerry.

Syncing Pictures and Videos

Also new to Desktop Software for Mac is the ability to sync your pictures and videos in the same way you sync your music.

Syncing Pictures

Under the **Media** heading in Desktop Software, you will see **Music, Pictures** and **Videos**.

1. Click on **Pictures** in the left column to see the **Picture** sync screen.

2. The Mac Desktop Software will attempt to determine which program(s) you have available for pictures and where your picture albums are stored.

3. In Figure 5-4, our Mac has the photos stored in iPhoto, so that is what is shown.

4. Place a check mark next to any picture, album or event listed and it will be synced to your BlackBerry.

Figure 5-4. Syncing specific pictures, albums or events in Desktop Software for Mac

Syncing Videos

You can sync video content from your Mac in a very similar fashion to pictures.

1. Under the **Media** heading, click on **Videos**. You will see a very similar screen for selecting video content from your Mac to be synced to the BlackBerry.

2. Assuming that iTunes is your primary method for handling video, the screen will ask you to simply select which videos from iTunes you wish to be transferred to your BlackBerry.

3. Click any of the videos shown (See Figure 5-5.) You cannot check dimmed items that have DRM next to them as these are protected to only run on your Apple devices.

Figure 5-5. *Syncing specific videos, albums or events in Desktop Software for Mac*

Why can some videos and songs not be synced? (DRM)

In Figure 5-5 you see a red **DRM** next to many of the videos. These videos are purchased or rented in iTunes and are **DRM** protected (Digital Rights Management), so they can only be synced to and played on Apple devices (iPhone, iPod or iPad) registered with your iTunes.

NOTE: If your videos are protected with **DRM** (digital rights management) you will not be able to copy them to the BlackBerry. Also, if you choose too many videos for your memory card, you will receive a **Memory Full** error message in the lower right hand corner as shown above.

Importing Pictures and Videos from Your BlackBerry

On the main screen of the BlackBerry Desktop Software, under the **Device Options** button is an **Import Media** option.

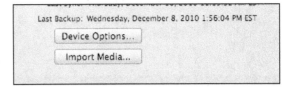

Import Media will show you all the new media on your BlackBerry – from songs purchased to pictures and videos taken and give you the option of importing this media to your Mac.

Click the **Import Media** button and select which media items you want imported to your BlackBerry (see Figure 5-6).

Figure 5-6. Import Media from your BlackBerry to your Mac

Using Wireless Music Sync

New to Desktop Software for Mac is Wireless Music Sync. Wireless Music Sync lets you keep your synced playlists up to date on your BlackBerry using your home Wi-Fi network.

Setting up Wi-Fi Music Sync

Click on **Device Options** and then on the Media tab. You will see a box next to **Wi-Fi Music sync**.

Check the box and you will be prompted that **Wi-Fi Music Sync** needs to be installed on the BlackBerry.

Wireless Music Sync will be installed on the BlackBerry. Once installation is complete, the BlackBerry will need to be restarted and then an information screen will appear. You will also be reminded to make sure your router is working and that your computer is turned on and connected to the same Wi-Fi network as your BlackBerry.

You will be reminded to turn on Wi-Fi on your BlackBerry (see the "Wi-Fi Connections" section of Chapter 1 for help).

Using Wi-Fi Wireless Music Sync on Your BlackBerry

After you setup the **Wi-Fi Music Sync**, you will notice that some songs, playlists and albums appear grayed out or dimmed in your BlackBerry **Music** app.

> **NOTE**: If you are not connected to the Wi-Fi network, you will see a "waiting for connection to desktop…" message. If you see that, make sure you connect to the Wi-Fi network. You may be prompted to connect to the Desktop Software once again with the USB cable the first time you enable Wi-Fi.

These songs are in your computer library but not on your BlackBerry. If you click on any of these dimmed items, you can request that they be synced to your BlackBerry (see Figure 5-7).

> **TIP:** You can even request songs, artists or playlists when you are away from your home Wi-Fi network. What happens is that these requests are logged and when you return home the items are synced wirelessly and automatically behind the scenes!

The next time you come in contact with the Wi-Fi network where your computer is located (and your computer is turned on), you will receive the requested songs wirelessly via your Wi-Fi network.

Figure 5-7. *How Wireless Music Sync works in the* **Music** *app on your BlackBerry.*

NOTE: If the Wi-Fi Music Sync does not work, the wireless connection was most likely not made. Try the following:

On your device, in the browser, type the following URL: **http://***type your computer IP address here:***4481/mediasync/music**. If you are prompted, accept the certificate warning. If the webpage displays the text "Wireless music sync", then your device is connected to the same network as your computer. If you receive a display error, your device is not connected properly to the same network as your computer or there might be a firewall issue or routing issue.

If your computer, router, or wireless network has a firewall, verify that ports 4481 and 4482 are open for TCP and UDP, and that the BlackBerry Desktop Software is allowed by the firewall. For more information and instructions, see the documentation for your firewall software and/or router.

If your router has UDP broadcast, verify that UDP broadcast is turned on. Most routers support this feature and do not mention it, but your router might need special configuration. For instructions, see the documentation that came with your router.

Verify that your gateway IP address is the same on both your device and your computer, and that both your device and computer IP addresses are on the same subnet.

Tip Courtesy of www.blackberry.com - Copyright 2010 Research In Motion Limited. All Rights Reserved.

Some Songs Cannot Be Wirelessly Synced

You will notice that when you try to click on a dimmed song from your **Music** app, you will see a couple of different error messages.

Unsupported Format – this means the media is not playable on your BlackBerry or that it has been protected with Digital Rights Management (DRM).

Cannot be found – this means the song cannot be located on your main music library on your computer.

In both cases, you cannot sync these songs to your BlackBerry. Try checking to see if you can play these songs on your computer. Some of these songs may have been purchased in iTunes and are protected to only play on your Apple device.

USB Drive Mode Transfer for Your Media Card

This works whether you have a Windows or a Mac computer. We will show images for the Mac computer process, but it will be fairly similar for a Windows PC. This transfer method assumes you have stored your media on a MicroSD media card in your BlackBerry.

1. To get to this screen, click the **Search** icon from your **Home** screen and type "storage."

2. Click the **Options** icon and click on **Storage**.

3. Make sure **Media Card Support** for your media card is checked (turned on), and other settings are as shown.

4. Now connect your BlackBerry to your computer with the USB cable. Choose **USB Drive** from the three options shown on the screen.

5. Your media card will look just like another hard disk to your computer (similar to a USB flash drive).

TIP: If you choose the **Sync Media** option then the Desktop Software will open and attempt to sync media using the options described earlier in this chapter.

Using USB Drive Mode

NOTE: You will need to install Desktop Software for Mac in order to be able to use this mass storage option. This is because Desktop Software contains drivers required to connect your BlackBerry to your Mac.

Once connected, your Mac will see your BlackBerry as a mass storage device and mount it as an external drive.

The BlackBerry will also be visible if you click the **Finder** icon in the dock. It will be listed under **Devices**.

> **NOTE**: In the image to the right, there are two devices listed – one is the internal memory for the BlackBerry called "BlackBerry 1," and "No Name" is the Media Card.

Exploring the Drive

Right-click the icon for the BlackBerry or Media Card and choose **Open**—or double-click on the **Desktop** icon and open the drive (see Figure 5-8).

Now you can explore your BlackBerry as you would any drive. You can copy pictures, music, and video files by just dragging and dropping to the correct folder, or you can delete files from your BlackBerry by clicking the appropriate folder, selecting files, and dragging them to the trash.

> **NOTE:** Your music, video, ring tone, and picture files are located in the folder called **BlackBerry**.

Figure 5-8. Finding media on the BlackBerry

Copying Files Using USB Drive Mode

After your BlackBerry is connected and in USB Drive Mode, just open up your computer's file management software. On your computer, start your Finder. Look for another hard disk or BlackBerry model number that has been added.

NOTE: You will see your own BlackBerry model number (e.g., BLACKBERRY_9800) or another way of identifying your BlackBerry like BlackBerry 1.

When you plug your BlackBerry into your Mac, it will identify the main memory and the contents of the MicroSD card as two separate drives, and place them right on your desktop for easy navigation.

On your computer, click the **Finder** icon in the lower-left corner of the dock. On Windows, click the disk drive letter that is your BlackBerry media card. You will see your devices (including both BlackBerry drives) on the top and your places (where you can copy and paste media) on the bottom.

To copy pictures (or other items) from your BlackBerry, follow these steps:

1. Select the pictures from the **BlackBerry/pictures** folder using one of the following methods:

   - Draw a box around some pictures to select them.

   - Click one picture to select it.

   - Press **Command+A** to select them all.

   - Press the **Cmd** key and click to select individual pictures.

2. Once selected—Ctrl-click or right-click one of the selected pictures and select **Cut** (to move) or **Copy** (to copy) (see Figure 5-9).

Figure 5-9. *Status of copying files to your BlackBerry*

3. Click any other disk/folder on your computer (e.g., **Documents**), and navigate to where you want to move/copy the files.

4. Once there, right-click again in the right window where all the files are listed, and select **Paste**.

You can also delete all the pictures/media/songs from your BlackBerry in a similar manner. Navigate to a BlackBerry/(media type) folder such as **BlackBerry/videos**. Press **Command+A** on your computer keyboard to select all the files, and then press the **Delete** key to delete all the files.

You can also copy files from your computer to your BlackBerry using a similar method. Just go to the files you want to copy and select (highlight them). Then right- click **Copy** and paste them into the correct **BlackBerry/[media type]** folder.

> **NOTE:** Not all videos, images, or songs will be playable or viewable on your BlackBerry. Use Desktop Software for Mac to transfer the files; most files will be automatically converted for you.

Chapter 6:
Typing, Spelling, Search, and Help

In this chapter, we help you get typing as fast and accurately as possible on your BlackBerry, show you the useful **Word Substitution** feature (which was called "AutoText" in previous BlackBerry devices), look at the built-in **Spell Checker**, dig into the **Universal Search** and also show you how to find **Help** right on your BlackBerry.

The Trackpad – Scrolling and Clicking

Using the **Trackpad** is like using a mouse on a computer – you scroll using the **Trackpad** to highlight an item, then click or press the center of the **Trackpad** to select a highlighted item.

Scrolling is done by slowly "gliding" or quickly "swiping" over the **Trackpad** with your finger.

The "double-swipe" or "persistent-swipe" is useful on the **Home** screen when you are on a screen of icons and want to move a screen to the left or right. Just keep swiping on the trackpad that direction and eventually, usually on the second swipe, your screen moves to the next icon page. Similarly, if you are on the Home screen with only one or two rows of icons, keep swiping down and you will eventually open up the tray and see all your icons on that page.

Clicking and holding the **Trackpad** is sometimes referred to as a "long press." When you do this many times you will see a pop-up menu appear on the screen with some relevant options.

You can adjust the **Trackpad** to suit your own preferences, as we show you below.

Trackpad Sound and Sensitivity

The nice thing is you can adjust the speed of the **Trackpad** as well as whether or not it makes a soft clicking sound when you move it.

1. Click on the **Search** icon and type "trackpad."

2. Click on the **Options** icon (wrench).

3. Click on **Trackpad Sensitivity**.

4. Click on the **Horizontal Sensitivity** or **Vertical Sensitivity** number. The default is 70; higher is more sensitive, lower is less.

5. Check the box next to **Audible Roll** to hear a soft clicking sound as you move or glide the **Trackpad**.

6. Press the **Menu** key and select **Save**.

TIP: You may find that your Trackpad moves too quickly up or down lines. If so, then reduce the **Vertical Sensitivity** to 50 or lower.

Typing Tips for Your BlackBerry

In this section we get you started with a lot of good typing tips to help you save time and increase accuracy.

Press and Hold for Automatic Capitalization

Here's an easy way to get uppercase letters as you're typing:

On the keyboard, simply press and hold the letter to capitalize it.

Caps Lock and Num/Alt Lock

Using the keyboard, to lock the **Caps** key to TYPE ALL UPPERCASE, press the **Alt** key, then press the right **Shift** key. Click on the either **Shift** key to turn off **Caps** lock.

Using the keyboard, if you want to type only numbers or the symbols shown on the top of the keys, turn on **Num/Alt** lock by pressing the **Alt** key and then the left **Shift** key. Click on the either **Shift** key to turn off **Num/Alt** lock.

Automatic Period and Cap at End of Sentence

At the end of a sentence, just press the **Space** key twice to get a "." (period). The next letter you type will be automatically capitalized.

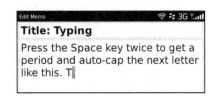

Typing Symbols

There will be times when you want to type the symbols shown on the keyboard, in this section we show you how.

Using the keyboard, you can type the symbols and numbers shown on the top of the keys by pressing the **Alt** key then the key on the keyboard. For example, to type an @, you would press **Alt** then press the **P/@** key.

To type symbols not shown on the keyboard, you need to press the **Sym** key just to the right of the **Space** key. Then you will see the first of two extra symbols screens. Roll the **Trackpad** to the left or right to switch between the two screens (see Figure 6-1).

Figure 6-1. Accessing symbols not shown on the keyboard

Select the symbol by pressing the associated letter or gliding and clicking the **Trackpad**. In the image above, if you press the letter **C** on your keyboard while viewing Page 1/2, you'd get the symbol for the Japanese Yen currency. Notice that Page 2/2 are simply the same symbols that you can easily access by pressing the **Alt** key.

Quickly Typing Accented Letters and Other Symbols

If you want to type common accented letters, you can do so quickly on the keyboard. The process is a little different as described below.

You can easily type standard accented characters such as Á by pressing and holding a letter on the keyboard and gliding the **Trackpad**.

Try this: Press and hold the letter **A** to scroll through these accented characters related to A: À Á Â Ã Ä Å Æ (both upper and lower case).

> Letters this trick works on are: E, R, T, Y, U, I, O, P, A, S, D, K, C, V, B, N, M.

> Letters that give you some other common characters: V key for ¿, T key for trademark symbol, C key for copyright symbol, R key for registered trademark symbol.

Editing Text

Making changes to your text is easy with the BlackBerry.

Click on anywhere on the screen or move your finger over the **Trackpad** to position the cursor.

Edit text using **Del** or **Alt+Del**.

Use the **Del** key to erase characters to the left of the cursor.

Hold the **Alt** Key and press **Del** to delete characters under the cursor.

The Mighty Space key

Like many of the keys on the BlackBerry, the space key can do some very handy things for you as you type.

Using the Space key While Typing an Email Address

On most handhelds, when you want to enter the @ or a period for an email address, you need a complicated series of commands—usually a **SHIFT** or **ALT** plus another key.

On the BlackBerry, you don't need to take those extra steps. When you're typing the email address, just press the **Space** key once after the user name (martin, for instance) and the BlackBerry will automatically insert the @— "martin@". Skip typing the dot as well. Another click on of the **Space** key will type the dot before **.com**.

Quickly Navigating Drop-Down Lists

The **Space** key is also great at moving you down to the next item in a list. In a minute field, for example, pressing **Space** jumps to the next 15 minutes. In an hour field, you jump to the next hour, and in a month field, you jump to the next month. In any other type of field, pressing the space key jumps you to the next entry.

Give it a try.

1. Click on your **Calendar** icon.

2. Start scheduling a new calendar event by clicking the **Trackpad** anywhere in **Day** view.

3. Glide down to the month and press **Space.** Notice you advance one month.

4. Glide over to the hour and press **Space.** You advance one hour.

5. Finally, glide to the minutes and press **Space.** Notice that you move 15 minutes forward.

These great tricks let you quickly reschedule calendar events.

Jump to First Letter Trick

You can use the letter keys on your keyboard to instantly jump to the first item matching either letter on the key (if there are two letters), or to jump to a matching menu item, or to a matching item in a list (like the long list that appears when you press the Options icon).

Using Number Keys to Type Dates and Times

You can use the number keys on your keyboard to instantly type a new date or time or to select an entry in a drop-down list with that number.

Examples include:

Typing 40 in the minute field to set the minutes to 40;

Typing 9 in the hour field to get to 9 AM or PM.

This also works in fields where drop-down list items start with numbers, as in the Reminder field in calendar or tasks. Typing a 9 immediately jumps you to the **9 Hours** setting.

Fine-Tuning Your Typing, Spelling and More

You can also customize how your BlackBerry handles your typing, spelling and related items.

1. From your **Home** screen, click the **Search** icon and type "**typing**."

2. Click on the **Options** icon.

3. Click on **Typing**.

You can select the following for your keyboard:

Select the style of typing –

Predictive – this is where the BlackBerry tries to guess the word you are typing and shows the guesses in a drop-down list for you to select.

Direct – this shows only the letters you type without any guessed words.

For the **Predictive** option, you can click on the **Advanced Style Options** button to see additional screens of options (see Figure 6-2).

Figure 6-2. Advanced Syle Options screens for Predictive typing.

Selecting Text to Copy, Cut or Delete

The fastest way to select text to copy, cut or delete is to place the cursor where you want (using the **Trackpad**.)

1. Press the **Shift** key to start selecting text.

2. Roll the **Trackpad** to highlight the text.

3. Once you have the text selected, press the **Trackpad** key and select **Copy** or **Cut**.

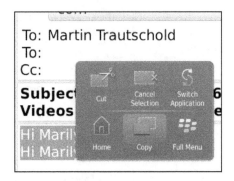

> **TIP:** Check out the "Copy and Paste" section of the Quick Start Guide for more on copying and pasting text between apps.

Save Time with Word Substitution (AutoText)

In this section, we show you some great tips and tricks to save time and increase accuracy for words and phrases that you may have to type many times. If you have used BlackBerry smartphones before, this feature was called **AutoText** on older devices. **Word Substitution** can help you by allowing you to skip typing the apostrophe in most contractions and automatically common spelling mistakes.

We will show you how to come up with useful **Word Substitutions** for just about anything you can imagine:

- An email you send frequently.

- Legal disclaimer text.

- Language describing your products or services.

- A phrase, paragraph or other text you commonly type.

- A set of directions to your home or office.

- Various different email signatures.

- Your home or office address.

- A special time stamp that automatically types today's date and time.

Just about anything that you might want to type frequently.

Standard Word Substitutions

Sometimes, typing on the little BlackBerry keyboard produces less than desirable results. Fortunately, for the more common misspellings, there are hundreds of standard or pre-loaded Word Substitutions. Below is a list of some of the more common and useful ones.

acn > can	Arent > Aren't	Cant > Can't	Wont > Won't
Didnt > Didn't	Dont > Don't	Teh > The	Hel > He'll
Wel > We'll	Wer > We're	Yr > year	Mn > Minutes
Hr > hours	Lt > current time	Ld > current date	Shel > She'll

TIP: Knowing **Word Subsituion** is there to help you get things right will allow you to type with greater abandon on your BlackBerry. Take a few minutes to browse the **Word Subsituion** pre-loaded entries, especially the contractions, so you can learn to type them without ever using the apostrophe.

In order to view the standard **Word Substitution** pre-loaded entries, follow these steps:

1. From your **Home** screen, click the **Search** icon and type "**word**."

2. Click on the **Options** icon.

3. Click on **Word Substitution.**

4. Scroll up or down or type a few letters to find a particular entry.

5. Press the **Escape** key or **Red Phone** key to back out to your

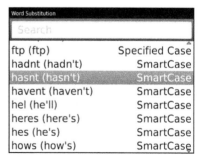

Home screen.

You can also create custom Word Substitutions for more advanced things like automatically typing an email signature, driving directions, a canned email, routine text describing your products or services, legal disclaimer text, anything!

Creating Custom Word Substitutions

To create your own custom **Word Substitutions**, navigate to the list of existing Word Substitutions as we described above.

To create a new entry, follow these steps:

1. From the list of **Word Substitutions**, press the **Menu** key and select **New**.

2. Under **Replace**, type the text you want to be replaced. In this example, we typed **homeaddr**.

> Word Substitution: New
> Replace:
> homeaddr
> With:
> Martin Trautschold
> Cell: 386 555 1253
> 25 Main Street Way
> Ormond Beach, FL 32177
> Using: SmartCase ▼
> Language: All Locales ▼

3. Under **With:** type the text you want to appear when you type your new word. In this case we type our name contact information and home address.

4. For **Using,** you can select **SmartCase** or **Specified Case.** **SmartCase** will replace the text whether or not the case matches exactly, for example **Homeaddr** would work as would **homeaddr**.

5. For **Language** you can select **All Locales** (default) or only specific languages such as **English** or **Spanish**.

6. Press the **Menu** key and select **Save**.

Now, you are ready to test out your new Custom Word Substitution. Open up a MemoPad or compose a new email message. Type your new word (**homeaddr**) and press the **Space** key to see the substitution (See Figure 6-3).

Figure 6-3. *Using your new Custom Word Substitution entry.*

Edit or Delete an Entry

You may need to edit or remove a **Word Substitution** entry. The steps to get this done are very similar to creating a new one:

1. Return to the **Word Substitution** list by repeating the steps shown above.

2. Type a few letters to find the entry you wish to change or delete.

3. Press the **Menu** key, and select **Edit** or **Delete**.

Advanced Features – Macros – Time Stamp

A very useful feature of Word Substitution is that you can actually insert macros or shortcuts for other functions such as the current time and date, your PIN, or owner information. You can even simulate pressing the **Backspace** or **Delete** keys.

Let's create a new entry called **ts** (**time stamp**) that will instantly show the current time and date.

1. Start by creating a new entry as you did above.

2. Type the **ts** under **Replace**.

3. Move the cursor down to under **With:**

4. Press the **Menu** key and select **Insert Macro.**

5. Now, scroll up or down and select the macro you want. In this case, we want a short date (%d) which is **mm/dd/yy**

format.

6. Press **Space**, type a hyphen (-), and then press **Space**.

7. Press the **Menu** key and insert the short time (%t) macro. The entry should now look like this image to the right.

TIP: You could also simply type the **%t** to save a few steps. Read below for a list of all the two-character macro shortcuts.

Now, whenever you want to insert the current date and time, just type your new

Title: Meeting ts

entry **ts**.

Press the **space** key to see the date/time.

Title: Meeting 1/31/2009 - 9:25a

Here's a list of the standard **Word Substitution Macros:**

%d	Short Date	
%D	Long Date	
%t	Short Time	
%T	Long Time	
%o	Owner Name	
%O	Owner Information	
%p	Your Phone Number	
%P	Your PIN	
%b	Backspace	
%B	Delete	
%%	Percent	

Title: Macros List

Short Date: 9/22/2008
Long Date: Mon, Sep 22, 2008
Short Time: 8:12p
Long Time: 8:12:29 PM
Owner Name: Martin Trautschold
Owner Info: If found, please contact Martin Trautschold office: 1-386-506-8224.
123 Main Street
Anytown, STATE 38928

Using Your Spell Checker

Your BlackBerry comes with a built-in Spell Checker.

Normally, your Spell Checker is turned on to check everything you type. Words that seem to be misspelled are underlined and suggestions are shown.

1. If you see the correct word just click on it or click on it with the **Trackpad**.

2. If you want to ignore the word, cancel the spell check or add this word to your custom dictionary, then press the **Menu** key.

3. From the menu select one of these options: **Ignore Once, Ignore All, Add to Dictionary** or **Cancel Spell Check**.

Using the Custom Dictionary

Sometimes, you may use unique words (such as the names of local places) in your emails that are not found in the standard dictionary. In this case, you may add these words to your own custom dictionary. The advantages of this are (1) that you will never again be asked to replace that word with something suggested and (2) if you misspell this custom word, you will be suggested the correct spelling.

Adding a Word to the Custom Dictionary

Let the Spell Check program notice the word that it believes is misspelled. In this example, we are using "Funfetti" (a brand of cake that Martin Trautschold's family enjoys) that is not in the standard dictionary.

The spell check program will suggest options for replacing the word.

1. Press the **Menu** key.

2. You will see options to **Ignore Once, Ignore All** or **Cancel Spell Check**.

3. Click the **Add to Dictionary** to add this new word to your own custom dictionary.

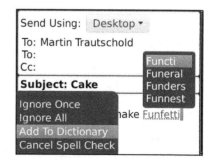

Next time we spell "Funfetti," it will not be shown as misspelled. Even better, the next time we misspell Funfetti (e.g. "Funfeti"); the spell checker will find it and give us the correct spelling.

Edit or Delete Words in the Custom Dictionary

Mistakes happen. Sometimes, you press the wrong menu item and inadvertently add incorrectly spelled words to the Custom Dictionary. The authors have done this plenty of times.

1. From the **Home** screen, click on the **Search** icon and type "Custom."

2. Click on the **Options** icon then **Custom Dictionary**.

3. Once you are viewing the **Custom Dictionary** words, click on any word to simply edit it.

4. To add, delete words or even clear out the entire dictionary, highlight the word by using the Trackpad to roll up or down, then press the **Menu** key and select **New**, **Edit**, **Delete** or **Clear Custom Dictionary**.

5. When done, press the **Menu** key and **Save**.

Universal Search

Your BlackBerry can hold so much information that it can sometimes be difficult to keep track of where everything is on the device. Fortunately, the BlackBerry comes with a comprehensive **Search** program (also known as "Universal Search") to help you find exactly what you might be looking for.

In this chapter, we will show you how use the **Search** program across your email, music, contacts, application names, options functions, and even across the web, as well as how to filter your search information to show only what you want.

> **TIP:** You can even use the **Search** program to search through your calendar events and answer questions such as the following:
>
> When is my next meeting with Sarah?
>
> When did I last meet with Sarah?
>
> For this feature to work, you need to type people's names into your calendar events as you enter them. For you example you might enter the following: **Meet with Sarah** or **Lunch with Tom Wallis**.

Understanding How Search Works

As you get used to your BlackBerry, you will begin to rely on it more and more. The more you use it, the more information you will store within it. It is truly amazing how much information you can place in this little device.

At some point, you will want to retrieve something – a name or a word or a phrase – but you won't remember exactly where you stored that particular piece of information. This is where the **Search** program can be invaluable.

> **TIP:** Check out the "Universal Search" section of the Quick Start Guide at the beginning of this book to learn how to enable automatic **Search** when you start typing letters from the **Home** screen.

By default, if you start typing letters from any home screen as shown to the right, you will see those letters appear in the Search field at the top.

If you don't see your letters appear automatically, then you have turned on your Application Shortcuts and need to click on the Search icon (magnifying glass) first before you start typing.

Notice that icons start appearing and changing at each additional character you type.

In the image shown above, three contacts appeared, email, text messages, calendar items, the Help app, and a number of other search apps appeared. If you click on any search app such as Search **Calendar**, the search phrase that you typed (in this case "help") will be searched in the appointments in the

Calendar app. Keep scrolling down and you will see that you can search the **App World**, **Facebook**, **YouTube** and even the web in general.

Examples of Searches

You can search for just about anything on your BlackBerry or on the web using the **Universal Search** app. Below are a few types of searches to get you thinking about what is possible.

- Find all videos on **YouTube** that have the word "baby" in the title or description.

- Find every contact in your **Contacts** app (address book) that live on a certain street or in a certain town.

- Find every appointment in your **Calendar** that has the word "dentist" in it – to help you find when your next dentist appointment is scheduled.

- Find all songs or artists in your **Pandora** app that have the word "love" in their song title or artist name.

- Find that **Text Message** where you or someone you were chatting with mentioned the phrase "best book."

- Do a **web search** for pizza in your town or postal code.

- Do a **web search** for the flight number of the person you are picking up at the airport to check to see if their flight is on time.

- Do a **web search** for 303 to understand where that area code is located.

Improving Your Search Quality

So far we've covered some of the things you might search for, as well as how to go about implementing a search. Next, we will cover some valuable tips and tricks that help you create more effective searches.

The more information you enter on your BlackBerry (or enter on your desktop computer and sync to your BlackBerry), the more useful your device becomes. Combining a great deal of useful information with this **Search** tool means you truly have a very powerful and useful handheld computer. As your BlackBerry fills up, however, the possible places where your information is stored increases. Also, a search might not turn up the exact information you are looking for due to inconsistencies in the way you store the information.

Try to be consistent in the way you type someone's name – for example, always use *Martin* instead of *Marty* or *M* or any other variation. This way, the **Search** program will always find what you need.

Occasionally, you should check your address book for contacts with multiple entries. It is easy to wind up with two or three entries for one contact if you add an email one time, a phone number at another time, and an address on still another occasion. Restricting your contacts to one entry each helps you stay organized – and helps you find what information you're looking for more easily.

TIP: It is usually easier to do this cleanup work on your computer, and then sync the changes or deletions back to your BlackBerry.

If you're not sure whether you are looking for *Mark* or *Martin*, just type in *Mar* and then perform your search. This way, you will find both names.

Do your best to put consistent information into calendar events. For example, if you want to find the next dentist appointment for Gary, you could search for *Gary Dentist* in your calendar and find it. But this only works if you made sure to enter the full words *Gary* and *dentist* in your calendar entry. In this case, it would be better to search only for the word, *dentist*.

Fine-Tuning Your Search

You can adjust the breadth of apps included in your **Search**. If you want to avoid searching all your email accounts, or only search specific accounts, you can. If you only wanted to search **Contacts** and **Calendar** items, you could do that as well. After you start a search, press the Menu key and select **Search Options**. Then you will be able to scroll up and down to check or uncheck specific items to include in your search (see Figure 6-4).

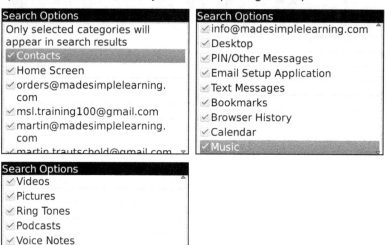

Figure 6-4. Customize your Search with the Search Options screens.

Using the BlackBerry's Built-in Help

There might be times when you don't have this book handy and you need to find out how to do something right away on your BlackBerry.

Two Ways to Get to Help

You can get into the BlackBerry built-in **Help** menus in two ways (see Figure 6-5). One is to press the **Menu** key from almost any app and select **Help** (it's usually near the bottom). The second way is to click on the **Help** icon (which is usually at the bottom of your **All** page of your **Home** screen). The built-in help can be pretty useful when you are in a bind and need to try and find something out in a hurry, but you will notice that the help is 90% text based with sparse directions.

Figure 6-5. Two ways to get to the Help on your BlackBerry.

Using the Help Menus

As we showed above, you can get to **Help** from the menu in most apps to see help about that application. For our purposes, we will take a look at the **Help** icon itself.

1. From your **Home** screen, scroll to the bottom and click on the **Help** icon.

2. The main help menu will look similar to this image. From here you can do a number of things:

- To search for a specific topic, start typing the word or phrase on your keyboard. You will instantly see results appear on the screen. Keep typing more words to narrow the search.

- To view the ten most frequently asked questions, click on **Top 10**.

- To learn about important keys on your device, click on **Find Important Keys.**

- To learn about common setup items such as Wi-Fi, email and more, click on **Start using your device**.

- Click on any other item in the Quick Help area to learn more.

- Scroll your finger down to view additional help topics (see Figure 6-6).

Figure 6-6. *Navigating the BlackBerry's built-in help function.*

3. Continue to click on topics you would like to learn about.

4. Press the **Escape** key to back up one level in the help menus.

5. As you delve deeper into help you will notice that there are usually links at the bottom for **Related Information**. These can be useful links to help you get a more complete picture of what you are trying to learn.

Help Tips and Tricks

Like pretty much every other feature on the BlackBerry, there are some tips and tricks when using **Help**.

1. **Use the Search**. The search built into the Help app is quite powerful and will quickly help you pinpoint the topic you are trying to find. For example, type "con call" to search for all conference call related topics.

2. **Use Related Information links**. At the bottom of most detailed help pages, you will see links to related topics. It can be quite helpful to use these links.

3. **Use the Contents link**. To get back to the main menu of the Help app, click on the **Contents** link you see at the bottom of most every screen.

4. **Use the Top 10**. From the main Help menu, these are the top 10 most frequently asked questions. Chances are, you will or may have already, asked these questions.

5. **Use other Quick Help items**. These can be quite useful to give you a basic overview of how to setup, customize and use your device when you don't have our book handy.

6. **Ask a Question Online**. At the bottom of most screens you will see the link **Ask a Question Online**. Click on this link to be brought to the online help section of BlackBerry.com. Here you can browser and learn more about help and even ask a question.

> **TIP:** When asking an online question, be very brief and only include the most important words. For example, instead of typing "How do I make a conference call?" type just "conference call."

Chapter 7: Personalize Your BlackBerry

In this chapter, you will learn some great ways to personalize your BlackBerry, like changing your Home screen wallpaper, moving and hiding icons, organizing with folders, setting your convenience key, changing your BlackBerry theme (look and feel), and adjusting font sizes and types.

You will also learn how to use the various **Home** screens available to you; **All**, **Favorites**, **Media**, **Downloads** and **Frequent**.

Setting Your Home Screen Preferences

The easiest thing to do to personalize your BlackBerry is to change your **Home** screen preferences which include the background wallpaper, rows of icons, and whether or not you see icons or upcoming calendar events, recent emails, and phone call logs.

Changing Your Wallpaper

You might want to change the background picture on your BlackBerry's Home screen from time to time. To do so, follow these steps:

1. From your **Home** screen, press the **Menu** key and click on **Options**.

2. Click the **Change Wallpaper** button.

3. If you want to take a picture right now to use as wallpaper, then click on the **Camera** at the top of the page.

    a. Snap a picture.

    b. After taking the picture, press the **Menu** key and select **Set As Wallpaper**.

    c. You can also click and hold the Trackpad image and choose **Set as Wallpaper** from the pop-up menu.

4. If you want to use a picture or pre-loaded wallpaper, navigate to a folder; either **Camera Pictures**, **Picture Library**, **Wallpaper**, **BlackBerry Messenger** or **other folder listed** and search for an item to use as your wallpaper.

5. Once you get to the image you want to use, press the **Menu** key and select **Set As Wallpaper**.

Changing the Location of Your Downloads

The default setting on your BlackBerry is to have the your newly installed application icons (your "downloads") go to the **Home** screen. You can customize where you want the **Download** to go by following these steps:

1. From your **Home** screen, press the **Menu** key and select **Options**.

2. Click the drop-down item under the **Downloads Folder** heading.

3. Choose **Home, Media, Instant Messaging, Applications** or **Games**.

4. Press the **Escape** key and Select **Save** on the next screen to save your changes.

Resetting Your Home Screen Preferences

If you find yourself wishing you had not made so many changes, or you just want to revert your Home screen preferences back to the defaults, follow these steps.

1. From your Home screen, press the **Menu** and click on **Options**.

2. Click on **Reset Settings.**

3. Select the items you want to reset by pressing and clicking on them. You can reset any of the following: **Wallpaper, Layout, Download Folder,** or **Icon Arrangement**.

4. Click on **Apply** when done.

Organizing Your Icons

You may not need to see every single icon on your **Home** screen, or you may want to move your most popular icons to the top row for easy access. The way you move and hide icons may vary a little depending on which Theme you have on your BlackBerry. Below we show you the standard way to move and hide icons.

Picking Favorites

New with BlackBerry OS 6, you can select your favorite icons and place them in the Favorites section of the Home screen.

1. Highlight the icon you wish to make a favorite and press and hold the **Trackpad** until you see the pop-up menu.

2. Select **Mark as Favorite** as shown.

3. Now the selected icon appears in the **Favorites** section of your **Home** screen for easy access.

> **TIP:** The icons you mark as **Favorites** appear at the bottom of the list of icons. You may want to click and hold the icon to **Move** it up to the top of the **Favorites** page.

4. If you want to remove a **Favorite** icon, click and hold it and select **Unmark as Favorite** from the pop-up menu.

Moving Your Icons within a Folder

Press the **Menu** key to see an array of all your icons. If the icon you want to move is inside a particular folder, like **Favorites**, **Media**, **Downloads** or **Frequent**, scroll to that **Home** screen.

1. Click and hold the icon you wish to move until you see the pop-up menu.

2. Select **Move** as shown.

3. Once you select **Move,** you will see arrows around the icon (as shown).

4. Use the **Trackpad** to move the icon to the desired location.

5. Finally, click to set the moved icon at the new location.

TIP: You can also press the **Menu** key and select **Mark as Favorite** to have the icon show up in the **Favorites Home** screen.

Hiding and Showing Icons

Hiding icons is fairly straightforward. Getting them back takes a few more steps.

How to Hide Icons

To hide an icon, follow these steps.

1. With the **Trackpad**, click and hold the icon you wish to hide until you see a menu pop-up in the middle of the screen.

2. Select **Hide** from the pop-up menu.

You're done – the icon is hidden.

How to Show Hidden Icons

To show a hidden icon, follow these steps.

1. Press the **Menu** key and select **Show All.**

2. The icons that are hidden appear dimmer or grayed out like the middle icon to the right.

3. Highlight the icon you wish to restore from being hidden.

4. Press the **Menu** key and select **Hide**. Notice that there is a checkmark next to the menu item; this shows the icon is currently hidden. Clicking **Hide** again will un-hide it.

5. Finally, if you want to get rid of all the other hidden icons, you need to turn off the **Show All**. Press the **Menu** key and select **Show All**.

When in a Folder

When you are in a folder, you see a little tabbed folder icon at the top of your screen and the name of the folder. In this image, we are in the **Applications** folder.

Moving Icons between Folders

Sometimes you want to move icons to your **Home** folder to make them more easily accessible. Conversely, you might want to move some of the icons you seldom use from your Home folder into another folder to clean up your Home screen.

Let's say we wanted to move our **Text Messages** icon from the **Home** screen to the **Applications** folder.

1. Highlight the **Text Messages** icon and click and hold the **Trackpad** until you see the pop-up menu.

2. Select **Move to Folder** as shown.

> **NOTE:** You can also press the **Menu** key after highlighting the icon and select **Move to Folder** from the menu.

3. We want to move this icon out of our **Home** folder into the **Applications** folder, so we click on **Applications.**

4. Notice that right after you move an icon, it appears at the bottom of the folder. **Text Messages** is now at the bottom of the list of icons in the **Applications** folder.

Use Top Row for Your Key Icons

Sometimes, you want to get your most used icons into the very top row of the **All** Folder on the Home screen.

1. If the icon is not in the **Home** folder, then use the **Move to Folder** function to move it to **Home**.

2. Then use the **Moving Icons** function to move it to the very top row of icons. As shown here, the **Calculator** is in the Home (All) folder at the top row for very easy access.

Working with Folders

On your BlackBerry, you can create or delete folders to better organize your icons. There are several folders created by default—typically, the **Media**, **Instant Messaging**, **Applications**, and **Games** folders. You can add your own folders and then move icons into your new folders to better organize them.

Creating a New Folder

> **NOTE:** At the time of publication, you could only create folders one level deep. In other words, you can only create new folders when you are in the Home folder, not when you are already inside another folder.

1. To create a new folder, first highlight any icon on the **Home** screen and then press the **Menu** key and select **Add Folder**. (you won't see this menu item unless you are on an icon)

2. After you select the **Add Folder** menu item, you will see this screen. Type your folder name.

3. Then, if you want to change the icon, click on it and select a new icon for your new folder.

4. Once you're done selecting the folder icon style, Click on it, and scroll down to Click on the **Add** button to finish creating your folder. Now you will see your new folder.

Editing a Folder

You can edit a folder by highlighting it, pressing the **Menu** key, and selecting **Edit Folder**. Then you can change the name and folder icon, and save your changes.

Deleting a Folder

Whenever you want to get rid of a folder, just highlight it, press and hold the **Trackpad** and select **Delete.**

Setting the Date, Time, and Time Zone

You can adjust the Date, Time, and Time Zone in the Setup Wizard, but there are times when you want to adjust it manually.

1. From your **Home** screen, type "time" in the Universal Search bar.

2. Click on the **Options** icon and select **Date and Time**.

3. The only way you can manually adjust the date or time is if you change **Update Time** to **Manual**.

4. You will then see **Set Time** and **Set Date** buttons appear.

5. Then, click on the time or date field to bring up the setting pop-up window. You can scroll up/down to change a value. Or, in number fields, you can click on the field to bring up the keyboard and type a number like "23." Typing digits can be faster and more accurate than scrolling.

6. If you prefer **12 hour** format (7:30 AM/ 4:30 PM) to **24 hour** format (07:30/16:30), you set that in **Time Format**. Click on the **space** bar to toggle between the two options.

TIP: You can force the BlackBerry to get updates to the time zone by pressing the **Menu** key and select **Get Time Zone Updates**.

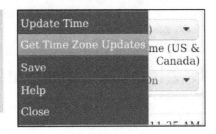

7. Click next to **Time Zone** to see a list of all the time zones and select the correct one.

8. If you leave the **Auto Update Time Zone** to the default **On**, then every time you move between time zones, your BlackBerry will automatically detect the new time zone from the cell towers and update your BlackBerry.

9. Finally, to save your changes, press the **Menu** key and select **Save**.

Changing Your Font Size and Type

You can fine-tune the font size and type on your BlackBerry to fit your individual preferences.

Do you need to see more on the screen and don't mind small fonts? Then go all the way down to a micro-size 7-point font.

Do you need to see larger fonts for easy readability? Adjust the fonts to a large **14-point font**.

To adjust your font, follow these steps:

1. Click on the **Options** icon. You may need to press the **Menu** key and **Open Tray** to find it.

2. Select **Display,** then select on **Screen Display** (Figure 7-2).

3. You can change the **Font Family**, **Font Size**, and **Font Style** on this screen. Click to change any item. Notice the preview of your currently selected style and size to make sure it will fit your needs.

4. When done, press the **Menu** key and select **Save**.

Figure 7-2. Changing your BlackBerry font family, size, and style

Themes - The Look and Feel

You can customize your BlackBerry to make it look truly unique. One way to do this is to change the **Theme** of your BlackBerry. Changing **Themes** usually changes the wallpaper, layout and appearance of your icons by and the font type and size you see inside each icon. There may be only one or a few themes pre-installed on your BlackBerry. The good news is that you can find hundreds of Themes available for download from various web sites.

CARRIER-SPECIFIC THEMES: Depending on your BlackBerry wireless carrier (phone company), you may see various customized Themes that are not shown in this book.

MORE STANDARD/GENERIC BLACKBERRY THEMES: Most of the Standard Themes shown below are on every BlackBerry (or can be downloaded from http://mobile.blackberry.com).

Downloading New Themes

CAUTION: The authors have downloaded many themes on their BlackBerry smartphones. Some themes can cause problems with your BlackBerry, such as the BlackBerry may stop working or freeze, or you may not be able to see everything on the screen. We recommend only downloading themes from a web site you know and trust.

Download from App World

Downloading **Themes** from **App World** is generally safer because these themes have undergone some basic testing in order to be a part of the **App World** store.

1. Start BlackBerry App World. See Chapter 20 for help getting **App World** running.

2. Click on the **Categories** soft key in the lower left corner.

3. Scroll down and click on the Themes category.

   Themes (769)

4. Click on the type of theme you would like to download.

5. In this example, we'll choose **Nature**.

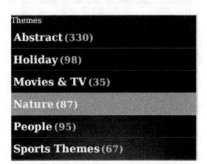

```
Themes
Abstract (330)
Holiday (98)
Movies & TV (35)
Nature (87)
People (95)
Sports Themes (67)
```

6. Now you see all the themes in the **Nature** category.

   Notice that there are FREE and paid themes.

7. Click on any theme to learn more about it, buy it, or download it.

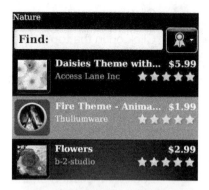

8. To learn more about the theme, check out the **Screenshots** and **Reviews**.

> **WARNING:** Some of the reviews may have explicit language and many have spelling errors.

9. If you are ready to try the Theme, click the **Download** button.

10. When the theme is downloaded, you may see a message asking if you want to activate it, if so click **Yes** to give the new Theme a try right now.

11. Here is an example of the new **Theme** activated.

You can't see it in the book, but the rose is animated. It opens and closes slightly, and the sparkles move around.

Download Themes, Wallpaper, and Ringtones from Other Web Sites

You can also find many Themes from BlackBerry-related web sites. To download these themes, follow the steps below:

1. Click on your **Browser** icon.

2. Click on in the top Address bar to type in one of the BlackBerry community web sites such as:

   ▪ BlackBerry Mobile Site: http://mobile.blackberry.com

   ▪ CrackBerry.com : http://www.crackberry.com

   ▪ BlackBerry Forums: http://www.blackberryforums.com

3. Click the Enter key on the keyboard.

4. Look for a section on the site that says something like personalize, themes, wallpapers or ringtones.

5. Follow the steps on the site to download the content to your BlackBerry.

CAUTION: Some of the items you find on these web sites may be explicit or offensive. Please view and download with care.

Selecting or Activating a Theme

1. Scroll and click on the **Options** icon on your BlackBerry. Once in **Options**, scroll down to **Display** and click and then click on **Screen Display**.

2. At the very bottom you will see **Theme.** If you have more than one theme installed, they will be listed one under the other.

3. If no other themes are listed, just press the **Menu** key and choose **Download Themes**.

4. Inside the **Theme** screen, just scroll and Click on the Theme you want to make **Active**. Your currently selected Theme is shown with the word (Active) next to it.

5. Then click the **Activate** key and then the **Escape** key to get back to the Home screen to check out your new theme.

Changing Your Convenience Keys

The key on the left side and the key on the right side under the volume keys are programmable keys called **convenience** keys (named so because the keys can be set to conveniently open any app on your BlackBerry, even new apps that you add to your BlackBerry).

1. Click on the **Universal Search** icon (magnifying glass) on the top left of your **Home** screen and type the characters "conv."

2. Click the **Options** icon.

3. Click **Convenience Keys**.

4. To change the application that these keys open, just click on the item to see the entire list. Then click on the icon you want.

5. Then press the **Menu** key and select **Save** to save your changes.

TIP: We recommend setting your right convenience key to open the **Camera**. It makes it that much easier to just take a picture when needed.

Now give you newly set convenience keys a try.

> **TIP:** The Convenience keys **work from anywhere**, not just the **Home** screen.
>
> **TIP:** You can set your Convenience keys to open any app, even newly installed ones!
>
> After you install new apps, you will notice that they show up in the list of available icons to select in the Screen/Keyboard options screen. So if your newly installed stock quote, newsreader, or game is important, just set it as a convenience key.

The Blinking Light - Repeat Notification

One of the features that BlackBerry users love is the little LED that blinks in the upper right hand corner. It is possible to have this light blink different colors:

- Red when you receive an incoming message (MMS, SMS or Email) or calendar alarm rings

- Blue when connected to a Bluetooth device

- Green when you have wireless coverage

- Amber if you need to charge your BlackBerry or it is charging

Red Flashing Message or Alert LED

By default, whenever you receive a new email message or your calendar or other alarm rings, the red LED on the top of your BlackBerry will also flash. The red light can be pretty bright, especially in the dark, so you might want to turn it off. You can disable the red LED feature by following the steps below:

1. Click on your **Sounds** icon.

2. Scroll down to **Change Sounds and Alerts** and click.

3. Scroll down to **Profile Management** and click.

4. Click on the profile you wish to adjust. (Most often, **Normal** is the profile that is highlighted.)

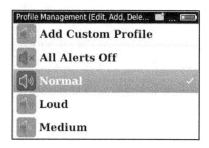

5. To edit email accounts, click on Messages. You will see each of your email accounts listed as Email [(your email address)], and Level 1, PIN, Text, etc.

6. To edit Calendar and other alerts, click on the **Events -Reminders** section.

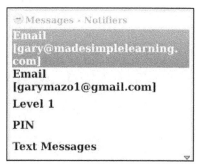

7. Click on any account or app you wish to modify.

8. Set the LED to **Off** to disable the red flashing light.

9. Press the **Menu** key and select **Save**.

Bluetooth Flashing Blue LED

In order to disable or enable the blue flashing LED when you are connected to a Bluetooth device, follow these steps:

1. Click on the very top status bar (with the time) from your **Home** screen to open your **Manage Connections** screen.

2. Scroll down and click on **Bluetooth Connections**.

3. Press the **Menu** key and select **Options.**

4. To turn on the blue indicator, check the box next to **LED Connection Indicator**. To turn this off, uncheck the same box.

5. Press the **Menu** key and **Save** your settings.

Coverage Flashing Green LED

To enable or disable the green coverage flashing LED, follow these steps:

1. Click on your **Options** icon.

2. Scroll to **Display** and click.

3. Click **Screen Display** and then Scroll down to **LED Coverage Indicator** and place a check in the radio box

4. Press the **Menu** key and **Save** your settings.

Sounds: Ring and Vibrate

Your BlackBerry is highly customizable—everything from Ringtones to vibrations to LED notifications can be adjusted. Traveling on an airplane but still want to use your calendar or play a game without disturbing others? No problem. In a meeting or at a movie and don't want the phone to ring, but you do want some sort of silent notification when an email comes in? No problem.

Virtually any scenario you can imagine can be dealt with preemptively by adjusting your Sound Profile settings.

Preloaded Sound Profiles

By default, the BlackBerry is set to a **Normal** sound profile, meaning that when a call comes in, the phone rings; when a calendar alarm rings, you will see an alert on the window (without any sound or vibration); and when a message comes in, you hear a sound and the phone may vibrate. The currently selected sound profile has the word "(Active)" next to it. Seven preloaded sound profiles are available on your BlackBerry.

All Alerts Off will turn off all notifications.

Normal is the default Active profile; in it, the phone rings and messages beep and vibrate.

Loud increases the volume for all notifications.

Medium adjusts all notifications to mid-level volume.

Silent will display notifications on the display and via the LED only.

Vibrate Only enables a short vibration for all alerts. (Great for meetings, movies, family dinners, or other places where cell phone rings are discouraged.)

Phone Calls Only will turn off all notifications except incoming calls.

Selecting a Different Preloaded Sound Profile

You can quickly change your sound profile from your **Home** screen.

1. Click on the **Speaker** icon in the upper left portion of the Home screen.

2. Click on to select a new **Sound Profile** (see Figure 7-3).

3. The new profile will be shown by a change in the **Speaker** icon.

Figure 7-3. Selecting a different preloaded sound profile

If you don't see the speaker icon on your home screen, then follow the steps below to adjust your **Sound Profile**:

4. Roll or swipe down on your **Trackpad** until you see all the icons. (You need to be in the **All** folder of your Home screen.)

5. Locate and click on the **Sounds** (Speaker) icon.

6. As shown in Figure 7-3, click on the new sound profile you wish to activate.

NOTE: You can also scroll to the bottom of the profile menu to where it says Change Sounds and Alerts. Then scroll to Profile Management and click to get to the next screen where you can make individual adjustments for each profile.

Customizing a Sound Profile

There may be some situations where you want a combination of options that one preloaded profile alone cannot satisfy. The BlackBerry is highly customizable, so you can adjust your profile options for virtually any potential situation. The easiest way to accomplish this is to choose a profile that is closest to what you need and edit it as shown below.

1. Click on **Sounds** icon (speaker).

2. Select **Change Sounds and Alerts** button near the bottom of the list by clicking it.

3. Now, scroll down to **Profile Management** and click.

4. Then click on a profile that is close to what you want as a custom profile. In this case, we want to tweak the **Normal** profile. If you wanted to adjust a different profile, simply click on it instead.

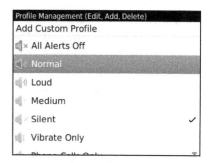

5. Click on the category of alert you wish to edit. In this case, we want to edit the Calendar, so we click on **Events-Reminders** to see the Calendar listed below.

6. Click on **Calendar**.

7. The default for the calendar does not vibrate or ring, and we want to change it. You can adjust virtually every aspect of how the Calendar alerts you when a calendar alarm rings. We changed the **Volume** from **Silent** to **5,** set **Play Sound** to **Always,** and set the **Vibration** to **On**.

8. Press the **Menu** key and select **Save**.

TIP: Make sure to leave the **Vibrate with Ring Tone** to **Off**. This will give you a few seconds of vibration before the alarm starts ringing, giving you a chance to keep the phone silent if necessary.

9. If you want to adjust your email notifications, click on **Messages** to expand that section, then click on your **Email** account to see the image shown.

10. You will see settings for **In Holster** and **Out of Holster**. A holster may be supplied with your device or sold separately and is essentially a carrying case that clips to your belt and uses a magnet to notify your BlackBerry it is **In Holster**.

NOTE: If you make e-mail sound profile changes **before** you set up individual e-mail accounts, you won't need to adjust each one individually.

Changing Your Phone Ring Tone

Please see Chapter 8: "Phone and Voice Dialing," to learn how to change your ring tone. See Chapter 16: "Your Music Player," to learn how to use a song on your BlackBerry as a ring tone.

Downloading a New Ring Tone

You may find that your stock ringtones just are not loud enough for you to hear, even when you turn the volume up to loud. Sometimes, you just want a fun Ringtone. We have found that you can download a new ringtone from **mobile.blackberry.com** (among other web sites) to help with this problem.

1. Open your **Web Browser**.

2. If you can't see a place to type a web address, then **Menu** key and select **Go To...**

3. Type in **mobile.blackberry.com** and press the **Enter** key.

4. Then scroll down and click on the

link called **Personalize**. Then, just Click on **Ringtones.** You may need to **Accept** the agreement.

5. You should see featured ringtones at the top of the list, or you will see categories of ringtones when you scroll down.

6. When you click **Download**, you can **Open** (listen/play it) or **Save** it on your BlackBerry.

7. Go ahead and **Open** a few to test them out. To get back to the list and try more ringtones, press the **Escape** key.

8. If you like the ringtone, then click **Menu** key after you listened to it and select **Save** from the menu. (You can also select **Set as Ringtone** if you select **Save** instead of **Open** after you click **Download**.)

9. This time, scroll down and check the box at the bottom that says **Set as Ringtone**, then select **Save.**

10. You are done. Next time you receive a phone call, the new ringtone should play.

TIP: New Ringtones are available on many BlackBerry user Websites like:

www.crackberry.com

www.blackberryforums.com

www.blackberrycool.com

View some examples of ringtones for sale (see Figure 7-4).

Figure 7-4. Other sources for ringtones for your BlackBerry.

Unique Ring Tones for Contacts

Would you like to know who is calling, emailing, or sending a SMS text message without having to look at the screen?

You can do this by setting what is called a **Contact Alert** on your BlackBerry. You can set these up in two places on your BlackBerry: in the **Sound Profile** app (Speaker icon) and in the **Contacts** app.

Using the Sound Profile App

Since the Sound Profile app is to easy to get to, you might want to use this method:

1. Click on your **Sounds** icon.

2. Scroll down and click on **Change Sounds and Alerts**.

3. Click **Sounds for Contacts** and select **Add Contact Alert** to choose a contact for which this new profile will apply.

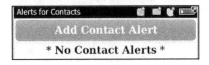

4. Type a name for the Contact alert. In this case, we typed **Gary**.

5. Next, click the box under where is says **Contacts**.

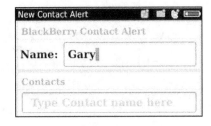

6. Type a few letters of the person's first and last name to find them in your Contact list.

7. Then click on their name to select it.

8. Now, you can adjust the custom alerts for this person for both Messages (e-Mail, SMS, etc.) and the Phone by clicking on **Messages** or **Phone**.

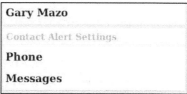

9. Now, make the adjustments for this person. In this case, we want a different ring tone, so we changed it to **Adventurous** and changed the **Volume** to **10**.

10. We also adjusted the **Vibration** to **On** and the Vibrate with **Ring Tone** to **Off**.

11. Press the **Menu** key and select **Save**.

Using the Contact List

You can also set up custom ringtones and alerts for contacts directly in your Contacts icon.

1. Start your **Contacts** app.

2. Type a few letters to find a contact to customize.

3. Click on the contact name you wish to edit, press the **Menu** key and select **Edit**.

4. Scroll down until you see the **Custom Ring Tones/Alerts** section.

5. Click on **Phone** or **Messages** to adjust either one.

6. Make your changes to Ring Tones, volume, vibration, and more on this screen.

7. Press the **Menu** key and select **Save** to return to the contact edit screen.

8. Press the **Menu** key and select **Save** again to finish editing the contact.

Accessibility Options

Your BlackBerry offers some "tweaks" to the accessibility options – which can change the look and feel of your **Home** screen, color contrast and event sounds.

1. Click on your **Options** icon and then scroll down to **Accessibility** and click.

2. To change the **Home Screen Grid Layout**, just click the dropdown and choose from the default up to 4 columns of icons in the **Home Screen** grid.

3. Here is an image showing the **Home** screen with **2 columns** set.

4. The change the contrast (to make the screen more visible) click the dropdown and choose from **Normal, Reverse Contrast** or **Greyscale**. **Reverse Contrast** is shown to the right. Experiment with this to see that gives you the best viewing experience.

5. Finally, you can choose to have **Event Sounds** be **On** or **Off**.

Chapter 8:
Phone and Voice Dialing

In this chapter, we dig into the many ways your BlackBerry is a powerful and full-featured phone. You will learn how to quickly make phone calls, use your call logs, and call people from your **Contact** list. You'll also learn quick ways to dial voice mail, use speed dial, and add new contacts from the phone calls you place or receive. Finally, you will learn how to use voice dialing on your BlackBerry.

Two Phone Views

When you open the phone the first time, you may not notice the small soft key in the upper right corner. Clicking this soft key will switch you between the two phone views: **Call Logs** view, and your **Contact** list view. (see Figure 8-1).

Figure 8-1. The two phone views on your BlackBerry.

Phone Basics: Keys and Buttons

It helps to get a feel for how the phone works by looking at all the keys, buttons, and on-screen icons shown in Figure 8-2. Your main phone keys are the **Green** and **Red Phone** keys on the bottom of the device.

Figure 8-2. Phone keys and buttons on your BlackBerry.

Placing a Call

Making phone calls is easy. There are many ways to place a call: you can dial a number, use your call logs, or dial by name from your contact list.

Dialing a Phone Number

1. Press the **Green Phone** key at any time to get into the **Phone**.

2. Press the **number keys** on your keyboard to dial the number.

3. Press the **Green Phone** key to start the call.

TIP: To re-dial the last number you called, simply press the **Green Phone** key. If you are not in the Phone, just press the **Green Phone** key twice to dial the last number.

Dial from Call Logs

You can quickly dial from your **Call Logs** (calls you have placed, received, or missed).

1. Start the **Phone** by pressing the **Green Phone** key.

2. If you don't see the **Call Logs**, then click the **Call Log** icon in the upper left corner.

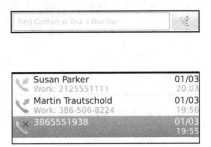

3. Once in the call log screen, just scroll to the call log you wish to use and press the Green Phone key to call that exact number, or press the Trackpad to call another number for that person.

TIP: If you want to call a person, but not the number shown on the Call Log (e.g. "Work" is shown, but you want to call "Mobile"), highlight the call log and click the **Trackpad**. Then, select from the additional phone numbers shown.

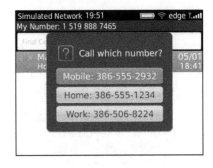

Dialing a Contact by Name

You can quickly dial anyone in your Contact list by following these steps.

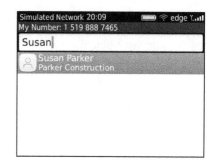

1. Start the **Phone** by pressing the

    Green Phone key.

2. Once in the **Phone** screen, start typing a few letters of a contact's first, last, or company name to find them.

3. Click on the contact's name.

4. If the contact has more than one phone number, you will be prompted to select from the available numbers.

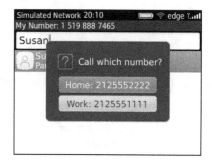

Answering a Call

Answering a call couldn't be easier. When you call comes in, the number will be displayed on the screen. If you have that particular number already in your **Contact** list, the name and/or picture will also be on the screen (if you have entered that information into that particular contact.)

When a call comes in:

Press the **Green Phone** key to answer the call.

If you are using a Bluetooth Headset, you can usually press a button on the headset to answer the call (see Chapter 1)

TIP: Just press the **Volume Down** key to stop the ringing. Press the **Red Phone** key to instantly send the caller to voice mail.

Ignoring Phone Calls

Sometimes you can't take a call. In such cases, you need to make a decision to ignore the call or mute the ringing. Both of these options can be achieved quite easily with your BlackBerry.

When the phone call comes in, press the **Red Phone** key to ignore it.

= Ignore call, send to voice mail, and stop the ringing.

TIP: Need to silence the ringer but still want to answer the call?

Just Click on the **Ringer Off** button on the bottom of your screen. If the ringing or vibrating had started while your BlackBerry was still in the holster (carrying case), simply pulling the BlackBerry out of the holster should stop the vibrating and ringing, but still give you time to answer.

Ignoring a call will immediately send the caller to your voice mail.

The **Missed Call** icon will be displayed on your Home screen; it's an icon that

shows a phone with a red X next to it. The number shows the total number of missed calls.

You can immediately call back the missed caller by doing the following:

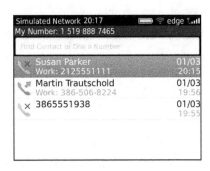

1. Press the **Green Phone** key.

2. If you are not already viewing the call logs, press the **Call Log** soft key (top right).

3. Locate and click on the missed call—usually it will be the top entry, as shown in the image.

Using the Mute Button to Turn Off the Ringing Phone

Besides pressing the **Ringer Off** button, you can also mute the call via the mute key on the top of your BlackBerry.

If you would prefer not send the call immediately to voice mail and simply let it ring a few times on the caller's end, but you don't want to hear the ring (perhaps you are in a movie theatre or a meeting), press the **Mute** key on the very top edge of your BlackBerry. On the Bold the **Mute** key is on the top right, on the Curve it is in the top middle (Play/Pause/Mute).

This will silence the ring. You may still pick up the call or let the caller go to voice mail.

Dialing Numbers, Taking Notes, and Jumping to Other Apps

When you are on a call, you will notice some soft keys at the bottom of the screen that allow you to do a number of useful things. You may want to click on

the **Speaker** soft key [Speaker] or press the **Speaker** key [icon] on your keyboard, before pressing any of these keys so you can hold the BlackBerry away from your face.

If you need to dial numbers on a phone call, simply press the numbers on your keyboard.

You don't need to press and hold **ALT** to dial numbers while on a call. If you do press the **ALT** key, you will be able to type the letters on the keys instead of numbers.

Taking Notes While On a Call

Have you ever hung up the phone and asked yourself, "What was it that I promised to do?" If so, the **Notes** feature on your BlackBerry is a perfect solution to keep track of exactly what was said or promised during a phone call.

You can take notes, save them, and even email them to yourself or others.

The notes you take while on a call are attached to the call log, also known as **Call History**.

1. In order to take the phone away from your ear so you can type notes, either click the **Speaker** key or use your headset.

2. Press the **Menu** key and click on **Notes**.

3. Now, you can type your notes using the keyboard.

4. If you need to get back to the phone screen, then press the **Escape** key. (Your notes will be saved.)

5. When done, you can simply hang up with the **Red Phone** key.

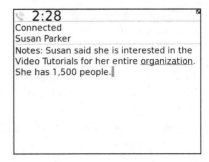

View, Edit, Delete, or Send Call History and Notes

1. From the Call Log screen, highlight the log entry, press the **Menu** key and scroll to **View** and select **Call Notes**.

2. Highlight the item with the notes you wish to view and click the **Trackpad** to view the notes.

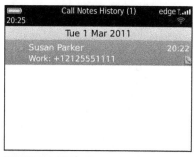

3. From this screen, you can also do the following:

Press the **Menu** key and select **Compose** to write a note for any call history entry.

Press the **Menu** key and select **Delete** to remove the Call History item and related note.

Press the **Menu** key and select **Forward** to send these call notes as an email message as shown in this image.

You can also select **Open, Call, Compose Email or View Contact information** and then perform one of the desired actions from the menu.

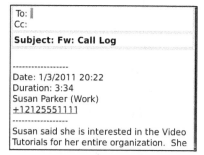

Adjusting the Volume on Calls

There may be times when you have trouble hearing a caller. The connection may be poor or you may be using a headset. Adjusting the volume is easy. While on the phone call, simply use the two volume keys on the right hand side of the BlackBerry to adjust the volume up or down.

What's My Phone Number?

You have your new phone, and you want to give your number to all your friends—you just need to know where you can get your hands on that important information.

1. Press the **Green Phone** key to

start the phone.

2. Read your phone number next to **My Number** at the top of the screen.

3. In the image to the right, the number is **1-519-888-7465**. (You may have to wait a second for it to appear.)

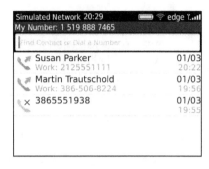

TIP: To quickly dial your Voice Mail -- Press and hold the **1** key.

Changing Your Ring Tone

You can change your main phone ring tone inside the Phone app by following these steps:

1. From any Phone screen, press the **Menu** key (see Figure 8-3).

2. Scroll down and select **Phone Ring Tones**.

3. Then click on the button under **Ring Tone** to select a different tune.

4. You can adjust other properties, such as volume, vibration, length and count.

5. Click the **Try It** button to check out your new settings.

6. Press the **Menu** key and select **Save**.

Figure 8-3. Changing your ring tone from the Phone

234

Calling Voice Mail

 The easiest way to call voice mail is to press and hold the number **1** key from the keyboard. This is the default key for voice mail.

If it is not working correctly, read below for some troubleshooting help or call your phone company technical support for help in correcting it.

To setup voice mail, just call it and follow the prompts to enter your name, greeting, password, and other information.

Voice Mail Control Keys

While voice mail systems vary, here are some typical control keys that may be available to you on your BlackBerry:

1= Start playing message if at main menu.

1= Rewind currently playing message

1,1= Play current message from beginning

2= Stop or start message playback

3= Fast forward current message

3,3= Jump to end of message

#= Skip current message, start playing next message

7= Delete current message

*= Go to main menu, or disconnect, if at main menu

When Voice Mail Doesn't Work

Sometimes, pressing and holding the **1** key or selecting **Call Voice Mail** from the menu will not correctly dial voice mail. This happens if the voice mail access number is incorrect in your BlackBerry.

You will need to call your phone company (wireless carrier) and ask them for the local voice mail access number. This sometimes happens if you move to a different area or change cell phones, then restore all your data onto your BlackBerry.

Once you have the new phone number from the carrier, you need to enter it into your BlackBerry.

1. Start your Phone by pressing the **Green Phone** key.

2. Press the menu key and select **Options**, then select **Voice Mail**.

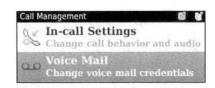

3. Enter the phone number you received into the Voice Mail **Access Number**.

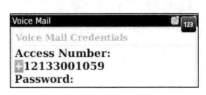

TIP: You can even enter your voice mail password if you like.

Using Your Call Logs

The Call Log is an especially useful tool if you make and receive many calls. Besides being able to quickly dial them, you can use the call log to add contacts to your Contact list, add notes, forward, and view details.

For instance, you can't remember if you added an individual to your Contact list, but you definitely remember that they called yesterday. Here is a perfect situation: use your Call Log to access the call, add the number into your address book, and place a return call.

Checking Your Call Logs

The easiest way to view your call logs is to do the following:

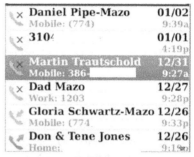

1. Press the **Green Phone** key.

2. Initially, you should see the **Call Log**. The default setting is to show most recent entries at the top of the list.

3. Use the **Trackpad** to highlight a call log entry. Then, either press the **Menu** key to see your options or click and hold the **Trackpad** to bring up a short menu on the screen shown here.

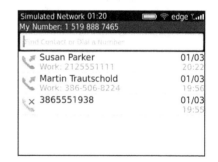

See Both Names and Numbers

You will see both phone numbers and names in your phone call logs.

When you see a name instead of a phone number, you know that the person is already entered in your BlackBerry contact list.

It is easy to add entries to your contacts right from the phone call log screen. We show you how below.

Add New Contacts from Call Logs

If you see just a phone number in your call log screen, there is a good chance you will want to add that phone number as a new **Contact** entry.

NOTE: Call log entries are generated whenever you place, receive, miss, or ignore a call from your BlackBerry.

Get into the call log screen by clicking the **Green Phone** key once.

1. Highlight the call log phone number you want to add to your address book.

2. Press the **Menu** key and select **Add to Contacts**.

TIP: You can also press and hold the number with the **Trackpad** and select **Add to Contacts** from the pop-up menu.

3. Notice that the phone number is automatically placed in the **Work** phone field but you can also change it by clicking the phone label as shown.

4. Fill in as much information as possible, press the **Menu** key, and select **Save.**

Copy and Paste Phone Numbers

For Underlined Phone Numbers:

With underlined phone number like 313-555-1212, or phone numbers in call logs, simply highlight the call log and press the **Menu** key and select **Copy** to copy it.

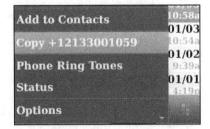

TIP: This trick works on any underlined

email address or PIN as well!

Move to where you want to paste, press the **Menu** key, and select **Paste**.

To Show Your Call Logs in the Messages App

It might be useful to show calls made, received, and missed in your message list (inbox) for easy accessibility. This allows you to manage both voice and message communication in a single unified inbox.

1. Press the **Green Phone** key to see your call logs.

2. Press the **Menu** key and select **Options**.

3. Scroll to **Call Logs and Lists** and click. Under **Show These Call Log Types in Message List** select either:

    ▪ **Missed Calls** (see only missed calls)

    ▪ **All Calls** (see all placed, missed, received)

    ▪ **None** (this is the default; don't see any calls)

4. Press **Menu** and select **Save**.

Benefits of Adding People to Your Contact List/Address Book

- Call any number for this person (that is entered into your address book)

- Send them an email (if this person has an email address entered)

- Send them an SMS text message

- Send them an MMS Message (multimedia message with pictures or other media like songs)

- Send them a PIN message

- View the contact information

- Add a Speed Dial for the contact.

Speed Dial

Speed dialing is a great way to call your frequent contacts quickly. After you setup speed dial, press and hold a number key from the dial pad to have their phone number automatically dialed. There are a couple of ways to set up speed dialing on your BlackBerry.

Set Up from Call Logs

1. Press the **Green Phone** key and then select call logs using the soft key at the top.

2. Use the **Trackpad** to highlight the call log entry (either phone number or name) that you want to add to speed dial and press the **Menu** key.

3. Click on **Add Speed Dial**.

4. You will be asked to confirm that you want to add this speed dial number with a pop-up window.

5. In the **Speed Dial** list, the number defaults to the first unused spot or sometimes to the first letter of the name of the contact if that is free.

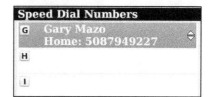

6. Click on any other number and vacant spot to select that spot instead.

7. Press the **Escape** key to exit the **Speed Dial** list.

Set Up using Keyboard Letters

Simply press and hold any unassigned letter to assign that letter as a new speed dial entry. Follow the same steps as shown above to complete the process (see Figure 8-4).

1/W Key
Press and hold
to speed dial
voice mail.

Assign Speed Dial
Press and hold unassigned
keys on keyboard to set up
as Speed Dial letters.

Q Key
Press and hold to
change sound profile to
Vibrate mode.

A Key
Press and hold to
Lock the keypad
and screen.

Figure 8-4. *Setting New Speed Dial Entries from the Keyboard*

Give your newly created speed dial numbers and letters a try by pressing and holding the same key you just assigned on your keyboard.

Edit, Move or Delete a Speed Dial Number

You can adjust or delete speed dial numbers.

1. Press the **Green Phone** key to start the phone.

2. Press the Menu key and select **View** then **Speed Dial List**.

3. Highlight the number you want to adjust.

4. Press the **Menu** key and select **Edit** to change the number, select **Move** and click on the space to move to or select **Delete** and confirm your choice to remove this entry.

5. Press the **Escape** key to exit the **Speed Dial** list.

Using Your Speed Dial Entries

To use any speed dial entry, press and hold the key on the keyboard.

Voice Dialing Basics

Now that you know how to use Speed Dialing, we help you understand another way to save time – using the **Voice Dialing** program that allows you to voice dial and perform other simple commands. Voice dialing provides a safe way to place calls without having to look at the BlackBerry and navigate through menus. Voice dialing does not need to be trained like on other smartphones—just speak naturally.

Voice Dialing a Contact

The **Convenience** key is usually set for the **Camera** app but you can also set it for Voice dialing. Your BlackBerry has two convenience keys – a right and a left. Try pressing that key. If you have set the key for another program, press the

Menu key and select the **Applications** folder. Then click the **Voice Dialing** icon to start the **Voice Dialing** app.

> **TIP:** We show you how to set or change your convenience keys in the "Convenience Key" section of Chapter 7.

The first time you use this feature, the BlackBerry will take a few seconds to scan your Contact list.

When you hear **Say a Command**, just speak the name of the contact you wish to call using the syntax "Call Martin Trautschold."

If this contact has more than one phone number, you will then be prompted with **Which number?**

Again, speak clearly and say **Home**, **Work**, or **Mobile**

Say **Yes** to confirm the selection and the BlackBerry will begin to dial the number.

Voice Dialing a Number

Start **Voice Dialing** by pressing the icon from the **Home** screen, or, if you've set it, the **Convenience** key.

When you hear **"Say a command,"** say **"Call"** and the phone number. Example: **"Call 386-506-8224."**

Depending on your settings, you may be asked to confirm the number you just spoke or it will just start dialing.

Other Voice Dialing Commands

You can use the **Voice Dialing** app to perform other functions on the BlackBerry. These are especially useful if you are in a position where you can't look at the screen (while driving) or in an area where coverage seems to fade in and out.

The most common are:

- **Call Extension** will call a specific extension.
- **Call Martin Home** will call the contact at their home number.
- **Check Battery** will check the battery status.

- **Check Signal** will let you know the strength of your wireless signal and whether you have No Signal, Low Signal, High Signal, or Very High Signal.

- **Turn Off Voice Prompts** will turn off the "Say a command" voice and replace it with a simple beep.

- **Turn On Voice Prompts** turns the friendly voice back on.

Changing Voice Dialing Options

You can control various features of Voice Dialing by going into your **Phone Options** by pressing the **Green Phone** key and scrolling to **Options** and selecting **Voice Dialing.**

Change the **Choice Lists** if you do not want to be confronted with lots of choices after you say a command. Your options are **Automatic** (default), **Always On**, or **Always Off**.

Audio Prompts can be set to **No Prompts**, **Basic Prompts** (default), and **Detailed Prompts.** With Detailed Prompts, you will hear more detailed questions and confirmations back from the BlackBerry after you speak. Use Detailed Prompts if you find that you are misdialing a great deal.

Adapt Voice in Voice Dialing

In order to teach the BlackBerry how you speak, you will need to use the **Voice Adaptation** function (which used to be called Adapt Digits on earlier BlackBerry software versions).

1. From the Voice Dialing options screen click the Start button under **Voice Adaptation.**

2. It helps to be in a quiet room and then you will have to repeat 15 sets of prompts (see Figure 8-5).

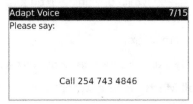

Figure 8-5. Training your Voice Dialing

3. After about 15 screens, you will see a message that the device is working to adapt your voice.

4. When it's done, you will be placed back into the Voice Dialing options. Press the **Red Phone** key to jump back to the Home screen.

Now, give your newly trained **Voice Dialing** a try.

Voice Dialing Tips and Tricks

There are a few ways to speed up the voice dialing process. You can also customize the way Voice Dialing works on the BlackBerry.

Make Voice Dialing Calls More Quickly

When using Voice Dialing, give more information when you place the call. For example, if you say "**Call Martin Trautschold, Home**," the Voice Dialing program will only ask you to confirm that you are calling him at home.

The call will then be placed.

Give your Contacts Nicknames

Make a **Nickname** entry for a contact, especially one with a long name.

In addition to my **Gary Mazo** contact, I might also edit his contact entry to add a Nickname field and then add **GM** as the Nickname.

I would then say: "Call GM."

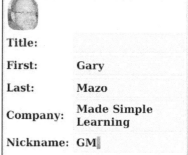

Title:	
First:	Gary
Last:	Mazo
Company:	Made Simple Learning
Nickname:	GM

Changing Your Voice Dialing Language

If you need to speak in a different language on Voice Dialing, you can change the Voice Dialing language in the Options icon. Start the **Options** icon (usually a wrench), then click on **Typing and Input** and then click on **Language** to see the screen shown here.

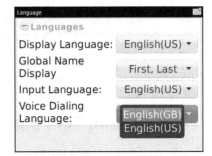

NOTE: If you do not see all of these languages displayed, it is likely they were removed during the Setup Wizard process and will need to be re-installed. If you are a Windows PC user, you can use Desktop Software to add back languages in the Application Loader section. If you are a Mac user, use BlackBerry Desktop Software for the Mac.

Setting your Phone Ring Tone

The BlackBerry supports using many types of audio files as Ringtones. You can set one general ringtone for everyone or set up individual tones for your important callers.

You can change ringtones from various places:

- The **Phone** itself
- The **Sound** profile (Speaker icon) app,
- The **Music** app
- The **Ringtones** app

Important: Place Ringtones in Ringtone Folders

In some BlackBerry smartphones, when you are attempting to set a ringtone for a specific person in the Contact list or in Profiles, you can only browse to the Ringtone folder, not the Music folder. If this is the case, then you must copy your music ringtones to the Ringtone folder using the methods to transfer media found in this book.

Changing Your Ring Tone from the Phone

We will show you a few ways to set your ringtone starting with the **Phone** app itself.

1. Press the **Green Phone** key to start the phone.

2. Press the **Menu** key and select **Phone Ring Tones**.

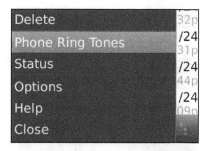

3. Click the drop-down under Ring Tone to select a new ring tone.

4. From this screen you can also adjust the ring tone **Volume** and when it is played (**Play sound**). There are other adjustments below with the **LED** and **Vibration**.

5. When you're done changing things, you can try out your new settings by clicking the **Try It** button at the bottom.

6. Press the **Menu** key and **Save** your settings.

7. Next you will see a question about which Sound Profile to change. You can select **All Profiles** to set this for every profile or **Normal Profile Only** to select this new ring tone only for the Normal sound profile.

Changing Your Ring Tone from Other Places

Music app: To change your ring tone from your **Music** app, highlight to the song you want to use from the list on the screen. Press the **Menu** key and select **Set as Ring Tone**.

Ringtone app: Start the Ring Tone app, select a ring tone you want to use and follow the same procedure as described for music.

Sounds app: Click on the **Sounds** app (speaker icon). Click the button at the bottom called **Changes Sounds and Profiles**. Click the **Phone Ring Tone** at the top. Click on the Ring Tone drop down list and select a new ring tone.

TIP: Unique Ringtones for Callers

Set up unique ringtones for each of your important callers. This way you will know when each of these people is calling without looking at your BlackBerry screen.

Set a Custom Ring Tone for a Caller

We covered how to do this in the "Setting Different Ring Tones for Contacts" in Chapter 7: "Personalize Your BlackBerry."

Call Waiting – A Second Caller

Like most phones these days, the BlackBerry supports call waiting, call forwarding, and conference calling – all useful options in the business world and in your busy life.

If you are on the phone with someone, and a second person calls, you can do any of the following:

- Answer the second caller by pressing the **Green Phone** key. This will put your first caller on hold.

- Ignore the second caller and send them to voice mail by pressing the **Red Phone** key.

Join a Conference Call or Swap

After you have two callers on the phone, you can join them in a conference call or toggle between them (called **Swap**) see Figure 8-6.

Figure 8-6. Working with two callers on your BlackBerry

1. To swap between the callers (put one on hold and talk to the other), just click the **Swap** key (or the **Green Phone** key).

2. To join the two callers together in a conference, click the **Join** key.

3. To split the call, press the **Menu** key and select **Split Call** from the menu.

4. Then choose which call to separate from the conference call first.

Conference Calling

Conference Calling is a very useful option for talking with more than one person at a time.

> **TIP:** In your Calendar, you can pre-load conference call dial-in information so you don't have to dial it every time. This works well if you use the same conference call service regularly. See Chapter 11 for details.

Sometimes conferencing several parties together is the faster (and safer) way to transfer necessary information.

For instance, one author was leasing a new car and the car dealer left a voicemail to call the insurance company to approve the proof of insurance being faxed to the dealer.

The author called the insurance company, expecting they already had received the dealer's fax number.

Unfortunately, the insurance company did not have the fax number.

Instead of hanging up and calling the dealer, asking for the fax number, and calling the insurance company back, the author used the BlackBerry conference call feature.

Over the course of the conference call, the dealer's fax number was relayed, along with any special instructions.

To Set Up a Conference Call

Place a call as you normally would.

While on the call, press the **Green Phone** key (or click the **Add Participant** button on the screen) and either choose a contact from your Contact List or type in a phone number.

Choose which number (if the contact had more than one) that you wish to conference.

Figure 8-8. Conference call setup

If you add more than two callers to the conference call (Figure 8-8), just repeat the process starting with another **New Call** (press the **Green Phone** key).

Join the calls as you did above. Repeat as needed.

To speak with only one of the callers on a Conference Call:

1. Press the **Menu** key and select **Split Call** or select **Split Call (name).**

2. Select the caller to whom you want to speak privately.

3. The other caller will be placed on hold.

To End or Leave a Conference Call

To hang up on everyone and end the conference call for all, press the **Red Phone** key or press the **Menu** key and select **Drop Call** to just disconnect from one caller.

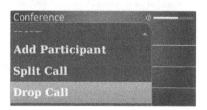

Advanced Dialing (Letters, Pauses, and Waits)

You may want to do some advanced dialing whether you are on the phone or entering a phone number in your Contact list. How to dial letters and how to add pauses and waits when a phone number is dialed are all covered in this section.

Dialing Letters on a Phone Call

Sometimes you call a company with a **Dial by Name** directory that will ask you to "Dial a few letters of the person's last name to look them up."

Simply press the **ALT** key and start typing letters from the keyboard. It's that easy!

Dialing Phone Numbers with Letters in your Contact List

Typing phone numbers with letters in your Contact list:

If you had to enter **800-CALLABC** into your address book you would follow these steps:

1. Type in **800**

2. Using the keyboard, press and hold **ALT** while typing the letters.

Adding Pauses and Waits in Phone Numbers

Sometimes you want to type a phone number that has preset pauses and waits.

A **Pause** is a 2-second pause, and then dialing continues. If you need more than 2 seconds, just put more than one pause in the phone number.

Press the **Menu** key and select **Add Pause.**

A **Wait** waits for you to press the screen before continuing to dial.

Press the **Menu** key and select **Add Wait.**

If you need a variable amount of time to wait, then you should use a **Wait** instead of a **Pause**.

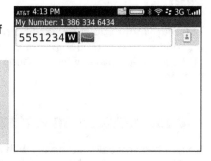

> **TIP:** This is a great way to enter a voice mail access number to quickly check voice mail on a work or home number.

More Phone Tips and Tricks

Like most features on the BlackBerry, there is always more you can do with your Phone. These tips and tricks will make things go even quicker for you.

- To dial the previous call, press and hold the **Green Phone** key when in the **Phone** app.

- To insert a **plus** sign when typing a phone number, hold the number zero 0.

- To add an extension to a phone number, press the X key and then type the extension number. It should look like this: **8005551212 x 1234.**

- To check your voice mail, press and hold the number 1.

- To view the last phone number that you dialed, scroll to the top of the Phone screen, and press the **ENTER** key. Press the **Send** key to dial the number.

Chapter 9:
Email Like a Pro

The newer BlackBerrys, even though small and stylish, are BlackBerrys to the core—they are powerful email tools. This chapter will get your up and running with your email. In minutes, you will be an emailing pro.

> **NOTE:** If you have not yet set up your email accounts, please see the "Set Up Email Accounts" section of Chapter 1: "Getting Started."

Composing Email

The BlackBerry, like all BlackBerry smartphones, gives you the freedom to email on the go. With the cellular network, you are no longer tied to a Wi-Fi hotspot or your desktop or notebook; email is available to you at all times almost anywhere in the world.

Send Email from Messages

This first option is perhaps easiest for learning how to initially send an email.

1. Click on the **Messages** icon. You will have an icon for each email address that you have set up in addition to the overall **Messages** icon.

2. You have a few ways to start composing a new message:

NOTE: You will see options based on installed apps on the BlackBerry. So, if you have **Facebook** and **Twitter** installed, they should appear in the **Compose** list.

▪ Press the Email Shortcut key letter **C** (for Compose) on your keyboard.

TIP: Learn all the shortcut keys in Part 4 at the end of this book.

▪ Click on a date row separator gray bar and select **Compose** or other message type from the pop-up window (see image to above and right).

▪ Press the **Menu** key and scroll down to select **Compose Email**.

3. Type in the recipient's name or email address in the **To** field. If the BlackBerry finds a match between what you are typing and any **Contacts** entries, they are shown in a selectable drop-down list.

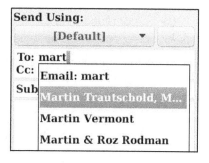

4. Select the correct name by clicking it. If there is more than one email address stored for that particular contact, just choose the correct address.

TIP: Press the **space** key for the @ and "." in the email address. EXAMPLE: To type susan@company.com, you would type "susan" **space** "company" **space** "com"

5. Repeat to add additional **To:** and **Cc:** addressees.

6. If you need to add a Blind Carbon Copy (Bcc:), then press the **Menu** key and select **Add Bcc:**

7. Then type the **Subject** and **Body** of your email message.

8. When you are done, click the **Trackpad**, then select **Send**. Or, you may press the **Menu** key and select **Send**. That's all there is to it.

Send Email from Contacts

After you have entered or synced your names and addresses to your BlackBerry, you may send emails directly from your **Contacts** list.

1. Click on your **Contacts** icon.

   Begin to type a few letters from your person's first or last name to find them. Then click his/her name to see the contact details.

2. To compose a new message you could do any of these actions:

   ▪ Click on on the **email address** to compose a new message.

   ▪ Press the **Menu** key and select **Email (the person's name)**.

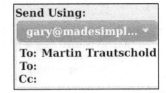

Selecting a Different Email Address to Send From

If you have several email addresses integrated with your BlackBerry, you can select which one to send your email from.

1. Click on the field that shows **your email address** or **[Default]** at the top of email compose screen under **Send Using**.

2. Scroll up or down to click on another **Email Account** to use.

Click on the Name for More Options

When you receive email on your BlackBerry, you will often see the person's name (e.g. Margaret Johnson) and not their email address in the **From** field.

You can see the email address and can also contact them in a number of different ways (assuming they are in your **Contacts** list), by clicking on their name with the **Trackpad**.

- Roll up with the Trackpad to highlight the person's name and click the **Trackpad**. You can then **Copy**, **Show Name** or **Email Address**, **Email**, **Call**, **View Contact**, **Text**, **Switch Application** (Multitask), **Home** (jump to the **Home** screen).

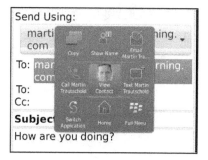

TIP: You can also highlight the name/email address and press the letter **Q**.

Replying To Messages

Once you get the hang of emailing on your BlackBerry, you will quickly find yourself checking your email and wanting to respond quickly to your emails. Replying to messages is very easy on the BlackBerry.

1. Click on the **Messages** icon.

2. Click on the message you wish to reply to.

3. Press the **R** key (shortcut for Reply) or press the **Menu** key and select **Reply**.

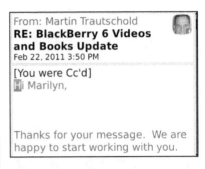

From: Martin Trautschold
RE: BlackBerry 6 Videos and Books Update
Feb 22, 2011 3:50 PM

[You were Cc'd]
Hi Marilyn,

Thanks for your message. We are happy to start working with you.

TIP: Check out all the Messages keyboard shortcuts in Part IV at the end of this book.

4. The recipient is now shown in the **To** field.

5. Type in your message.

6. Click the **Menu** button and select **Send** from the **Short Menu**. You can also   press the **Menu** key and select **Send**.

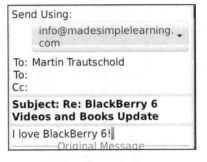

Send Using:
   info@madesimplelearning. com

To: Martin Trautschold
To:
Cc:
Subject: Re: BlackBerry 6 Videos and Books Update
I love BlackBerry 6!
————Original Message

Navigating Around and Other Tidbits

There are a few useful things to know when you are working with your **Messages** inbox. You may also notice some blank spots in email messages you receive where pictures should be located. In this section, we show you how to retrieve those images. There are times you want to change the importance level from **Normal** to **Low** or **High** depending on the situation. Also, you will want to know how to turn on **Spell Checking** for every email you compose and send from your BlackBerry.

Email Shortcut Keys

You can use special keys on your keyboard to quickly move around your inbox. For example, pressing the letter **T** will jump to the top of your inbox, **B** will jump to the bottom, **N** will go to the Next day and **P** will go to the previous day. There are many more shortcut keys listed at the end of this book.

TIP: See the all **Email Shortcut keys** in Part 4 of this book at the very end.

Navigating Your Inbox

You can use the scroll motion with your finger on the **Trackpad** to move around in your email inbox.

- To move to the next message, swipe your finger on the **Trackpad** from right to left.

- To move to the previous message, swipe from left to right.

- Once you get back to the first message, swiping from left to right will bring you back to the message list.

You can also highlight and click the date row separator with the **Trackpad** to bring up the pop-up menu shown here.

Getting Rid of Blank Spots (Missing Graphics)

On some email messages, you may see blank spaces where images should be. If you see this, follow these steps to see all your images:

1. Press the **Menu** key.

2. Select **Get Image** to retrieve just one image or **Get Images** to retrieve them all.

3. You may see a warning message about exposing your email address; you need to Click on **Ok** or **Yes** in order to get the image.

TIP: To set your BlackBerry so that it automatically loads the images every time, you can set an option. Start **Messages**, press the **Menu** key and select **Options**. Select **Email Preferences** and make sure to check the box next to **Download Images Automatically** for each email account.

Setting the Importance Level of the Email

Sometimes you need your email to be noticed and responded to immediately. The BlackBerry lets you set the importance level so that the recipient can better respond.

Begin composing a new email message, then press the **Menu** key.

Select the **Options** menu item.

TIP: Pressing the letter key that matches the first letter of the menu item a couple of times will jump you down to that item.

In the **Options** screen, you will see a line that says **Importance** and the default **Normal** at the end of the line. Click on the word **Normal** and you see the options **High** or **Low**.

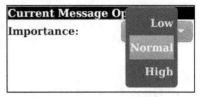

Just click on on the appropriate option. Press the **Menu** key and **Save** your choice to return to the email message. Then press the **Menu** key and **Send** the message.

Finally, you will see high importance and low importance messages marked with special icons in your messages list (Inbox):

 High = Exclamation point

 Normal = Nothing

Low = Arrow pointing down

Spell Checking Email Messages

Please see later in this chapter about how to enable spell checking on email messages you type and send. The spell checker may not be turned on when you take your BlackBerry out of the box the first time.

Flag for Follow Up

After receiving an email message, have you ever found yourself thinking:

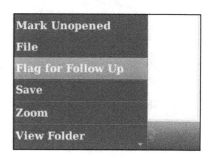

"This is important, I don't want to forget about it, but I can't deal with it right now."

"I need to spend more time before I reply to this message."

"I need to give them a call about this message on Wednesday."

If so, then the **Flag for Follow Up** can be a great feature for you.

You can set flags of many types and colors with or without due dates from the main email inbox or while you are reading a particular message.

Setting a New Flag

To set a flag, follow these steps:

1. Press the **Menu** key and select **Flag for Follow Up**.

2. You can set various **Flag Properties** on this screen. As you set these properties, keep in mind that you can use the messages **Search** command to find flags or specific colors of flags.

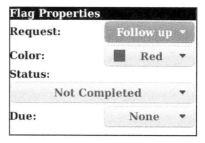

3. **Request type**: There are quite a few types of follow-ups that you can select. Click on the Request field to see them all. In some cases, you might even want to select **No response necessary**.

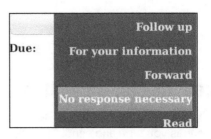

4. **Color:** You can change the color of the flag, which can help you locate the flagged items later with the email search feature.

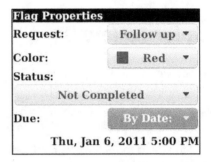

5. **Status**: Is either **Not Completed** or **Completed**

6. **Due**: Is either **None** or **By Date** and it lets you specify a due date.

7. Press the **Menu** key and select **Save**.

Changing or Editing a Flag

Once you set the flag, you will see it in the top of the message under the addresses and subject information.

1. Click on the flag itself in an email or press the **Trackpad** or the **Menu** key and select **Flag Properties**.

2. This will allow you to change all the properties.

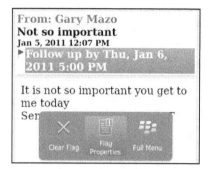

Finding Flagged Items

1. In your email inbox (Messages), press the **Menu** key and select **Search**

2. Scroll down to the bottom where it says **Type** and select **Email With Flags**.

3. Notice you can also select a specific **Color** or **All colors**.

TIP: Set a Hotkey for your Search

Before you execute your Search, press the **Menu** key and select **Save**. This allows you to name your search and set a hotkey combination ALT + some letter.

Try **ALT + Q**

Now, in your email inbox, you can quickly find all flagged items by pressing **ALT + Q**.

Flag Alarms

When a flagged item alarm rings, you will see a pop-up screen similar to the one shown.

You will also notice a flag on your top status bar with a number next to it showing how many flag due dates have passed.

Attaching Contacts, Files, and Pictures

There may be times you want to send a Contact entry to someone who asked for your colleague's mailing address or phone number. There are other times you want to share a picture, a word processing file, or a spreadsheet file. For this, you would attach a file to a message. In this section we show you how to do these things.

Attaching a Contact Entry

If you need to send someone an address that is contained in your **Contacts** list:

1. Start composing an email.

2. Press the **Menu** key and click on **Attach** and then choose **Contact** from the menu.

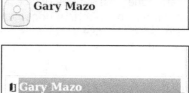

Show Symbols	Picture
Send	File
Save Draft	Video
Flag for Follow Up	Music
Attach	Voicenote
Add Bcc:	Contact

3. Either scroll to the contact you want to add or use the keyboard to type in the first few letters of the desired contact and then click on the highlighted name.

Select Contact

Gar|

New Contact
Create a new contact named...

Gary Mazo
Made Simple Learning

Gary Mazo

4. You will now see the attached contact shown as a little address book icon at the bottom the main body field of the email.

Gary Mazo

Attaching a File, Picture, Video, or Voice Note

There may be times you want to send a spreadsheet, document, picture, video, music or voice note from your BlackBerry via email. For this, you will need to attach a file (much like you would do on your computer) to the email you send from your BlackBerry.

1. Start composing an email message and press the **Menu** key.

2. Select **Attach** and choose **File** from the menu.

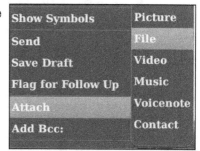

Show Symbols	Picture
Send	File
Save Draft	Video
Flag for Follow Up	Music
Attach	Voicenote
Add Bcc:	Contact

3. Next, locate the directory in which the file is stored. Your two initial options are **Device Memory** or **Media Card.**

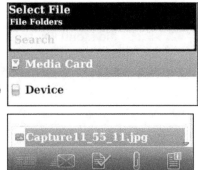

4. Navigate to the folder where the file is stored. Once you find the file, simply Click on it and it will appear in the body of the email at the bottom of the screen.

Working with Email Attachments

One of the things that makes your BlackBerry more than just another pretty Smartphone is its serious business capabilities. Often, emails arrive with attachments of important documents: Microsoft Word files, Excel spreadsheets or PowerPoint presentations. Fortunately, the BlackBerry lets you open and view these attachments and other common formats wherever you might be.

Your BlackBerry also comes with the **Documents to Go** program from DataViz. This is an incredibly comprehensive program that allows you to not only view but also edit Word, PowerPoint and Excel documents and it preserves the native formatting. This means that the documents can open on your BlackBerry and look just like they do on your computer.

Supported Attachment Formats

Your BlackBerry can open and view the following document and image formats:

- Microsoft Word (DOC)
- Microsoft Excel (XLS)
- Microsoft PowerPoint (PPT)
- Corel WordPerfect (WPD)
- Adobe Acrobat PDF (PDF)
- ASCII text (TXT)
- Rich Text Format files (RTF)
- HTML
- Zip archive (ZIP)
- (Password protected ZIP files are not supported)
- MP3 – Voice Mail Playback (up to 500Kb file size)

- Image Files of the following types: JPG, BMP, GIF, PNG, TIFF

NOTE: Multi-paged TIFF files are not supported.

NOTE: Additional file types may be supported in newer versions of the system software running on your BlackBerry.

Features available in attachment viewing:

- Images: Pan, Zoom, or Rotate.

- Save images to view later on your BlackBerry.

- Show or hide tracked changes (e.g. in Microsoft Word).

- Jump to another part of the file instead of paging through it.

- Show images as thumbnails at the bottom of the email message.

The Email Attachment Icon

How do you know if you have an email attachment?

You will see an envelope with a paperclip, as shown.

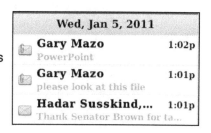

Wed, Jan 5, 2011	
Gary Mazo PowerPoint	1:02p
Gary Mazo please look at this file	1:01p
Hadar Susskind,... Thank Senator Brown for ta...	1:01p

 = Has Attachment

= No Attachment (or it has an attachment that cannot be opened by the BlackBerry)

Opening Attachments

Navigate to your message with the attachment icon showing (paperclip on envelope) and Click on on it.

At the very top of the email, in parenthesis, you will see **[1 Attachment.]** or **[2 Attachments]**, depending on number of attachments.

1. Click on the Attachment (or click the Trackpad) and select **Open Attachment(s).**

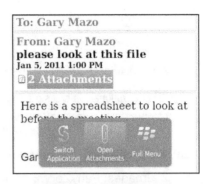

2. If the document is a Microsoft Office document format, it will then be presented with the option of **View** or **Edit with Documents to Go.**

   ▪ For a quick view without true document formatting, select **View.**

   ▪ To really see the document the way it was meant to be seen, we suggest you select **Edit with Documents to Go.**

3. If you get an error message such as **Document Conversion Failed**, it is very likely that the attachment is not a format that is viewable by the BlackBerry Attachment Viewer. Check out the list of supported attachment types up above.

Editing Attachments with Documents to Go

Once you select **Edit with Documents to Go** the document will open on your screen.

1. You can scroll through just like you were reading a Word Document on your computer.

Figure 9-1. *Editing a document with Documents to Go*

2. If you want to make changes to the document, just press the **Menu** key and select **Edit Mode** from the menu (Figure 9-1).

3. If you want to adjust the Formatting of the document, just press the **Menu** key and select **Format** (right image of Figure 9-2).

Figure 9-2. *Formatting options in Edit Mode*

4. Alternatively, you may press and hold text or selected text to see the formatting pop-up menu (see left portion of Figure 9-2).

Standard Document Viewer

You may decide you don't want to use the **Documents to Go** app.

1. Click on the attachment in the email message.

2. Select the **View** option (Figure 9-3).

3. You will see the document open with the standard document viewer. The document won't have the same look, but you will be able to navigate through it quickly.

Figure 9-3. Using the standard document viewer to view a Word document

Sheet to Go and Slideshow to Go

Following the same steps you did earlier when you opened the word processing document you can edit a spreadsheet with **Edit with Documents to Go** and a presentation file with **Edit with Documents to Go** (see Figure 9-4).

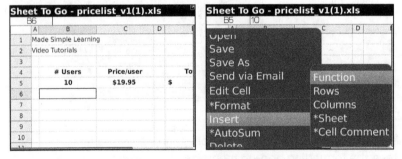

Figure 9-4. Viewing and editing a spreadsheet with Documents to Go

Open a Picture

1. Open a message with pictures attached.

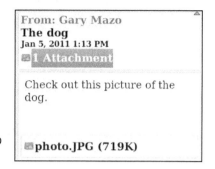

2. Either click on the **[1 Attachment]** or **[2 Attachments]**, etc. at the top of the email message or the attachments listed at the bottom.

3. Select **Open Attachment** or **Download Attachment** (to save it on your BlackBerry).

4. Then click on the image file names to open them.

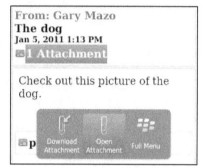

TIP: Once you have opened the pictures, the next time you view that email, you will see the thumbnails of all the pictures at the bottom of the message. You can then just scroll down to them and click on them to open them.

5. To save the picture, press the **Menu** key select **Save Image**. The picture will be saved where you specify, either on your Media Card or the main Device Memory (Figure 9-5). You can also **Set As Wallpaper** at the same time by checking the box at the bottom.

Figure 9-5. Viewing and saving an image on your BlackBerry

6. Other menu options include the following:

    ▪ **Zoom** - to expand the image

    ▪ **Rotate** - to rotate the image

    ▪ **Send** - Then choose how you would like to send it; Email, Text Message, Messenger Contact, Twitter, Group or Facebook.

    ▪ **Retrieve Info** - Retrieves image type, size and other pertinent information.

7. To save the image as a Caller ID picture, follow these steps:

    ▪ Press the **Menu** key and select **Assign to Contact**.

    ▪ Begin to type in the contact name to find the contact.

    ▪ Navigate to the correct contact and save as prompted.

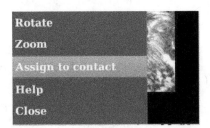

Searching for Messages (Email, SMS, MMS)

You might find that you use your messaging so often, since it is so easy and fun, that they really start to collect on your BlackBerry.

Sometimes you need to find a message quickly, rather than scroll through all the messages in your in box. There are three primary ways to search through your messages; searching the entire message through any field, searching the sender, and searching the subject (see Figure 9-6).

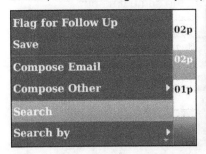

Figure 9-6. Various ways to search your Messages Inbox

The General Messages Search Command

This is the easiest way to search for a message if you are not sure of the subject or date:

1. Click on your **Messages** icon, press the **Menu** key and select **Search**.

2. Enter in information in the **Search** box at the top of the screen. When you are done, click the **Trackpad** or press the **Enter** key.

The messages that match the search criteria are then displayed on the screen.

Search Sender or Search Recipient

The easiest way to search through your emails is to search by either **Sender** or **Subject**. The **Search By** command from the Menu makes this very easy to accomplish.

Search Subject

Find an email with a subject you wish to search for in other messages. Press the Menu key and scroll down to Search by and choose Subject.

The search results will then be displayed as shown in (Figure 9-7).

Figure 9-7. Search by subject.

Search Sender or Recipient Menu Command

TIP: The Search, Search Sender, Search Recipient, and Search Subject work on SMS messages, e-mail, MMS —anything in your Messages Inbox!

Sometimes, you only want to see the list of your communication with a particular individual. Say that you want to find a specific message from Gary and you have lots of messages from Gary on your device.

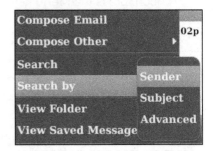

Highlight one of the messages and press the **Menu** key.

Scroll to **Search** by and choose **Sender** from the options.

All the messages from Gary will now be displayed.

Only the list of messages sent by that particular person (in this case, Gary) is now displayed. Just scroll and find the particular message you are looking for.

Chapter 10:
Your Contact List

Your BlackBerry excels as a contact manager. You will most likely turn to your **Contacts** app more than any other app on the device. From a contact, you can email, send a text message, call, fax, or even "poke" on Facebook.

One rule of thumb you will hear from us often is to add anything and everything to your contacts. Whenever someone calls, add him or her to your contacts. Add contacts from emails and messages—that way they are always available for you later.

The Heart of Your BlackBerry

Your address book is really the heart of your BlackBerry. Once you have your names and addresses in it, you can instantly call, email, send text (SMS) messages, PIN-to-PIN BlackBerry messages, or even pictures or Multimedia Messages (MMS). Since your BlackBerry came with a camera, you may even add pictures to anyone in your address book, so that when they call, their pictures show up as Picture Caller ID (as we see here with Gary's picture).

Ways to Get Your Addresses on Your BlackBerry

You can manually add contact addresses one at a time as we show you in this chapter. You can also sync your computer's contacts with your BlackBerry.

If your BlackBerry is tied to a BlackBerry Enterprise Server, the synchronization is wireless and automatic, see Chapter 1 for steps to connect to an "Enterprise Account."

Otherwise, you will use either a USB cable or Bluetooth wireless to connect your BlackBerry to your contacts and calendar on computer to keep it up to date. For Windows PC users, see Chapter 2: "Windows PC Set Up;" Apple Mac computer users, see Chapter 4: "Apple Mac Set Up."

If you use **Gmail** (Google Mail), you can use the Google Sync program to wirelessly update your contacts on your BlackBerry with your address book from Gmail for free!

Learn how in the "Using Google Sync for Contacts and Calendar" section at the end of Chapter 11: "Manage Your Calendar."

When Contacts is Most Useful

Your Contact list is most useful when two things are true:

- You have **many names** and addresses in it.
- You can **easily find** what you need.

Our Recommendations

We recommend keeping two rules in mind to help make your contacts most useful.

Rule 1: Add anything and everything to your contacts.

You never know when you might need that obscure restaurant name/number, or that plumber's number, etc.

Rule 2: As you add entries, make sure you think about ways to easily find them in the future.

We have many tips and tricks in this chapter to help you enter names so that they can be instantly located when you need them.

Transfer SIM Card Contacts into Your Contact List

If you are using your SIM (Subscriber Identity Module) card from another phone in your BlackBerry and have stored names and phone numbers on that SIM card, it's easy to transfer your contacts into your contact list.

Start your **Setup app**; it should be in the **All** Home Screen.

Scroll down to Personalization

Click the **SIM Contacts Sync** icon.

The BlackBerry will then sync the SIM card contacts to your device **Contacts** app.

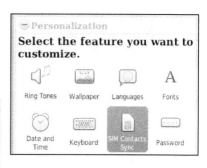

> **TIP:** Your SIM card contains only the bare minimum—**name** and **phone number**. You should review your imported contacts and add in email addresses, mobile/work phone numbers, and home/work addresses to make your BlackBerry more useful.

How to Easily Add New Addresses

On your BlackBerry, since your address book is closely tied to all the other icons (Messages/Email, Phone, and Web Browser) you have many methods to easily add new addresses:

- **Option #1:** Add a new address inside the **Contacts** app.

- **Option #2:** Add an address from an email in **Messages**.

- **Option #3:** Add an address from a phone call log in the phone.

- **Option #4:** Add a new address from an underlined email address or phone number anywhere (web browser, email, tasks, MemoPad, etc.).

- **Option #5:** (If your BlackBerry is tied to an Enterprise Server) Perform a Remote Lookup of your organizations main address list and add the resulting contacts to your **Contacts** list.

Option #1: Type an Address into Contacts

The most obvious way of adding a contact is to use New Contact and type in the information. To do this:

1. Click the **Contacts** icon.

2. You can either click on the **New**   OR

Contact tab at the top of the list or press the **Menu** key and select **New Contact.**

> New Contact
>
> New Group
>
> Filter

3. Add as much information as you can because the more you add, the more useful your BlackBerry will be!

TIP: Press the **Space** key instead of typing **@** and "." in the email address.

> Edit Contact
>
> **Add Field**
>
> Email Addresses
>
> Email: martin@ madesimplelearning. com
>
> Email: martin.trautschold@ gmail.com
>
> Email:

TIP: If you add someone's work or home address, you can easily map his or her address and get directions right on your BlackBerry.

TIP: Finding Restaurants

Whenever you enter a restaurant into your contact list, make sure to type the word **Restaurant** into the **Company Name** field, even if it's not part of the name. Then when you type the letters "**rest**," you should instantly find all your restaurants!

Up to Three Email Addresses

While you are adding or editing their contact entry, just click the **Email** field (there are three of them.)

Add up to three email addresses per contact.

Be sure to save your changes by pressing the **Menu** key and selecting **Save.**

> Email Addresses
>
> Email: martin@ madesimplelearning. com
>
> Email: martin.trautschold@ gmail.com
>
> Email: info@ madesimplelearning. com

Phone Numbers with Letters

Some business phone numbers have letters, like "1 800-REDSOX1." These are easier than you might think to add to your BlackBerry address book (or type while on the phone).

Here is how to do this easily:

1. Press and hold the **Alt** or **Shift** keys while you type letters.

2. Type all the letters or combination of numbers and letters as shown to the right.

> **TIP:** Do you need to enter a phone number with pre-set **pauses** or **waits** (like the pause before entering a voice mail password)? See the "Adding Pauses and Waits" section of Chapter 8: "Phone and Voice Dialing" for more information.

Option #2: Add Contacts from Email Addresses

Another easy way to update your address book is to simply add the contact information from email messages that were already sent to you.

1. Open up an email message in your inbox.

2. Highlight any email address for the contact you want to add.

3. Press the **Menu** key and select **Add to Contacts**.

4. Add the information in the appropriate fields, press the **Menu** key, and **Save**.

Option #3: Add Contacts from Phone Call Logs

Sometimes you will remember that someone called you a while back, and you want to add his or her information into your address book.

1. Press the **Green Phone** button to bring up your call logs.

2. Use the Trackpad to highlight the number you want to add to your address book.

3. Press the **Menu** key and select **Add to Contacts**.

4. Add the address information, press the **Menu** key, and select **Save**.

Call From Contacts	12/13
	9:55a
Call Voice Mail	12/11
	10:32p
Contact +12027094387 ▶	12/11
View ▶	5:05p
	12/10
Add Speed Dial	11:18a
	12/08
Delete	3:59p
	12/04
Add to Contacts	9:07a

Option #4: Add Contacts from Underlined Numbers, Email Addresses and Street Addresses

One of the very powerful features of the BlackBerry is that you can really add your contacts from just about anywhere.

Whenever you see an underlined phone number, email address or physical street address, you can click on it to bring up a short menu and select **Add to Contacts**.

Here is an example with an underlined street address.

Notice that with this address, the menu also allows you to:

- View On Map

- Navigate to Here

Option #5: Perform a Remote Lookup (If your BlackBerry is tied to an Enterprise Server)

If your BlackBerry is connected to a BlackBerry Enterprise Server (See "Enterprise Account Set Up" of Chapter 1), then you can perform a **Remote Lookup**. This allows you to search your corporate or enterprise-wide database stored on the central server for names of people in your organization. Once you locate these people, you can easily add them to your local **Contacts** list with a menu command.

TIP: This **Remote Lookup** also works from the **Universal Search** on the Home screen. All you need to do is type a few letters of someone's first or last name in the **Search** window and click on on the **Remote Contact Lookup** icon (shown here).

1. Click on your **Contacts** icon.

2. Type a few letters of someone's first name (you can also type a few letters of their last name if you end up finding too many people).

3. Click on **Remote Lookup** as shown.

4. Now, the BlackBerry will search the remote list of all the names in your organization for matches. In this example, there were 23 matches for "Gary." Press the **Menu** key and select **Get More Results**.

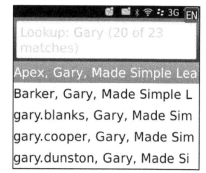

5. To add one name to your **Contacts** list, select **Add to Contacts** from the menu. To add everyone of the names listed, select **Add All to Contacts.**

6. Notice that you can also **Delete the Lookup** from the menu (lookups are saved until you delete them).

Easily Find Names and Addresses

Once you get the hang of adding contact information to the **Contacts** app, you will begin to see how useful it is to have all that information at your fingertips. The tricky part can be actually locating all the information you have input into the BlackBerry.

Using the Find Feature in Contacts

Contacts has a great Find feature at the top of the Contacts startup page that will search for entries that match the letters you type into one of these fields:

- **First Name**
- **Last Name**
- **Nickname**
- **Company Name**

1. Inside **Contacts**, just type a few letters of a person's first name, last name, nickname, and/or company name (separated by spaces) to instantly find that person.

2. Press the letter **M** to see only entries where the first name, last name or company name start with the pressed letter. Press more letters to get a closer match.

3. You can also press one letter and then the **Space** key and type another letter, like **T**, to further narrow the list to people with an **M** and a **T** starting their first, last, or company name.

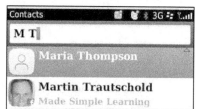

4. In this case, I can easily find what I am searching for: "Martin Trautschold."

Finding and Calling Someone in the Phone

Sometimes, you just want to make a phone call to someone in your contacts.

1. Press the **Green Phone** key to start your phone.

2. Type a few letters of someone's first name, last name, nick name, or company name, and the BlackBerry immediately starts searching for matching entries from your contacts.

3. Click on the person's name and a call is started to them. If they have more than one phone number, you are asked to select a number.

Managing Your Contacts

Sometimes, your contact information can get a little unwieldy, with multiple entries for the same individual, business contacts mixed in with personal ones, etc. There are some very powerful tools within the **Contacts** application that can easily help you get organized.

Editing Contacts

One of the first things to do is to make sure that all the correct information is included in your contacts. To do this, you will follow the steps to select and edit your contact information.

1. Click on the **Contacts** icon.

2. Type a few letters of the first, last, or company name to find the contact, or just scroll through the list.

3. Highlight the contact you want to manage and click.

4. Press the **Menu** key and choose **Edit** to access the detailed Contact screen and add any information missing in the fields.

For Facebook Users

If you use Facebook, once you load it on your BlackBerry (see Chapter 14) all your Facebook contacts will have their Facebook profile photos loaded, and you can do some cool things right from your contact list to your Facebook friends.

Friend Photos Simply Appear

All your Facebook contacts will automatically have their Facebook profile photos placed in their contact entries. You know it is a Facebook photo because of the little f in the lower right corner of the picture.

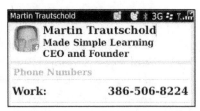

Poke!, Send a Message, or Write on a Wall

You can also Poke! your Facebook friends, send them a Facebook message, or even write on their walls right from your BlackBerry contact list!

To do this, highlight a Facebook friend in the contact list, press the **Menu** key and select **Facebook.**

Then you can **Poke!, Send Message** or **Write on a Wall.**

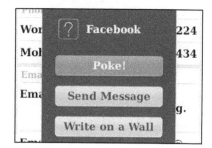

Adding a Picture to the Contact for Caller ID

Sometimes it is nice to attach a face with the name. If you have loaded pictures onto your media card or have them stored in memory, you can add them to the appropriate contact in your contacts. Since you have a BlackBerry with a camera, you can simply take the picture and add it as a **Picture Caller ID** right from your camera.

1. Select the contact to edit as you did previously.

2. Scroll down to the **Picture** icon, and click.

3. Choose the folder containing the picture you would like to use. You will see **Camera Pictures**, **Picture Library**, **Avatars** and possibly **BlackBerry Messenger**.

You can also choose Camera at the top to take a new picture with the built in camera.

If you want to use a stored picture, then navigate to the folder in which your pictures are stored by scrolling the screen up/down and clicking the correct folder.

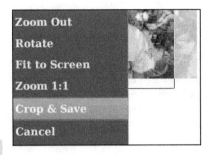

Once you have located the correct picture, click it, and then click Crop and Save.

NOTE: If you choose a small icon like an Avatar, you won't have to crop and save.

You can use the camera instead to take a picture right now. To do this, click the camera, and take the picture. Move the viewing box to the center of the target of the photo, click, and select **Crop and Save**.

The picture will now appear in that contact whenever you speak to him or her on the phone.

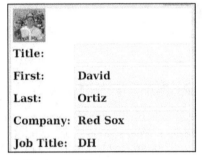

Changing the Way Contacts Are Sorted

You can sort your contacts by first name, last name, or company name.

1. Click your **Contacts**.

2. Press the **Menu** key and select **Options**.

3. Click **Contact Display Actions**.

4. In the **Sort By** field, click the First Name selection (it may say Last Name or Company if you have changed it) and choose the way you wish your contacts to be sorted. You may also select whether to allow duplicate names and whether to confirm the deletion of contacts from this menu.

Using Categories

Sometimes, organizing similar contacts into categories can be a very useful way of finding people. What is even better is that the categories you add, change, or edit on your BlackBerry are kept fully in sync with those on your computer software.

1. Find the contact you want to assign to a category, click to view the contact, click it again, and select **Edit** from the short menu.

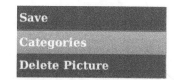

2. Click the **Menu** key and select **Categories**.

3. Now you will see the available categories. (The defaults are **Business** and **Personal**.) If you need an additional category, just press the **Menu** key and choose **New**.

4. Type the name of the new category, and it will now be available for all your contacts.

5. Scroll to the category to which you wish to add this contact, and click.

TIP: You can assign a contact to as many categories as you want!

Filtering Your Contacts by Category

Now that you have your contacts assigned to categories, you can filter the names on the screen by their categories. So, let's say that you wanted to quickly find everyone who you have assigned to the business category.

1. Click your **Contacts**.

2. Press the **Menu** key, scroll up, and select **Filter.**

3. Click on any category to select it.

4. Once you do, only the contacts in that category are available to scroll through.

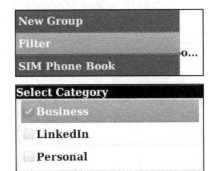

Knowing when Your Contacts Are Filtered

You will see a black bar at the top of your Contact list with the name of the category. In this case the category is **Business**.

> **TIP:** If you filter by a category where you have no contacts assigned, or just a few assigned, it may appear as if you have lost your entire address book. To fix this issue, see how to un-filter the Contact list in the next section.

Un-Filtering Your Contacts

Unlike the Find feature, you cannot just press the **Escape** key to un-filter your categories. You need to reverse the filter procedure.

Inside your contacts, press the **Menu** key. Select **Filter**, scroll down to the checked category, and uncheck it by clicking it or pressing the **space** key when it is highlighted.

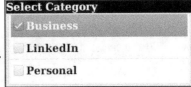

Using Groups as Mailing Lists

Sometimes, you need even more organizing power from your BlackBerry. Depending on your needs, grouping contacts into mailing lists might be useful so that you can send mass mailings from your BlackBerry.

Examples

- Put all of your team members in a group to instantly notify them of project updates.

- Let's say you're about to have a baby. Put everyone in the notify list into a "New Baby" group. Then you can snap a picture with your BlackBerry and instantly send it from the hospital!

Creating and Using a Group Mailing or SMS List

1. Start the contact list (address book) by clicking the **Contacts** icon.

2. Press the **Menu** key, scroll to **New Group**, and click.

3. Type a name for your new group.

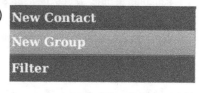

4. Press the **Menu** key again, and click **Add Member**.

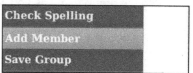

TIP: You can make both an SMS text group and an email group. Make sure each email group member has a **valid email address** and each SMS text group member has a **valid mobile phone number**, otherwise you will not be able to contact them from the group.

1. Scroll to the contact you want to add to that group and click.

2. Choose which Address to use.

3. Continue to add contacts to that group or make lots of groups and fill them using the previous steps.

TIP: You can add either mobile phone numbers (for SMS groups) or email addresses for email groups. We recommend keeping the two types of groups separate. In other words, have an SMS-only group and an email–only group. Otherwise, if you mix and match, you will always receive a warning message that some group members cannot receive the message.

Sending an Email to the Group

Just use the group name as you would any other name in your address book. If your group name was "My Team" then you would compose an email and address it to "My Team." Notice that after the email is sent, there is a separate **To** field for each person you have added to the group.

Chapter 11:
Manage Your Calendar

The BlackBerry calendar is both intuitive and powerful. In this chapter we will show you how to add events, schedule individual and recurring appointments, accept meeting invitations, and search and utilize all the features of your **Calendar** app.

Organizing Your Life

For many of us, our calendar is our lifeline. Where do I need to be? With whom am I meeting? When do the kids need to be picked up? When is Martin's birthday? The calendar can tell you all these things and more.

The calendar on the BlackBerry is really simple to use, but it also contains some very sophisticated options for the power user.

Ways to Get Your Calendar on Your BlackBerry

You can manually add calendar appointments one at a time as we show you in this chapter. You can also sync your computer's calendar with your BlackBerry.

If your BlackBerry is tied to a BlackBerry Enterprise Server, the synchronization is wireless and automatic, see Chapter 1 for steps to connect to an "Enterprise Account."

Otherwise, you will use either a USB cable or Bluetooth wireless to connect your BlackBerry to your contacts and calendar on computer to keep it up to date. For Windows PC users, see Chapter 2: "Windows PC Set Up;" Apple Mac computer users, see Chapter 4: "Apple Mac Set Up."

Google calendar If you use **Gmail** (Google Mail), you can use the Google Sync program to wirelessly update your calendar on your BlackBerry with your address book from Gmail for free!

Learn how in the "Using Google Sync for Contacts and Calendar" section at the end of this chapter.

Switching Views and Days

The calendar is where you look to see how your life will unfold over the next few hours, days, or weeks (see Figure 11-1). It is quite easy to change the view if you need to see more or less time in the Calendar screen.

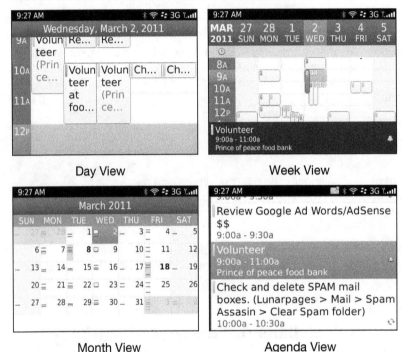

Day View   Week View

Month View   Agenda View

Figure 11-1. *Day, Week, Month and Agenda views in the* **Calendar** *app*

Swiping to Move Between Days

Navigate to your **Calendar** icon, and click. The default view is the Day view, which lists all appointments for the current calendar day.

Glide the Trackpad left or right to a previous day or an upcoming day.

Notice the date changes at the top of the screen.

Calendar Keyboard Shortcuts

You can enable one key shortcuts that allow you to switch between views and do other functions on your calendar. If you want to switch views quickly and like using your keyboard, then you will want to turn on these shortcuts.

1. Start your **Calendar**.

2. Press the **Menu** key and select **Options**.

3. Select **Calendar Display and Actions**.

4. Scroll down and **uncheck** the box next to **Enable Quick Entry**.

Now, you can use all the keyboard one-letter shortcuts. Here are a few of the more common ones: **D** = Day View, **M** = Month View, **A** = Agenda View, **W** = Week View, **N** = Next Day, **P** = Previous Day.

> **TIP:** Check out the **Calendar Keyboard Shortcuts** in Part 4 at the end of this book for a complete listing of these **Calendar** shortcuts as well as other useful shortcuts on your BlackBerry.

Scheduling Appointments

Putting your busy life into your BlackBerry is quite easy. Once you start to schedule your appointments or meetings, you will begin to expect reminder alarms to tell you where to go and when. You will wonder how you lived without your BlackBerry for so long!

Quick Scheduling

It is amazingly simple to add basic appointments (or reminders) to your calendar.

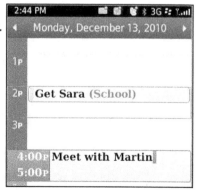

1. In Day view, move the cursor to the correct day and time by scrolling with the **Trackpad** to move the selected hour.

2. Start **Quick Scheduling** by pressing the **Enter** key on your keyboard.

3. Simply type your event in the Day View screen.

4. To change the start time, press the Shift key and glide the **Trackpad**.

5. To change the end time, glide the **Trackpad**.

6. When you're done, press the **Enter** key to save the new event.

TIP: Quick Scheduling is so fast you can even use your calendar for reminders like:

Pick up the dry cleaning, Pick up Chinese food, Pick up dog food

---

Detailed Scheduling

1. Click the **Calendar** icon.

2. Click on a time slot to start scheduling. Or, in any view, press the **Menu** key and select **New Appointment** to get into the New Appointment screen.

3. Type the subject and optional location. Click **All Day Event** if it will last all day, like an all-day conference.

Figure 11-2. Adjusting Time or Duration in the New Appointment screen

4. Click the field you need to change, and then just glide the **Trackpad** up or down to change the field (see Figure 11-2).

> **TIP:** Just use your keyboard and type numbers to set specific dates or times.

5. Alternatively, you can skip changing the end time of the appointment, and instead just change the length of the appointment by scrolling to the **Duration** field and putting in the correct amount of time.

6. Set a reminder alarm by clicking **Reminder** and setting the reminder time for the alarm from five minutes prior to nine hours prior.

> **TIP:** The default reminder time is usually 15 minutes, but you can change this by going into your Calendar Options.

7. If this is a recurring appointment, do the following: Click **Recurrence** and select **None**, **Daily**, **Weekly**, **Monthly**, or **Yearly**. Adjust the additional settings below like how many days per week, interval of the recurrence as well as when the meeting stops recurring.

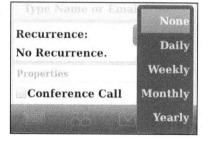

8. Mark your appointment as Private by selecting the **Mark as Private** check box.

9. If the meeting is a conference call, just put a check in the conference call box. You can then add the phone number and access code as well as participants.

10. If you would like to include notes with the appointment, simply input them at the bottom of the screen.

11. Press the **Menu** key and select **Save**.

Customizing Your Calendar

You can change a number of things to make your calendar work exactly the way you need using Calendar Options.

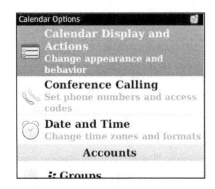

1. From the **Calendar**, press the **Menu** key and select Options.

2. Next, click **Calendar Display and Actions** at the top of the screen.

Changing Your Start and End Time on Day View

If you are someone that has early morning or evening appointments, the default 9am–5pm calendar will not work well. You will need to adjust the **Start of Day** and **End of Day** fields in the Options screen. These options are up at the top of the screen, under **Formatting**.

> **TIP:** If you use your keyboard, then you may also use the number keys on your keyboard to type the correct hours (e.g., type **7** for 7:00 and **10** for 10:00).

Changing Your Initial View

If you prefer the **Agenda** view, **Week** view, or **Month** view, instead of the default **Day** view when you open your calendar, you can set that in the Options screen. Click the drop-down list next to the **Initial View** field to set these.

Default Reminder (Alarm) and Snooze Times

If you need a little more advanced warning than the default 15 minutes, or a little more snooze time than the default 5 minutes, you can change those also in the **Options** screen.

Scheduling Conference Calls

The BlackBerry has some very useful built-in features for scheduling and joining conference calls. You can actually pre-load the conference call participant or moderator dial-in and access code numbers so when the alarm rings as shown, you can simply click the **Join Now** button.

How do you make this happen?

It's easy—in the **Appointment Details** screen when you schedule a new appointment, select the **Conference Call** check box. Then you can type the access numbers as shown.

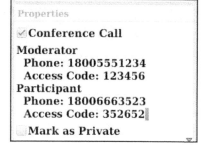

> **TIP:** You might want to set the reminder at "**0 Min.**" so you are reminded to dial-in right on time, instead of 15 minutes early (the default reminder).

TIP: If you use the same conference call dial-in service regularly, then you should pre-load the information in your Calendar Options screen.

From the calendar, press the **Menu** key and select **Options**.

Then select **Conference Calling**.

Type in the moderator and participant basic information. This is used to pre-load the conference call numbers on all scheduled appointments. If it changes, then you can alter the individual appointment.

Conference Calling	123
Moderator	
Phone: 18005623568	
Access Code: 1234	
Participant	
Phone: 3865552323	
Access Code: 2356	

Copy and Paste Into Calendar

The beauty of the Blackberry is how simple it is to use. Let's say that you wanted to copy part of a text in your email message and paste it into your calendar. A few good examples are:

- Conference call information via email
- Driving directions via email
- Travel details (flights, rental cars, hotel) via email

Please check out the "Copying, Pasting and Multitasking" section of the Quick Start Guide at the beginning of the book for detailed steps showing how to copy and paste text between applications.

Copying and pasting text into your calendar makes it available exactly when you need it. Gone are the days of hunting for the conference call numbers or driving directions, or asking yourself "What rental car company did I book?"

Dialing a Scheduled Conference Call

What is really great is that if you put a phone number into the conference call field of a **Calendar** appointment, it is very easy to call that number.

If you want to call the number before the alarm rings, open the event and then click the underlined phone number. Or select Call from the menu as shown.

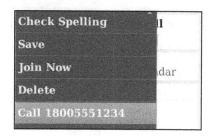

If you place the phone number in the conference call field and wait for the alarm to ring, then you can click the **Join Now** to call the number.

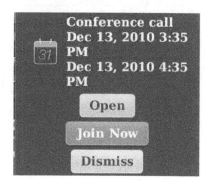

> **TIP:** You can also set a calendar event as a conference call so that you get a **Join Now** menu item.

Changing the Alarm Sound

In the "Customizing a Sound Profile" section we show you the basics of how to adjust your BlackBerry sounds. You can adjust how your device notifies you when a calendar alarm rings. The default is that the device only shows an on-screen alert, which can be easy to miss if you are not looking at your BlackBerry or it is hidden in your pocket or purse.

> **TIP:** We recommend adding at least a vibration and maybe even a sound to the Calendar alert.

Snoozing a Ringing Calendar or Task Alarm

When a calendar or task alarm rings, you can open it, dismiss it or snooze it.

To make sure you have the Snooze option active:

1. Open the **Calendar** application (see Figure 11-3).

2. Press the **Menu** button and scroll down to **Options**.

3. Click **Calendar Display and Actions** .

4. Look under the **Actions** sub-heading and click in the **Snooze** field.

 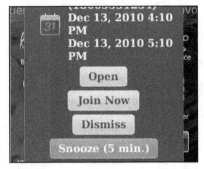

Figure 11-3. Snoozing a Calendar appointment

If you don't see a **Snooze** button as in the right screen of Figure 11-3, then you need to change the setting in your Calendar or Task options screen to some other value than **None**.

Clicking the **Snooze** option does just that—it will snooze five minutes, ten minutes, or whatever you have set in the Calendar or Task options screen.

Working with Meeting Invitations

Now with your BlackBerry you can invite people to meetings and reply to meeting invitations. If your BlackBerry is connected to a BlackBerry Enterprise Server ("BES"), you may also be able to check your invitees' availability for specific times as well.

Inviting Meeting Attendees

1. Create a new appointment in your calendar or open an existing meeting by clicking it.

2. Click in the field under **Attendees**, follow the prompts to find a contact, and click that contact to invite them. Just start typing their name and click on the appropriate email address.

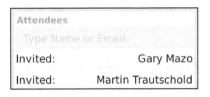

3. Follow the same procedure to invite more people to your meeting.

4. Click the **Menu** key and select **Save**.

Viewing Availability of Invitees

If your BlackBerry is connected to a BlackBerry Enterprise Server, then you will also see a button under the Attendees called **View Availability**.

1. Click on **View Availability** to see when the people you want to invite are available (based on their corporate calendars on the server).

2. From this screen, you will see a list of the availability of all the invited attendees. From this screen you can:

   - Scroll left or right using the **Trackpad** to see more of the time line. Scheduled events are shown as blocks in the time line for each person.

   - Click on **Next Available Time** to search the calendars to see the next time everyone might be free.

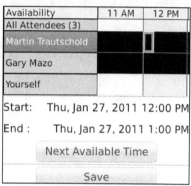

3. When done, click on **Save**.

Respond to a Meeting Invitation

You will see the meeting invitation in your messages (email inbox).

Open the invitation by clicking it, and then press the **Menu** key.

Several options are now available to you. Click either **Accept** or **Accept with Comments**, or **Tentative** or **Tentative with Comments**, or **Decline** or **Decline with Comments.**

Changing the List of Participants for a Meeting

1. Click the meeting in your **Calendar** application.

2. Navigate to the **Accepted** or **Declined** field and click the contact you wish to change.

3. The options **Invite Attendee**, **Change Attendee**, or **Remove Attendee** are available. Just click the correct option.

Sending an Email to Invitees

1. Navigate to the meeting in your calendar and click it to open it.

2. Click **Email all Attendees** and compose your email message.

3. Click the **Menu** key and select **Send**.

Using Google Sync for Contacts and Calendar

CAUTION: You can sync your Google contacts and calendar using the BlackBerry Internet Account Email Setup (see Chapter 1). We would strongly suggest that you **use the Google Sync app described in this section** to sync your Google Contacts and Calendar. We have seen problems with the Contacts sync portion of the BlackBerry Internet Account sync described in Chapter 1 (in our case the first line of the street address disappeared from all our Google Contacts!).

The great thing about using **Google Sync** for BlackBerry is that it provides you a full two-way wireless synchronization of your BlackBerry Calendar and Contacts with your Google Calendar and Address Book. What this means is anything you type in your Google Calendar/Addresses "magically" (wirelessly and automatically) appears on your BlackBerry Calendar/Contacts in minutes! The same thing goes for contacts or calendar events you add or change on your BlackBerry—they are transmitted wirelessly and automatically to show up on your Google Calendar and Contacts.

NOTE: Calendar events you have added on your BlackBerry prior to installing the Google Sync application don't get synced. However, contacts on your BlackBerry prior to the install are synced.

This wireless calendar update function has previously been available only with a BlackBerry Enterprise Server (whether in-house or hosted).

Getting Started with Gmail and Google Calendar

First, if you don't already have one, you must sign up for a free Google mail (Gmail) account at www.gmail.com.

Then, follow the great help and instructions on Google to start adding address book entries and creating calendar events on Gmail and Google Calendar on your computer.

Installing the Google Sync Program

1. Click your BlackBerry **Browser** icon to start it.

2. Type this address in the address bar on the top: http://m.google.com/sync.

3. Then click the **Install Now** link on this page.

NOTE: This page may look slightly different when you see it.

4. And click the **Download** button here.

NOTE: The version numbers and size will probably be different when you see this page.

After you download and install it, you can run it or just click **OK**. If you clicked **OK** and exited the browser, you may need to check in your **Downloads** folder for the new **Google Sync** icon.

After you successfully login, you will see a page similar to this one describing what Google Sync will sync to and from your BlackBerry.

You will see some sync status screens.

Notice at the bottom of this screen, you will see details on which fields (or pieces of information) from your BlackBerry will be shared or synchronized with your Google address book.

Finally, click **Sync Now** at the bottom of this page.

Then, finally, you will see a screen like this. Click **Summary** to see the details of what was synced.

From this point forward, the **Google Sync** program should run automatically in the background. It will sync every time you make changes on your BlackBerry or at a minimum every two hours.

From both the BlackBerry **Calendar** and **Contacts** icons, you will see a new **Google Sync** menu item. Select that to see the status of the most recent sync.

You can also press the **Menu** key from the Sync status screen to **Sync Now** or go into **Options** for the sync. If you are having trouble with the sync, check out Chapter 23: "Troubleshooting" or view Google's extensive online help.

How The Sync Looks

Here are views of the same calendar items in Google and BlackBerry.

Google Calendar on the computer:

BlackBerry Calendar:

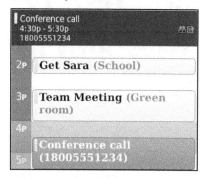

Notice the calendar events from Google Calendar are now on your BlackBerry. Anything you add or change on your BlackBerry or Google calendar will be shared both ways going forward. Automatically!

Google Address Book on your computer:

BlackBerry Contact List:

Notice all contacts from your BlackBerry contact list are now in your Gmail address book. Also, all contacts from your Gmail address book are now in your BlackBerry.

Chapter 12:
Text and MMS Messaging

As you may be aware, a key strength of all BlackBerry devices is their messaging abilities. We have covered email extensively and now turn to Text and MMS messaging. In this chapter, we will show you how to send and view both text messages (SMS) and multimedia messages (MMS.) We will show the various apps from which you can send a message and offer some advice on how to keep your messages organized.

Text and Multimedia Messaging

SMS stands for Short Messaging Service (text messaging) and MMS stands for Multimedia Messaging Service (sometimes called "Picture Messaging" or "Video Messaging"). MMS is a short way to say that you have included pictures, sounds, video, or some other form of media right inside your email message (not to be confused with regular email when media is an attachment to an email message). BlackBerry is beautifully equipped to use both of these services — learning them will make you more productive and make your BlackBerry that much more fun to use.

> **TIP:** SMS and MMS sometimes cost extra! Many phone companies charge extra for text messaging and MMS multi-media messaging, even if you have an "unlimited" BlackBerry data plan. Typical charges can be $0.10 to $0.25 per message. This adds up quickly!
>
> The solution is to check with your carrier about bundled SMS/MMS plans. For just $5–10 per month you might receive several hundred or thousand or even unlimited monthly SMS/MMS text messages.

Text Messaging

Text messaging has become one of the most popular services on cell phones today. You are hard pressed to find a teen ager (or their parents) who do not communicate via text messages these days!

The concept is very simple. Instead of placing a phone call, send a short message to someone's handset. It is much less disruptive than a phone call, and you may have friends, colleagues, or co-workers who do not own a BlackBerry—so email is not an option.

One of the authors uses text messaging with his children all the time—this is how their generation communicates. "R u coming home 4 dinner?" "Yup." There you have it—meaningful dialogue with an eighteen-year-old—short, instant, and easy.

Composing Text Messages

Composing an SMS message is much like sending an email. The beauty of an SMS message is that it arrives on virtually any handset and is so easy to respond to.

Sending from the Text Messages or Messages App

1. Click your **Text Messages** icon. (You can also send from the **Messages** app.)

2. Press the **Menu** key and choose **Compose Text Message**. Or, you can click on the **Date Row Separator** and select **Text Message**.

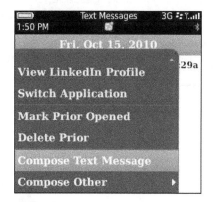

3. Begin typing in a contact name or simply type someone's mobile phone number. If you are typing a name, when you see the contact appear, Click it.

4. If the contact has multiple phone numbers, the BlackBerry will ask you to choose which number.

5. In the main body (where the cursor is) just type your message like you were sending an email message.

CAUTION: SMS messages are **limited to 160 characters** by most carriers. If you go over that in the BlackBerry, two separate text messages will be sent.

6. If you want to add some fun to your text message, click the smiley face to bring up a list of potential emoticons.

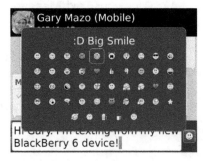

7. Click on the emoticon you want to use. Note at the top of the screen there are also the text shortcuts for each emoticon. For example, the shortcut for the "Big Smile" face is **:D.**

8. To send the message, just press the **Enter** key or **Trackpad** or press the **Menu** key and select **Send**. That's all there is to it.

Sending from the Contact List

1. Click your **Contacts** icon.

2. Type a few letters to find the person to whom you want to send your SMS message.

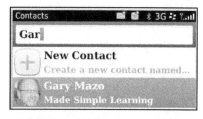

3. With the contact highlighted from the list, press the **Menu** key and you will see one of your menu options is **Text**, followed by the contact name.

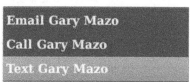

Text Messaging Menus

As with the email feature, there are many options via the menu commands in **Text** messaging.

The BlackBerry adds an **Text Messages** icon to the Home screen. One way to initiate SMS messaging is to click the icon.

> **NOTE:** On some other BlackBerry models, the icon says **SMS and MMS**.

On the Compose Text screen, when you are typing your text message, press the **Menu** key. The following options are perhaps to most popular ones you would use shown in Figure 12-1 are available to you.

Switch Application	Brings up the Switch Applications pop-up window so you can select another icon for multitasking (see Chapter 1)
Add Smiley	Add an emoticon to your Text message.
Attach	Click to add a Picture, Video, Location, Audio, Voice Note, Contact or appointment.
View Contact	Click to see the full contact information for the recipient.
Edit	Allows you to change or add recipients to the message.

Recipients

Options   Brings up the SMS option menus

Switch   Allows you to type your SMS message in another language
Input
Language

Close   This is the same as pressing the **Escape** key. It closes your
           Text window and asks if you want to save changes.

Figure 12-1. Text Messaging menu commands

Once you actually start typing your Text message and press the **Menu** key, a new option appears—**Check Spelling**—giving you the power of the BlackBerry spelling checker in your SMS messages.

Opening and Replying to Messages

Opening your Text messages couldn't be easier—the BlackBerry makes it simple to quickly keep in touch and respond to your messages.

1. Navigate to your waiting messages from either the **Text Messages** icon on the **Home** screen or your **Messages** app, and click the new Text message.

2. If you are in the midst of a dialogue with someone, your messages will appear in a threaded message format, which looks like a running discussion.

3. Press the **Menu** key if you want to edit or change or add

recipients to the message.

4. The cursor appears in a blank field—type your reply, click the **Menu** key, or the trackpad, and select **Send**.

TIP: Need to find a Text or MMS message? Go to the "Searching for Messages" section of Chapter 9: "Email Like a Pro."

MMS Messaging (Picture Messaging)

MMS stands for multimedia messaging, which includes pictures, video, and audio.

NOTE: *Not all BlackBerry devices or carriers support MMS messaging, so it is a good idea to make sure that your recipient can receive these messages before you send them.*

Sending MMS from Messages

Perhaps the easiest way to send an MMS message is to start the process just like you started the Text Message process earlier:

1. Compose a new text message from the **Messages**, **Text Messages** or **Contacts** apps.

2. Press the **Menu** key and select **Attach**. Now you can select from one of the following: **Picture**, **Video**, your **Location**, **Audio**, **Voice Note, Contact** or **Appointment**.

3. If you selected a picture, video, audio or voice note, then you will need to navigate to the item you want to attach and select it.

4. Here we see the selected picture of the new car has been sent in this multi-media message.

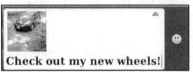

5. You can add a subject and text in the body of the MMS. When finished, just press the **Menu** key and click **Send** or press the trackpad and select **Send**.

Sending a Media File from the Media Icon

This might be the easier and more common way for you to send media files as MMS messages.

1. Scroll to the **Media** section of your **Home** screen Where you will see your Music, Videos, Pictures and other media files.

2. Click **Pictures**, and find the picture either on your device or media card that you wish to send.

3. Choose the folder that contains the picture you are looking for. Just highlight the picture (no need to click it) and press the **Menu** key.

4. Scroll down to **Send**, and click. You will then be directed to choose the method for sending the picture; either **Email**, **Text Message**, **Messenger Contact**, **Twitter** or other services that may be installed.

5. Once you select the method of delivery, choose your recipient as you did above.

TIP AND CAUTION: If you do not have a specific MMS or Picture Messaging plan, then you may be charged significantly more than a basic Text Message to send your Picture message. (Could be $0.50 or $1.00 for each picture message sent).

6. Type a subject and any text in the message, press the **Menu** key or the trackpad, and send it.

Advanced MMS Commands

While you are composing your MMS message, press the **Menu** key and scroll down to **Options**.

Scroll down to **MMS**.

From this screen you can set your phone to always receive multimedia files by setting the **Multimedia Reception** line to say **Always**.

You can also set your **Automatic Retrieval** to occur **Always** or **Never**.

You can adjust the importance at the bottom of the option screen to **Low**, **Normal** or **High**.

You can also select to **Reject Anonymous Messages** (messages without a return phone number, these are usually ads) and **Reject Advertisements** by checking both boxes.

Messaging Troubleshooting

Here are a few simple things you can do to help get your messaging going again. If they don't work, then try out some more techniques in Chapter 23: "Troubleshooting."

Host Routing Table "Register Now"

These troubleshooting steps will work for MMS, SMS, email, web browsing—anything that requires a wireless radio connection.

Host Routing Table—Register Now:

1. From your Home screen, click the **Search** icon and type "**host**."

2. Click the **Options** icon and select **Host Routing Table**.

3. Press the **Menu** key, and then click **Register Now**.

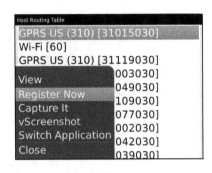

NOTE: This image shows "GPRS US." You may see your own wireless carrier name on the screen.

Perform a Soft Reset (Reboot)

Press and hold three keys simultaneously (ALT + CAP + DEL) until you see your BlackBerry screen go off for at least 10 seconds. This will reboot or reset your BlackBerry and many times will help re-establish network connectivity to fix issues with texting and picture texting.

Perform a Hard Reset (Battery Pull)

While the BlackBerry is still on, do a battery pull. Take off the back of the casing, remove the battery, wait 30 seconds, and then re-install it. Once the BlackBerry reboots, you should be all set for Text and MMS messaging.

TIP: The Quick Start Guide at the beginning of the book has more detailed steps with pictures showing how to remove the battery.

Chapter 13: BlackBerry Messenger, PIN Messaging and More

You already know that your BlackBerry is an amazing messaging device. What you may not realize is that there are so many more ways to use "messaging" on the BlackBerry. In this chapter, we will look at the famous **BlackBerry Messenger** (BBM), **PIN** messaging (using the unique identifying PIN for each BlackBerry) and other instant messaging.

> **TIP:** PIN messages are always free, whereas other SMS text and MMS (multimedia messages) may be charged under an extra service plan by your phone company.

BlackBerry Messenger

BlackBerry Messenger is really designed from the ground up to be both a messaging application and a group collaboration software. We show you the group functionality later in this chapter.

> **TIP:** If you cannot find the **BlackBerry Messenger** icon, what to do.
>
> First, click on the Search icon and type Messenger to see if it appears. Then touch and hold the icon to make it a Favorite so you don't lose it again!
>
> If the icon does not appear, then go to BlackBerry App World and download it. Check out Chapter 20 for help with this.

Setting Up BlackBerry Messenger (BBM)

BlackBerry Messenger offers you a little more secure way of keeping in touch quickly with fellow BlackBerry users. Setup is very easy.

If you don't see the **Blackberry Messenger** icon, then press the **Menu** key, look for the **Instant Messenger** folder, and click it.

1. Click the **BlackBerry Messenger** icon after accepting the legal agreement.

2. Type your **Display Name** (the name that others will see) and click OK.

3. You will then be asked which is your contact your **Contact** list. This allows better functionality in BBM.

Adding Contacts to BlackBerry Messenger

Once your user name is setup, you need to add contacts to your BlackBerry Messenger group. In BlackBerry Messenger, your contacts are fellow BlackBerry users who have the BlackBerry Messenger program installed on their handhelds.

1. Navigate to the main **BlackBerry Messenger** screen and press the **Menu** key.

2. Select **Invite Contact**.

3. Then you will be asked if you want to invite the person via PIN or email message, scan a barcode or add a contact by text messaging. (We show you the barcode scanning later in this chapter.)

4. Start typing someone's name or email address to invite them. Adjust your **Send using** email account, if you desire.

5. Click on **Send**.

6. The message request shows up in your **Pending** group, under **Contacts**.

7. When the person finally accepts your invitation, they appear in the Contacts section of BlackBerry Messenger main screen as shown with **Gary M** here.

Invite Using Barcodes

Perhaps the most innovative feature of the new BlackBerry Messenger is the use of a unique barcode as a means of connecting to someone as a Messenger contact.

Each BlackBerry can generate its own unique barcode. To find your barcode, just start up the **Messenger** application, press the **Menu** key, and select **View My Profile**.

NOTE: You can also just click on your display name at the top of your main screen.

Scroll to **PIN Barcode** and click on **Show**. The screen will now show your unique barcode. Any other BlackBerry user (with BlackBerry Messenger 5.0 or 6.0 installed *and* a camera on his or her BlackBerry) can snap a picture of the barcode.

What needs to be done is for the other BlackBerry Messenger user to choose **Invite Contact** from their menu and then choose **Invite by scanning a PIN barcode**. This will activate their camera and they can take a picture of your code.

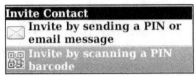

Responding to BlackBerry Messenger Invitations

You may be invited to join another BlackBerry user's Messaging group. You can either accept or decline this invitation.

You will receive your invitations via email or you can see them directly in BlackBerry Messenger.

1. Click your **BlackBerry Messenger** icon.

2. Scroll to your **Requests** group, highlight the invitation, and click.

3. A menu pops up with three options: **Accept**, **Decline**, or **Remove**.

4. Click **Accept** and you will now be part of the Messaging group. Click **Decline** to deny the invitation or **Remove** to no longer show the invitation on your BlackBerry.

BlackBerry Messenger Menu Commands

Open BlackBerry Messenger, go to your main screen, and press the **Menu** key.

Switch Application – Press this to multitask or jump to another application while leaving the **Messenger** application running.

New Multiperson Chat – Choose several BBM contacts to chat with at one time.

New Broadcast Message – Broadcast a quick message to as many BBM Contacts as you wish.

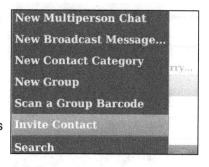

New Contact Category – Create a New Category for one or more BBM contacts.

New Group – Click to add a new messaging group such as Work, Family, or Friends.

Scan a Group Barcode – Member can display a group barcode from the **Group Details Screen.** You can scan the code to join the group.

Collapse All – This hides all group members.

Invite Contact – Use this to add people to your BBM directory.

Expand – This simply expands the dialogue screen, if the screen is already open. The menu command reads **Collapse All.**

> **TIP:** Clicking the main conversation screen does the same thing.

View My profile – View and/or change your name, change barcode settings, change status and display what you are listening to..

Options – Click to bring up your Options screen.

Close – Exit the **Messenger** application.

BlackBerry Messenger Options and Backup, Restore

If you wanted even more control of Messenger, you would press the **Menu** key and select **Options** (See Figure 13-1). On the Messenger Options screen, you can set the following:

1. Whether your BlackBerry will vibrate when someone **PING**s you (the default is **Yes.**)

2. Replace BlackBerry Contact pictures with BBM Pictures.

3. Whether your requests can be forwarded by other people (the default is **yes.**)

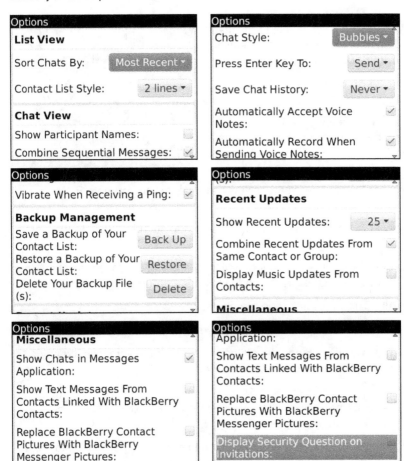

Figure 13-1. BlackBerry Messenger options

Finally, you can also set **Backup Management** options. You can **Backup**, **Restore** contacts from a previous backup or **Delete** backup files from the **Options** menu.

Conversations and Emoticons

While messaging is a lot like text messaging, you actually have more options for personal expression and the ability to see a complete conversation with the Messaging program.

Active **Chats** are shown at the top of the screen above all your contacts.

Click any active chat to continue the conversation.

Click on any **Contact** to start a new conversation.

Just type the new message and press the Enter key to send it. You can also click the **Trackpad** and select **Send Message**.

To add an emoticon to your message, click the **Emoticon** soft key button and use the **Trackpad** to move to the emoticon you wish to use (see Figure 13-2).

Just click the desired emoticon and it will appear in the message.

> **TIP:** You can also type the characters shown to get the emoticon you want—e.g., ":)" = Smile and "<3<3" = Love Struck.

Figure 13-2. Emoticon options in BlackBerry Messenger

Sending Files to a Message Buddy

In the midst of your conversation, you can send a file very easily (at the time of publication, you could sent pictures, voice notes, files and your location).

1. Click the contact in your Conversation screen and open the dialogue with that individual.

2. Press the **Menu** key and select **Send**. Choose whether you wish to send a **Picture**, **Voice Note**, **File**, or **Location**.

3. Navigate to where the image or audio file is stored on your BlackBerry, and select it.

4. Selecting the file will automatically send it to your message buddy.

NOTE: When you select **Voice Note**, the **Voice Note Recorder** will start. Just record a message and then choose **Send**.

Some BlackBerry providers (phone companies) may limit the size of file you can send via Bluetooth to a small size, such as 15 kilobytes (kb). Most pictures maybe 300kb or more, and full songs might be 500kb or more.

Pinging a Contact

Let's say that you wanted to reach a BlackBerry Messenger contact quickly. One option available to you is to ping that contact. When you ping a BlackBerry user, their device will vibrate once to let them know that they are wanted/needed immediately.

TIP: You can set your BlackBerry to vibrate or not vibrate when you receive a ping in your BlackBerry Messenger Options screen.

1. Open a conversation with a contact from the Contact screen.

2. Press the **Menu** key and scroll down to **Ping Contact**.

3. The dialogue screen will reflect the ping by showing PING!!! in capital red letters.

4. The ping recipient will notice that his or her BlackBerry vibrates and indicates that you have pinged it.

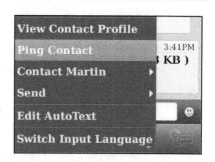

Set Availability (My Status)

Sometimes, you might not want to be disrupted with instant messages. You can change your status to unavailable, and you won't be disturbed. Conversely, one of your contacts might be offline, and you want to know when he or she becomes available. You can set an alert to notify you.

1. Navigate to your main Messaging screen and highlight your name at the top and then press the **Trackpad**.

2. You can also press the **Menu** key and scroll to **View My Profile** and click.

TIP: You can even show what music you are listening to by checking the box next to **Show What I'm Listening To**.

3. Scroll to My Status and choose either **Available** or **Busy**.

4. You can set a personalized status by clicking on **Personalize Status**.

5. Type in your status and that will be available to all your BBM contacts.

Multi-person Chat with BlackBerry Messenger

One very cool feature on BlackBerry Messenger is the ability to have a multi-person chat with two or more of your Messenger contacts.

To start a multi-person chat, just go to the main screen of the BlackBerry Messenger app, press the Menu key and select New Multi-person chat.

Start up a conversation as you did before. Now, let's say we wanted to invite another person (Martin) to join the conversation; we would press the **Menu** key and select **Invite Others** (see Figure 13-3).

Figure 13-3. Inviting a third party to a BlackBerry Messenger conference

I then find the contact from my Messenger list I want to invite—in this case, Martin.

An invitation is sent for him to join us. When she accepts, it will be noted on the Messenger screen and all three of us can have our conversation.

Using Groups

Another great feature of BlackBerry Messenger is the ability to create and use groups. Groups can be very useful for the following things:

- Chat with a private group at once

- Share pictures, and allow group members to comment on them (like Facebook comments)

- Create To-Do Lists and assign items to group members

- Share a group calendar

Create a New BBM Group

1. From your main Messenger screen, just click the **BlackBerry Groups** tab.

2. If you don't have any groups, you will see only the **Create a New Group** option.

3. Give your group a name and description, and even choose a new **Group** icon if you wish.

4. From your new group, click **Members** and then click **Invite a new member** to begin to choose members for your group. Follow the same steps as you did before to invite people.

Group Chats, Pictures, Lists and Calendar

Click on the group you just formed to see this Group main screen.

From here you can select:

Members to add or remove members.

Chat to talk with everyone in the group at once.

Pictures to upload pictures or comment on pictures others have uploaded.

Lists to create or manage to-do lists created for the group.

Calendar to view or add to the calendar shared among all group members.

Picture Comments:

Here is an example of a comment placed on a shared group picture. You get the idea – using BBM to share and comment on pictures can be very useful. This can give you and the entire group instant feedback and reactions to any picture – saving on countless phone calls and meetings!

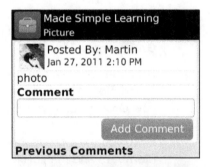

Shared To-Do Lists:

You can also share task lists among all group members and even talk about the tasks with the **Discuss List** feature you see here.

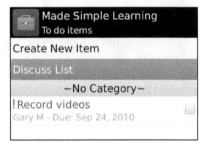

PIN Messaging

BlackBerry handhelds have a unique feature called PIN-to-PIN, also known as PIN Messaging or Peer-to-Peer Messaging. This allows one BlackBerry user to communicate directly with another BlackBerry user as long as you know that user's BlackBerry PIN number. We'll show you an easy way to find your PIN

(Figure 13-4), send an email message to your colleague, and a few good tips and tricks.

Figure 13-4. PIN messaging on your BlackBerry

Compose an email message to your colleague. In the body type of the email message, type the code letters **mypin** and hit the **space** key as shown in Figure 13-5—you will then see your pin number in the following format "pin:XXXXXXX," where the XXXXXXX is replaced by your actual PIN. Press the **Menu** key and select **Send**.

Subject: PIN messaging	Subject: PIN messaging
This is my PIN number: mypin	This is my PIN number: pin:22FAAC0A

*Figure 13-5. Typing **Mypin** to display your PIN*

Just press the **Menu** key and select **Send** to deliver an email message with your PIN number.

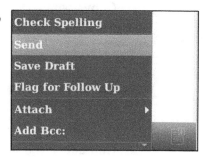

Replying to a PIN Message

Once you receive your PIN message, you will see that it is highlighted in red text in your inbox.

To reply to a PIN message, simply click the message to open it, click the **Menu** key, and select **Reply**, just like with email and other messaging.

Adding Someone's PIN to Your Address Book

Once you receive an email message containing a PIN number from your colleague or family member, you should put this PIN number into your contact list.

If you don't already have this person in your contact list, then do the following:

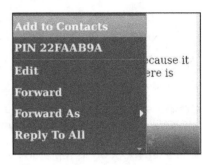

1. Highlight the **PIN** number

2. Press the **Menu** key.

3. Select **Add to Contacts** from the menu, and then enter the person's information.

4. Be sure to save your new entry.

If you already have this person in your contact list, then you should do the following:

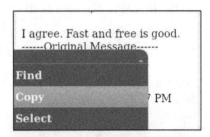

1. Select **Copy** from the menu and paste the PIN into the contact record.

2. Then press and hold the **Menu** key until you see the Switch Application pop-up window.

3. Select **Contacts** if you see it.

4. Select **Home** if you don't see **Contacts**—then click **Contacts** to start it from the **Home** screen.

5. Type a few letters of the person's first, last, or company name to find them, press the **Menu** key, and select **Edit**.

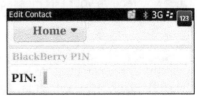

6. Scroll down to put the cursor in the **PIN** field, press the **Menu** key, and

select **Paste**.

7. Press the **Menu** key and select **Save**.

Now, next time you search through your contacts, you will have the new option of sending a PIN message in addition to the other email, Text, MMS, and phone options.

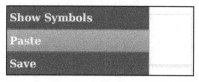

Using AIM, Yahoo, and Google Talk Messaging

After you get used to BlackBerry Messenger you will begin to see that it is a powerful way of quickly keeping in touch with friends, family, and colleagues. Realizing that many are still not in the BlackBerry world, you can also access and use popular IM programs like AOL Instant Messenger (AIM), Yahoo Messenger, and Google Talk Messenger right out of the box on the BlackBerry. Individual carriers do have some restrictions, however, and you will need to check your carrier web sites to see which services are supported.

Even More Instant Messenger Apps

It is likely you already have a number of Instant Messaging apps installed and we show you how to find them here. If you cannot find the one you want, visit **BlackBerry App World** and look for it there. It is likely that any popular IM application will be available for the BlackBerry.

1. First see if your carrier has placed an **IM** or **Instant Messaging** folder icon in your Applications directory (see Figure 13-6). This may already have the icons installed that you want to use.

2. Navigate to **Applications** and scroll for an icon that simply is called **IM**.

Figure 13-6. Other instant messaging icons on your BlackBerry

3. If you have an **IM Folder** icon, click it, and follow the on-screen prompts.

4. If there is no **IM** icon, click on BlackBerry App World and do a search for Instant Messenger apps or view the Instant Messaging category.

For more information to help you download and install third-party software, please check out Chapter 20: "BlackBerry App World" which is devoted to adding and removing software.

Chapter 14: Social Networking

BlackBerry smartphones aren't just for business executives anymore, but you already know that. Your BlackBerry can keep you in touch in ways beyond the messaging features shown earlier in this book.

Some of the most popular places to connect these days are social networking sites—places that allow you to create your own page and connect with friends and family to see what is going in their lives. Some of the most popular websites for social networking are Facebook, Twitter, and LinkedIn.

In this chapter, we will show you how to access these sites. You will learn how to update your status, "tweet," and keep track of those who are important or simply of interest to you.

We will also show you the new Social Feeds app which puts all your social networking and RSS feeds into one, easy to access place to quickly check up and check in.

Downloading Social Networking Apps

Check in your Applications folder or Social Networking folder for these apps. If you do not already see these apps on your BlackBerry, you can easily download them from **App World**.

1. Start **App World** by clicking on it.

2. Use the **Search** feature in App World and simply type the name of the app—**Facebook**, **Twitter**, **foursquare**, **Gowalla**, **MySpace**, **LinkedIn**, or **Flickr**—to quickly find each of these apps.

3. Download and install any
   app you want.

TIP: Follow the steps shown in Chapter 20 "BlackBerry App World" to get each app downloaded and installed.

As of publishing time, BlackBerry has its own very capable **Twitter** client. There are also more than half a dozen pretty good Twitter clients, many of them free. You might want to try out **UberTwitter** or one of the others.

Logging into the Apps

In order to connect to your account on **Facebook**, **Twitter**, and **MySpace**, you will need to locate the icon you just installed and click on it. We use the example of **Facebook** here, but the process is very similar for the rest of the apps.

There is a lot to like about having **Facebook** and these other social networking apps on your Blackberry. You can always stay in touch. Just log in as you do on your computer and you are ready to go anywhere, anytime from your BlackBerry.

NOTE: You might find your **Facebook** icon in your **Social Networking** folder, depending on your carrier.

Once **Facebook** is successfully downloaded, the icon in your **Downloads** folder should look something like this.

1. Click on the **Facebook** icon.

2. Enter your login information and click the **Login** link.

3. You are logged in. Usually, you will only have to log in one time to each of these apps.

Facebook

Facebook was founded in February of 2004. Since that time, it has served as the premier site for users to connect, re-connect and share information with friends, co-workers, and family. Today, over 400 million people use Facebook as their primary source of catching up with the people who matter most to them.

If you have the **Facebook** icon on your BlackBerry already, it will look like this:

1. Just click on the **Facebook** icon to start it.

2. Login if requested as shown above.

There is a lot to like about having **Facebook** on your Blackberry. All of your messages will be pushed to your device, just like your email, so you can always stay in touch. You also navigate the site in a very similar way to that on your computer.

Facebook Setup Wizard

1. After you login the first time, you will be taken through the **Setup Wizard** screens. (You can also get to these screens by **Menu > Options > Run Setup Wizard**.)

2. By default, all the boxes are checked. We recommend leaving them checked to have the best integration with your BlackBerry

apps.

3. Click on **Save** at the bottom to continue.

Some of the integration you will get with Facebook includes:

- See **Facebook Profile** pictures in your **Contacts** list.

- See Facebook calendar events on your BlackBerry **Calendar**.

- Receive a **Facebook** message in your **Messages** app when you or your friends poke you or do a status update.

- Receive a **Facebook** messages when anyone comments on photos you have uploaded.

- Replace existing **Contact** photos with **Facebook friend** photos.

Status Update and News Feed

Once you log on to **Facebook** for BlackBerry, you can to write you own status update.

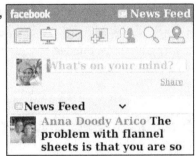

1. Click on **What's on your mind?**

2. Type your status update.

3. You can also see your **News Feed** from your friends.

Top Bar Icons

Along the top bar are icons for some of the most use features of Facebook. You will see icons for the **News Feed, Notifications, Messages, Upload a Photo, Friends, Search** or **Places**..

Notification/Email in Facebook:

Click on the Notifications icon (second from left) to see all your notifications in Facebook. The great thing is that these are fully integrated into your Messages Inbox icon. So every notification you receive in Facebook is also shown in Messages.

This saves you the step of going into Facebook to check for notifications.

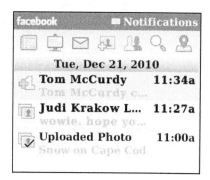

NOTE: If you choose to integrate your Facebook account into your Social Feeds, (see the end of the chapter) you will also see your notifications there.

Communicating with Friends

It is easy to communicate with your friends.

1. Click on the **Friends** icon to see a list of friends displayed.

2. If you have contact information or phone numbers in your **Contacts** app, the icons next to your friend's names will show that.

3. Click on the friend you wish to communicate with to see all the options available to you.

4. In this example, we clicked on Martin's name. Now we can:

    ▪ Send him a message

    ▪ Write on his wall

    ▪ Request his phone number

    ▪ Poke him

- View his profile
- View his BlackBerry profile
- Refresh contact info
- Disconnect his information from the BlackBerry profile

NOTE: We can also just highlight the same contact in our list and press the **Menu** key to see these same options.

Uploading Pictures to Facebook

An easy and fun thing to do with Facebook is to upload pictures. You can upload pictures from your BlackBerry to Facebook in using these methods:

- From the **Facebook** app - click on the small **Upload a Photo** icon.

- From your **Camera** app – snap a picture and upload it using **Send/Share** menu item or the **Send Picture** icon, then **Send to Facebook**.

- From your **Pictures** app – select a picture, press the **Menu** key, select **Send/Share**, and select **Send to Facebook**.

Once you select a photo to upload, you can specify a caption and a folder. You can also Tag the photo with a Facebook friend's name. We show you the steps from the **Facebook** app, but they are identical when you upload from any of the above options:

1. Click the **Upload a Photo** icon at the top of **Facebook**.

2. Navigate through the folders on your BlackBerry to locate the picture you wish to upload or choose **Camera** at the top to take a new picture.

3. Click on the picture to select it for upload.

4. Now you can write a **Caption**, select an Album for the photo (the default is **Mobile Uploads**), and **Tag This Photo** (left image in Figure 14-1).

5. Click on **Tag This Photo** to identify one or more people from the photo as your Facebook friends. You will be given a small cross-hair to identify the faces of your friends. After the photo is uploaded, your friends will be notified that they have been tagged (right image in Figure 14-1).

6. When you are done tagging, you can click **Upload** to send the picture.

Figure 14-1. *Uploading pictures to Facebook*

TIP: Immediately after you upload the photo from your BlackBerry, you can see it on both on your computer and on your BlackBerry Facebook page.

Twitter

Twitter was started in 2006. Twitter is essentially an SMS (text message)-based social networking site. It is often referred to as a "micro-blogging" site where the famous and not-so-famous share what's on their mind. The catch is that you only have 140 characters to get your point across.

With Twitter, you subscribe to "follow" someone who "Tweets" messages. You might also find that people will start to follow you. If you want to follow us, we are: @garymadesimple or @mtrautschold on Twitter.

Create a Twitter Account

Making a Twitter account is very easy. We do recommend that you first establish your Twitter account on the Twitter web site.

1. On your computer, go to www.twitter.com.

2. Click on the **Join Today** button.

When you establish your account, you will be asked to choose a unique user name and choose a password.

3. You will then be sent an email confirmation. Click on the link in your email and you will be taken back to the Twitter web site. You can choose people to follow, or post your own Tweets on the web site. You can also read Tweets from your friends.

Using Twitter for BlackBerry

To start using Twitter, follow these steps:

1. Click on the **Twitter** icon (it may be located in your **Downloads** folder).

2. The first time you start the app, log in with your Twitter **username** and **password**.

3. Click the checkbox next to **Remember me** to avoid re-entering your information.

4. Click **Sign In**.

5. The initial view in **Twitter** has a small box at the top of the screen that says "What's happening" where you can tweet (send messages) to those who are following you.

6. Under that are the tweets from those you are following.

7. Just scroll through the list of tweets to catch up on all the important news of the day!

Sending Out Tweets

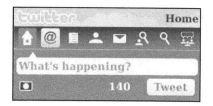

1. Click on in the box that says **What's happening?**

2. Type your Tweet about what is important to you (in 140 characters.)

3. Type your message and then click on the **Update** button to post your Tweet.

Twitter Icons

Along the top of the Twitter screen are eight icons; these are the quick links to the basic **Twitter** functions (see Figure 14-2).

Figure 14-2. Twitter icons at top of screen

Mentions

A "mention" in Twitter speak is a tweet that mentions your @username somewhere in the body of the tweet. These are collected and stored in your Mentions section of your Twitter account.

My Lists

You can create a custom list so that your followers cannot only follow everything you say, they can choose to follow a specific topic (a list) that you create. In this example, I created a list entitle "Made Simple Announcements" so that users can choose to only follow our special announcements if they choose.

My Profile

Just as it sounds, the My Profile icon will take you to your Twitter profile. You can see your followers, your tweets, and your bio. Just click on any field in your profile and a short menu comes up. To edit your information, just choose **Edit Profile** from the menu.

Direct Messages

Direct Messages are messages between you and another user on Twitter.

Click the **Direct Messages** icon to see your direct messages.

To compose a direct message click on the **Compose Message** icon.

Fill in the **To** field with the Twitter user name and then type your 140 character message in the box. When you are done, just click on the **Send** button.

Find People

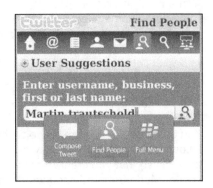

The **Find People** icon takes you to a search window where you can type in a user name, business name, or last name to search for someone who might be on Twitter.

1. Type in the name and your query will be processed. Press the trackpad to search.

2. Scroll through the results to see if you find what you are looking for. If so, just click on the entry that matches your search and scroll down.

You will be able to see the statistics of how many followers there are and if they have particular Lists to follow. You can also choose the select **Follow** or **Block** to either follow this contact on Twitter or block all tweets.

Search

 The **Search** icon takes you to another search window. Here you can type in any keyword to find opportunities to follow a topic or individual. For example, if you were to type in the word **golf**, you might find popular golf courses, golfers, or driving ranges that all use Twitter. You might also find thousands of individuals who just want to brag about their golf score.

> **TIP:** Be very specific in your search to help narrow down the search results.

Popular Topics

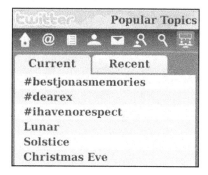 The **Popular Topics** icons will simply list those topics that are currently popular on Twitter. So, if you wanted to scroll through, you might find everything from the New England Patriots to the President's visit overseas. On Twitter, someone always has something to say about everything.

Twitter Options

To get to the Twitter options, follow these steps:

1. From your Twitter home screen, press the **Menu** key.

2. Scroll down to **Options**.

3. You will notice several boxes in which you can click to place or remove a check mark.

The available options are:

- Tweet refresh in background

- Automatic Tweet Refresh

- Notify on new tweets

- Notify on new replies and mentions

- Specify number of tweets per refresh

- Integrate in Messages app.

- Spell check before sending

- Show navigation bar

- Show tweet box on home screen

- Use system font settings

- Check tweets for personal information before sending

- Connect directly to Twitter when Wi-Fi is enabled

- Upload photos

Just put a check box in the corresponding box next to the option you would like to enable.

LinkedIn

LinkedIn has very similar core functionality to **Facebook** but tends to be more business and career focused, whereas **Facebook** is more focused on personal friends and games. With LinkedIn, you can connect and re-connect with past business associates, send messages, see what people are up to, have discussions, and more.

> **NOTE:** The **LinkedIn** app is available as a free download from the BlackBerry App World.

Download and Sign In

Locate and download **Linkedin** from BlackBerry **App World**.

Click on the icon, enter your **Email**, **Password** and click on **Sign In**.

Navigating LinkedIn

LinkedIn has a similar icon-based navigation as Facebook. The top of the home screen has a box for posting your profile update (similar to a status update on Facebook.)

Just type your message and then click on the **Post** button.

Icons

At the top of the LinkedIn home screen are six icons. The first one is the Network Updates icon that will return you to the home page with profile updates and the ability to update your own LinkedIn status.

Search

Click in the search box and LinkedIn will try to first match your search with contacts in your LinkedIn directory. Next, the search field will show individuals who match the search criteria who may be part of your "Network."

Note: LinkedIn uses a "Network" system. Someone who is a direct contact is considered a 1st degree connection in your network. Someone who is connected to one of your contacts (but not you) is considered a 2nd degree contact and so on.

Connections

The next icon along the top is the **Connections** icon, which shows you a listing of your LinkedIn connections. Scroll down and find the particular connection you are looking for.

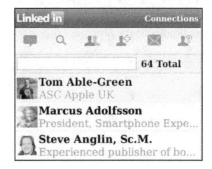

Tip: Press the **Menu** key on your BlackBerry when a connection is highlighted and scroll and click on **Link to BlackBerry Contact** in the menu. This will attach all contact information (including the LinkedIn picture) to your BlackBerry contact for that individual.

Invitation

Click on the Invitations icon to see if you have any pending invitations for connections. You can also press the **Menu** key and select **Compose New Invitation**.

Type in the email address of the individual you would like to add to your LinkedIn network.

Edit the text below the email field

Press the **Menu** key and select **Send**.

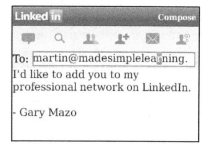

Note: Unlike the **LinkedIn** web based application, you don't have to say how you know the individual with whom you would like to connect. This makes it much easier to send an invitation from the mobile application.

Messages

The Messages icon is where you go for direct messages to your contacts. You can read messages that are sent to you here. You can also press the **Menu** key and select **Compose Message** to send a direct message to any of your **LinkedIn** contacts.

Reconnect

The Reconnect icon [   ] is where you click to see people you might know, people who might be in groups you belong to or people who might have common connections to you. It is a good way to expand your network and see interesting people you might have forgotten about.

LinkedIn Options

Press the Menu key from any section of the **LinkedIn** app and scroll to Options and click. You will notice a selection of radio boxes that you can check or uncheck depending on your needs and desires.

Select **BlackBerry Mail** to have LinkedIn messages displayed in your BlackBerry message list.

Select **BlackBerry Contacts** to have your LinkedIn contacts displayed as part of your Contact directory.

The bottom boxes let you specify your type of network and if you want BES integration of your LinkedIn account.

> **Note**: Some options like BES, Wi-Fi and WAP are only available if your BlackBerry is connected to those networks.

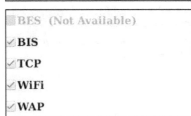

YouTube

A very fun site, **YouTube** lets you view short video clips on just about everything. Your new BlackBerry is able to view most of the **YouTube** videos without doing anything special. There are two ways to access YouTube on your BlackBerry, through the **YouTube** app or through the **YouTube** web site.

If the **YouTube** app is on your BlackBerry, it will usually be in the Media home screen. You can also go to BlackBerry App World and search for YouTube or go to mobile.blackberry.com and search for the YouTube app download.

The YouTube App

Navigate to the **YouTube** icon (usually in the **Media** home screen) and click. You will be prompted to either **Go to YouTube** or **Upload a Video**.

In this example, we will choose **Go to YouTube**. What you see is the standard mobile web based version of YouTube.

To access your **YouTube** account, sign in by clicking the **Sign In** button at the top right of the screen.

YouTube on the Web

If you don't see the **YouTube** app, you can still find it using your **Web Browser**. See Chapter 19 for more details on the **Browser**.

1. Click on your **Browser** icon.

2. Click on the top address bar and type in m.youtube.com.

3. Press **Enter** key on the keyboard.

4. You should now see a list of the most popular videos (Figure 14-3).

5. Click on the video image itself to start playing the video.

6. Click on the title of the video to learn more about it.

> **TIP:** Set a web bookmark in your Browser for YouTube by hitting the **Menu** key and selecting **Add Bookmark**. Go to Chapter 19 to learn how to set bookmarks

7. Once the video starts playing, click on the screen to show the controls. See the Chapter 18: "Fun with Videos" for more help about how to enjoy videos on your BlackBerry.

Figure 14-3. YouTube Mobile on the your BlackBerry

To search for any video on YouTube, just type anything in the search field. Type in your search and click the **Trackpad** and the search results will display for you.

YouTube Favorites

If you have a YouTube account, you can log in using the BlackBerry **YouTube** app or on the YouTube mobile web site.

Login with your YouTube user name and password. On the next screen, you will see your Videos, Favorites, Subscriptions and Inbox.

Just click on whichever of your items you wish to view. Your favorites are listed just like the popular videos on the YouTube home screen. Just click a video to start.

Social Feeds

With all the new Social Networking sites, you can find yourself inundated with messages, updates, feeds and status updates.

New to the BlackBerry in OS 6 is the ability to combine all your important Social Messaging apps into one Social Feed that is easy to quickly view. You don't "have" to use the Social Feed app, but it does make quick viewing of your feeds much more streamlined.

Getting Started with Social Feeds

Click the **Social Feeds** app on your BlackBerry. The app should be listed under the **All** Home Screen.

Usually, when you start the app for the first time you will see that you have no feeds associated with the app, so you will need to set them up.

You should see a Getting Started message under the Social filter. If you slide the screen to the left, you will see another filter for RSS feeds.

Adding Feeds

Touch the **Getting Started** button or just touch the Social filter heading and you will see all the options for the Social Feeds app. Initially you will see that you are not logged in to your Social Networking sites.

To add feeds to the Social Feeds app:

Click the **Social Filter** header.

Click on the account you want to add to the **Social Feed** app.

Log in to the appropriate app – either **Facebook, Twitter, BlackBerry Messenger, MySpace, Google Talk** or one of the other apps listed.

Adding RSS Feeds

RSS stands for "Really Simple Syndication." These are very short news feeds from popular web sites; snippets of full stories and a great way to quickly follow your favorite sites.

RSS feeds are usually viewed in an RSS reader like Google Reader or any other RSS app.

Once your Social feeds are set, just scroll with the **Trackpad** to the left and you will see the RSS filter. To add RSS feeds:

Click on the header for the **RSS Filter**.

If you have no RSS feeds, you will be prompted to search for a feed or to enter a URL of a web site you frequent. Most web sties have an RSS feed that you can "subscribe" to in order to get snippets of news.

You can also press the **Menu** key and select **New RSS Feed**.

Type in the web address to search for an accompanying feed.

Choose which of the feeds you wish to add to the **RSS Filter**.

In this example, we searched for MSNBC.com and found two available RSS feeds to which we could subscribe (see Figure 14-4).

Figure 14-4. Adding RSS Feeds to the **Social Feeds** app.

You can continue to add as many RSS feeds as you would like in this manner.

Using the Social Feeds App

Once the Social and RSS feeds are set up, using the **Social Feeds** app is quite simple. To use your Social Feeds app, just:

Click on the Social Feeds

To view your Social feeds, scroll through those listed under **Social Filter**.

To view your RSS feeds, slide the top status bar to the left and scroll through the feeds listed under the **RSS Filter** header (see Figure 14-5).

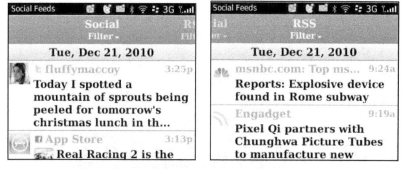

Figure 14-5 Social Filter and RSS Filter in the **Social Feeds** app.

Posting to All Social Apps at Once

One of the Great things about the Social Feeds app is that you can make one post and put in on BlackBerry Messenger, Facebook and Twitter at the same time. This certainly saves a bit of time if there is a status update you want to post on all three accounts.

To do this:

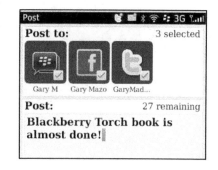

1. Make sure you are in the Social Filter.

2. Press the **Menu** key and select **New Post.**

3. Place check marks in the app to which you would like to post. In the example shows, we choose **BlackBerry Messenger, Facebook** and **Twitter**.

4. Type your post in the box provided and click on the **Post** button.

Managing RSS Feeds

While in one of the two filters, press the Menu key. In this example, we want to manage our RSS feeds.

Press the Menu key and select **Manage RSS Feeds**. The list of subscribed feeds will now be listed. Click on one of them. You can now edit the name of the feed or uncheck the Subscribe box and remove it from your filter (see Figure 14-6).

Figure 14-6 Managing RSS Feeds in the Social Feeds app.

Chapter 15:
Tasks and Notes

The Task Icon

 Like your contacts, calendar, and MemoPad, your task list becomes more powerful when you share or synchronize it with your computer. Since the BlackBerry is so easy to carry around, you can update, check off, and even create new tasks anytime, anywhere they come to mind. Gone are the days of writing down a task on a sticky note and hoping to find it later when you need it.

How Do You Get Your Tasks from Your Computer to Your BlackBerry?

You can mass load or sync your computer's task list with your BlackBerry **Task** app.

If your BlackBerry is tied to a BlackBerry Enterprise Server, the synchronization is wireless and automatic. Otherwise, you will use either a USB cable or Bluetooth wireless to connect your BlackBerry to your computer to keep it up to date. For Windows PC users, see Chapter 2; Apple Mac computer users, see Chapter 4.

Viewing Tasks

1. Click on the **Search** icon
    and type the word **Tasks**
    to find your **Tasks** icon.
    You could also click on the
    Applications folder to see
    the **Task** app within the
    folder as shown here.

2. The first time you start
    tasks on your BlackBerry,
    you may see an empty
    task list if you have not yet
    synchronized with your
    computer.

Adding a New Task

Press the **Menu** key and select **New** or just scroll and click the **Add Task** bar.
Then you can enter information for your new task in the screen in Figure 15-1.

TIP: Keep in mind the way the Find feature works as you name your task. For
example, all tasks for a particular "Proposal" should have "Proposal" in the name
for easy retrieval.

Figure 15-1. *New task screen*

Categorizing Your Tasks

Like Address Book entries, you can group your tasks into categories. And you can also share or synchronize these categories with your computer.

Assigning a Task to a Category

1. Highlight the task, click the screen, and open it (see Figure 15-2).

2. You can set the status of your task, as well as the priority and the due date, from this screen.

3. To categorize, press the **Menu** key and select **Categories** or touch the **Edit** button next to the **Categories** heading.

4. Select as many categories as you would like by checking them by clicking the screen or pressing the **Space** key.

Figure 15-2. Setting New Task status and priority

5. You may even add new categories by pressing the **Menu** key from the **Select Categories** screen and selecting **New**.

6. Once you're done, press the **Menu** key and select **Save** to save your category settings.

7. Press the **Menu** key and select **Save** again to save your task.

Finding Tasks

Once you have a few tasks in your task list, you will want to know how to quickly locate them. One of the fastest ways is with the Find feature. The same Find feature from the address book works in Tasks. Just start typing a few letters to view only those that contain those letters.

In the example here, if we wanted to quickly find all tasks with **Go** in the name Figure 15-3, then we type the letters **go** to quickly see them.

NOTE: If you have the **Universal Search** feature enabled (as it is by default) when you type in the search bar, your BlackBerry searches for matches outside of the current Task app as well.

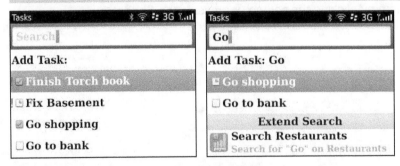

Figure 15-3. Finding exactly the task you are looking for

Managing and Checking Off Tasks

1. Scroll down to a task and use the **Trackpad** to highlight it. (Don't click it, unless you want to open it and make changes.)

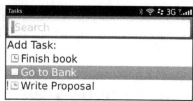

2. Once a task is highlighted, you can use the **Menu** key to manage the task.

   ▪ Mark it **Completed**.

   ▪ Mark it **In-Progress**.

   ▪ Or you can **Delete** it.

3. You can also simply hit the Space bar to mark the highlighted task **Completed** from the list.

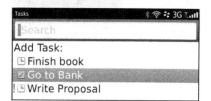

Sorting Your Tasks and Task Options

You may sort your tasks by the following methods in your Task Options screen: **Subject (default)**, **Priority**, **Due Date**, or **Status**.

You may also change the **Confirm Delete** field by simply placing a check in the radio box. You may also change the **Snooze** field from **None** to **30 Min**.

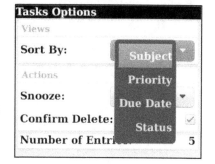

The MemoPad – Virtual Sticky Notes

One of the simplest and most useful programs on your BlackBerry is MemoPad. Its uses are truly limitless. There is nothing flashy about this program—just type your memo or your notes, and keep them with you at all times.

Using **MemoPad** is very easy and very intuitive. The following steps guide you through the basic process of inputting a memo and saving it on your BlackBerry. There are two basic ways of setting up memos on the BlackBerry: either compose the note on your computer organizer application and then synchronize (or transfer) that note to the BlackBerry, or compose the memo on the BlackBerry itself.

How to Sync Your MemoPad

You can also sync your computer's memo pad or notes list with your BlackBerry **MemoPad** app.

If your BlackBerry is tied to a BlackBerry Enterprise Server the synchronization is wireless and automatic. Otherwise, you will use either a USB cable or Bluetooth wireless to connect your BlackBerry to your computer to keep it up to date. For Windows PC users, see Chapter 2; Apple Mac computer users, see Chapter 4.

The sync works both ways, which extends the power of your desktop computer to your BlackBerry—add or edit notes anywhere and anytime on your BlackBerry—and rest assured they will be back on your computer (and backed up) after the next sync.

1,001 Uses for the MemoPad (Notes) Feature

OK, maybe we won't list 1,001 uses here, but we could. Anything that occupies space on a sticky note on your desk, in your calendar, or on your refrigerator could be written neatly and organized simply using the **MemoPad** app.

Common Uses for the MemoPad

- Grocery list
- Hardware store list
- Any store list for shopping
- Meeting agenda
- Packing list
- Made Simple Learning videos you want to watch
- Movies you want to rent next time at the video store
- Your parking space at the airport, mall or theme park

Adding or Editing Memos on the BlackBerry

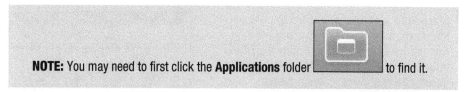

Locate the **MemoPad** icon (your icon may look different, but look for MemoPad to be shown when you highlight it).

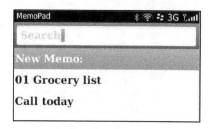

NOTE: You may need to first click the **Applications** folder to find it.

To add new memos to the list, simply click **New Memo** at the top of the list.

To open an existing memo, just scroll to it and click it.

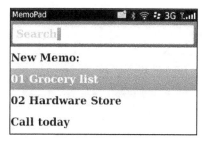

When typing a new memo, you will want to enter a title that will be easy to find later by typing a few matching letters.

1. Type your memo in the body section.

2. Press the **Enter** key to go down to the next line.

3. When you're done, press **Trackpad** and select **Save** or press the **Menu** key and select **Save**.

Notice, if you have copied something from

another app, like **Email**, you could paste it into the memo. (See the Quick Start Guide to learn more about Copy & Paste.)

Quickly Locating or Finding Memos

MemoPad has a Find feature to help you locate memos quickly by typing the first few letters of words that match the title of your memos. Example, typing **Gr** would immediately show you only memos matching those three letters in the first part of any word, like "grocery."

> **NOTE**: Because of the Universal Search feature of the BlackBerry, other items might show up on the search. The memos that mach the search criteria will appear first.

Ordering Frequently Used Memos

For frequently used memos, type numbers (01, 02, 03, etc.) at the beginning of the title to force those memos to be listed in order at the very top of the list. (The reason we started with zero is to keep memos in order after the tenth one.)

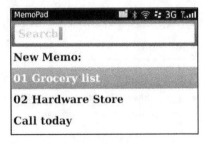

Separate Memo for Each Store

This can help eliminate the forgetting of one particular item you were supposed to get at the hardware or grocery store (and save you time and gas money)!

Viewing Your Memos

1. Scroll down with the **Trackpad**, or click in the **Search** field at the top to type a few letters to find the memo you want to view.

2. Click the highlighted memo to instantly view its contents.

> **TIP:** Typing **ld** (stands for "Long Date") and pressing the **space** key will insert the date "Tue, 28 Aug 2007," and "**lt**" ("Long Time") will enter the time: "8:51:40 PM" (in the local date/time format you have set on your BlackBerry).

Organizing Memos with Categories

Similar to your address book and task list, **MemoPad** allows you to organize and filter memos using categories.

> **TIP:** Categories are shared between your address book, task list, and **MemoPad**. They are even synchronized or shared with your desktop computer.

Similar to your **Contacts** and **Tasks** app, **MemoPad** allows you to organize and filter memos using categories.

First, you must assign your memos to categories before they can be filtered.

One way to be extra organized with **MemoPad** is to utilize categories so all your memos are filed neatly away.

The two default categories are **Personal** and **Business**, but you can easily change or add to these.

> **TIP:** Once you assign Memos to **Categories**, you can use the **Filter** menu command to view only Memos assigned to a specific category.

Switching Applications / Multitasking

From almost every icon on your BlackBerry, MemoPad included, pressing the **Menu** key and selecting **Switch Application** allows you to multitask -- leave your current icon open and jump to any other icon on your BlackBerry. This is especially useful when you want to copy and paste information between apps.

TIP: Pres and hold the **Menu** key to multitask.

Instead of using the **Switch Application** menu item, try pressing and holding the

Menu key. It's a good short cut!

Here's how you jump or switch applications:

1. Press and hold the **Menu** key until you see a little pop-up window with icons appear in the middle of the screen. This is called the Switch Applications window. You can also get to this window by pressing the **Menu** key and then selecting **Switch Application** from the menu (see Figure 15-4).

Figure 15-4. Multitasking on the BlackBerry

2. You will now see the Switch Applications pop-up window, which shows you every icon that is currently running.

3. If you see the app you want to switch to, just click it.

4. If you don't see the app you want, then click the **Home Screen** icon. Then you can locate and click the right app.

5. You can then jump back to **MemoPad** or the application you just left by selecting the **Switch Application** menu item from the icon you jumped to.

Press and hold the **Menu** key to jump back.

Forwarding Memos via Email, SMS, or BlackBerry Messenger

You might want to send a memo item via email, BlackBerry PIN message, or SMS text message to others. If so, you can use the **Forward As** command from the menu. Highlight the memo you want to send and press the **Menu** key.

1. Select **Forward As**, and then select whether you want **Email**, **Text Message, Group Message, Messenger Contact, PIN, Social Feeds**, or **Twitter** (see Figure 15-5).

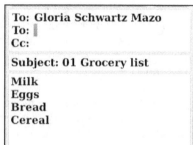

Figure 15-5. Forwarding a memo

2. Finally finish composing your message, press **Send** soft key at the bottom of the screen or the **Menu** key and select **Send**.

Other Memo Menu Commands

There may be a few other things you want to do with your memos. These can be found in the more advanced menu commands.

Start the **MemoPad** icon.

Some of these advanced menu items can be seen only when you are either writing a new memo or editing an existing one.

So you select either **New** and begin working on a new memo, or select **Edit** and edit an existing memo.

From the Editing screen, press the **Menu** key and the following options become available to you:

Switch Application – This is explained above.

Hide Keyboard – Use this to see more of the screen and temporarily hide the keyboard.

Find – If you are in a memo item, then this will allow you to find any text inside the memo.

Clear Field – This will erase the current contents of the memo you are working on - **USE WITH CAUTION!**

Paste – Suppose you have copied text from another program and want to paste it into a memo. Select and copy the text (from the calendar, address book, or another application) and select **Paste** from this menu. The text is now in your memo.

Select – This allows you to do just the reverse—click here and select text from the memo, press the **Menu** key again, and select **Copy**. Now, use the **Switch Applications** menu item to navigate to another application, press the **Menu** key, and select **Paste** to put the text in that application.

Check Spelling – This will run the BlackBerry spelling checker on the currently open memo item.

Save – This saves the changes in the memo.

Delete – This deletes the current memo.

Categories – This allows you to file this memo into either the Business or Personal categories. After selecting **Categories**, you can press the **Menu** key again and select **New** to create yet another category for this memo.

Switch Input Language – Changes to another installed language on the BlackBerry.

Close – This is similar to pressing the **Escape** key.

Chapter 16:
Your Music Player

Your BlackBerry is more than your phone and personal digital assistant, your email machine, and your address book. Today's BlackBerry smartphones are also very capable media players. With your BlackBerry, it is easy to carry your music, playlists, podcasts, and more. You can transfer playlists from iTunes and other media programs as well.

Listening to Your Music

One of the things that sets your BlackBerry apart from many of the earlier BlackBerry smartphones is the inclusion of multi-media capabilities and the ability to expand memory with the use of a media card. While some of the most popular formats of digital media are supported, you may have to take some steps to get all your music and videos working on the BlackBerry.

With a good-sized media card (e.g. 32 GB – gigabytes), the media capabilities of the BlackBerry, one might even suggest: **Why do I need an iPod? I've got a BlackBerry!**

Syncing Your Music and Playlists

The BlackBerry comes with internal memory, but the operating system (OS) and other pre-loaded programs take up some of that space. What's left over is usually not enough to store all your music.

STEP 1: Buy and insert a media card (if you don't already have one) to boost the memory available to store your favorite music—see the "Boosting Your Memory" section of Chapter 1 for help.

STEP 2: Transfer your music from your computer. If you are Windows user, please refer to Chapter 3. If you are an Apple Mac user, please refer to the information found in Chapter 5.

Playing Your Music

Once your music is in the right place, you are ready to start enjoying the benefit of having your music with you at all times on your BlackBerry.

The fastest way to get to your music is by swiping to the **Media** Home Screen and then touching or clicking the **Music** icon.

You are now presented with various preset options to find and play your favorite music.

All Songs: This shows you every song on your BlackBerry.

Artists: This shows you all artists. Then you can click an artist to see all of his or her songs.

Albums: This shows a list of all albums.

Genres: This shows a list of all genres on your BlackBerry (Pop, Rock, Jazz, etc.).

Playlists: This shows all playlists or allows you to create new ones.

Wi-Fi Music Sync: You can sync your music and playlists wirelessly if this is activated. See Chapter 3 for PC users and Chapter 5 for Mac users.

Shuffle Songs: Plays all your music in a shuffle mode or random order.

Finding and Playing a Song

1. Use the keyboard to search for a song. As soon as you start to type, the search box appears.

2. If you know the name of the song, then just type a few letters of any word in the song's name in the **Find** field at the top to instantly locate all matching songs.

3. In this case, we type **Rain** and see all matching songs. To narrow the list, press the **space** key and type a few more letters of another word in the name of the song.

4. Once you click a song, the music player will open and your song will begin to play.

5. Press the **Pause**, **Stop**, **Next Track**, and **Previous Track** keys.

6. Adjust your volume using the volume keys on the side of the BlackBerry.

TIP: Pressing the **Mute** key on the top of your BlackBerry will also pause or resume playback.

Music in the Background

You can keep your music playing while you are checking email, browsing the web, or doing just about anything else on your BlackBerry.

Get your music started, as shown previously. Then press the **Red Phone** key to jump out to your Home screen. Start up any icon you want: **Messages**, **Browser**, **Calendar**, **Facebook**, anything. Your music continues playing.

To quickly return to your music player and select another song or playlist, press the **Menu** key and select an item near the top called **Now Playing...** This will instantly jump you right back to the music player (see Figure 16-1).

Your music continues to play in the background.

Figure 16-1. Jumping from any app to the Now Playing screen

When a phone call comes in, the music automatically pauses for your call. When you hang up, the music automatically starts up again, picking up where it left off.

The fastest way to pause and silence the music is to click on the **Mute** key on the top- edge of your BlackBerry. (On the Bold this key is on the top right, and on the Curve, it is in the top middle.) Click on it again to re-start the music.

Using a Song as your Phone Ring Tone

1. Navigate to and play the song you want to use as a ring tone, as described previously.

2. Press the **Menu** key and select **Set as Ring Tone**.

3. Now, the next time you receive a call, your favorite song will be played. You can still set individual ring tones for your contacts – see Chapter 10.

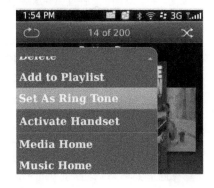

Playing All Your Music

Navigate to your music as just shown, and highlight the first song you wish to play. If you have not set up individual playlists, just highlight the first song, and then press the **Menu** key.

Scroll down to either **Play** or **Shuffle**, and the music player will begin to play all the songs listed.

If you select **Shuffle** (see Figure 16-2), then all the songs listed will be played in a random order.

Figure 16-2. Shuffling all of your music

Playing Your Playlists

1. To see the playlists on the BlackBerry, just scroll over to the **Music Player** icon, and click it.

2. Find the **Media** icon or Home Screen and touch or click the **Music** icon from the home screen.

3. Then scroll down to click **Playlists**.

4. You can see that the two playlists synced from iTunes are now listed right on the BlackBerry.

5. Simply click any playlist to begin playing the songs. In this example, we click the **Classic Rock** playlist.

Sync Playlists from Your Computer

Use the supported computer software (for example **iTunes** or **Windows Media Player**) on your computer to create playlists. Use the steps shown in Chapter 3 (PC users) or Chapter 5 (Mac users) to learn how to sync these playlists to your BlackBerry.

Creating Playlists on Your Device

1. From your Music app, click **Playlists** to get into the Playlists section.

2. Click **New Playlist** at the top of the screen.

TIP: You can also add any song that is

playing to one of the existing playlists or to a **New Playlist**. While a song is playing, press the **Menu** key and select **Add to Playlist** form the menu.

3. Now, you need to select **Standard Playlist** or **Automatic Playlist**.

4. Select **Standard Playlist** to select and add any songs already stored on your BlackBerry.

5. Then type your playlist name in the **Name** field at the top, press the **Menu** key, and select **Add Songs** to add new songs or just click the **Add Songs** button at the top of main screen.

TIP: To find your songs, you can just scroll up or down the list or type a few letters you know are in the title of the song, like and instantly see all matching songs.

6. When you find the song you want, just click it to add it to your playlist.

TIP: You can add songs to any existing playlist by just selecting the playlist and clicking **Add Songs** at the top of the **Playlist** screen.

TIP: The **Automatic Playlist** feature allows you to create some general parameters for your playlists based on artists, songs, or genres. See Figure 16-3 below.

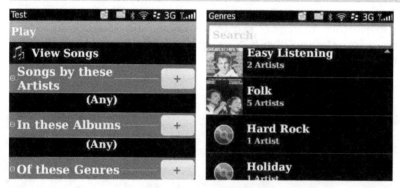

Figure 16-3. Generating automatic playlists on the BlackBerry

You can also add music to playlists by using the **Menu** key. This works when you are in the **Add Song** mode (Figure 16-4), or even when you just have a song playing and decide to add it to one of your existing playlists.

Figure 16-4. Adding individual songs to your playlist

Supported Music Types

The BlackBerry will play most types of music files. If you are an iPod user, all music except the music that you purchased with DRM (Digital rights Management) on iTunes should be able to play on the BlackBerry. However, if you burn your iTunes tracks to a CD (make a new playlist in iTunes, copy your iTunes tracks, and then burn that playlist.) The most common audio/music formats supported are the following:

- ACC - audio compression formats AAC

- AAC+, and EAAC+ AMR - Adaptive Multi Rate-Narrow Band (AMR-NB) speech coder standard

- MIDI - Polyphonic MIDI

- MP3 - encoded using MPEG

- WAV - supports sample rates of 8 kHz, 16 kHz, 22.05 kHz, 32 kHz, 44.1 kHz, and 48 kHz with 8-bit and 16-bit depths in mono or stereo. Other WAV file formats may not be supported.

TIP: You can pause (and instantly silence) any song or video playing on your BlackBerry by pressing the **Mute** key on the top of your BlackBerry. Press **Mute** again to resume playback.

Music Player Tips and Tricks

- To pause a song or video, press the **Mute** key.

- To resume playing, press the **Mute** key again.

- To move to the next item, click the **Next** button at the bottom of the screen.

- To move to a previous item (in your playlist or video library,) click the **Previous** button at the bottom left of the screen.

TIP: See all the Music and Media Player shortcuts and hot keys in Part 4 of this book.

Streaming Internet Radio

If you ever get tired of your music, try free internet radio. You can listen to personalized radio stations that play only the music you like. Select from hundreds of pre-set stations, or make your own new station based on your favorite artist.

There are several applications that allow you to set up and listen to streaming internet radio. There are now several great free applications for the BlackBerry. All work well. The two most popular are **Pandora** and **Slacker Radio**, both found in BlackBerry App World. Use the steps in Chapter 20: "BlackBerry App World" to locate and download these free apps.

After you set up your free account, specify the type of music you like and you should be streaming internet radio in minutes.

CAUTION: All internet radio programs are very data intensive. In other words, you should use them only if you have purchased an **unlimited data plan** from your wireless carrier. Without an unlimited data plan, you may be surprised with an extremely high wireless data charge on your next bill. Always use Wi-Fi when available so the data is not counted against your data plan.

Pandora Internet Radio

Pandora is an outgrowth of the Music Genome project. Essentially, Pandora is streaming internet radio where you control the radio stations. Essentially you build stations based around your favorite artists.

Installing Pandora

The easiest way to download Pandora is to go to **BlackBerry App World.** If the **Pandora** app is not part of the featured apps, you can find it in the Music section or by doing a search for Pandora.

Starting Pandora

Once loaded, you will see the **Pandora** icon, usually in your **Downloads** folder.

Applications Permissions

You may see one or two screens similar to the one shown here asking about Applications Permissions to http and https connections. Make sure to check both boxes and click on **Allow** so you won't be asked every time.

Pandora Account

When **Pandora** starts for the first time, you will be asked if you already have an existing account or if you would like to create a new account

Just type your email address and password (for an existing account) or input your email address and password to create a new account. The best thing about **Pandora** is that it is free!

If this is your first time using Pandora, you will be asked to create a new station.

If you have an existing Pandora account, (like shown here), you will see all your stations on the front page along with the **Create a New Station** and **QuickMix** options at the top.

NOTE: Pandora also works on your PC or Mac. You can create your stations, listen on your computer, and then just log in on the BlackBerry. All the stations created on the computer will appear.

Pandora Controls and Options

The interface of Pandora is very clean

and intuitive. To play or pause just press the **Play** button or **Pause**

button . (You can also press the **Mute** key on the top of your BlackBerry to **Pause** or **Play**.)

To skip to the next song on the station,

just click the **Next** button. Click the **Stations** button to return to your stations list.

Using "Thumbs Up" and "Thumbs Down"

Two buttons that you can click are the **Thumbs Up** and **Thumbs Down** buttons.

If you click the **Thumbs Up** button, a check mark is placed on the song letting Pandora know that you like this song and it can be used again.

Consequently, if you click the **Thumbs Down** button, a very quick check mark appears, and Pandora will skip to the next song and remember to not ever play that song again.

Slacker Radio

Conceptually, **Slacker** is very similar to **Pandora** internet radio. You build stations around your favorite artists or choose from hundreds of existing stations for your listening pleasure. **Slacker** seems to have a few more pre-programmed stations than **Pandora** and has a cache feature, which allows you to stream music to your computer, and then download the music to your BlackBerry media card. This allows you to listen to music without needing an internet connection—perfect for a long airplane trip or whenever you are out of radio coverage for a while.

Like **Pandora**, You can listen to **Slacker** Radio on your PC and Mac, as well as your BlackBerry.

Downloading and Installing

As you did with **Pandora**, you have two options for downloading **Slacker Radio**. You can find Slacker in BlackBerry App World, or you can also go to its website at www.slacker.com and download the latest build for BlackBerry. Follow the instructions for download and installation. Accept the license agreement and you will be Slacking in no time!

> **NOTE**: Slacker might ask you for permission to both personal information and connectivity resources. You will need to Save the permissions to continue.

Create Account or Log In

As with Pandora, your first screen will ask if you have an existing **Slacker** account or if you wish to create one.

Either log in or create a new account by clicking the **Create a new account** button at the bottom of the screen. As with Pandora, you can have Slacker running on your computer also!

If you have an existing account, you will see a screen with your favorite stations displayed.

If you are signing on for the first time, you have two options:

- Scroll down to check out stations by genre.

- Click **Search** at the top and build a new station with music created from your favorite artist (as you did with

Pandora).

In this example, we are creating a new station based on music by **John Legend**.

Choosing Your Station

Once you have some created stations, each time you log on to Slacker, you will be able to choose whether to listen to one of your **Favorites** or listen to other spotlight stations or genres in the Slacker library of music stations.

Slacker Controls

Slacker offers a few more controls and options than does Pandora. You can access the controls via the dock of buttons at the bottom. The Home button takes you back to the Slacker Home screen, where you can choose your station. Click the **Pause** button to pause or play the song. You can also use the **Mute** key on the top of your BlackBerry to do the same thing.

The **Next** or **Skip** button ![Next button] takes you to the next song in the station line-up. Notice that Slacker displays a picture of the next song or artist to the right of the album cover of the current song.

NOTE: in the free version of Slacker, you only get 6 skip in a day. The number of skips remaining is listed net to the **Skip** arrow.

If you like the artist or song, just click the **Heart** button for **Slacker** to remember your preferences.

If you don't want to hear this particular artist or song again, click the **Do Not Play** or **Ban** button.

Slacker Menu Commands and Shortcut Keys

Slacker offers some very cool commands in the menu. Just press the **Menu** button on your BlackBerry and you can:

Upgrade to Slacker Plus

See Song Info

Cache the Station

Share the Station

Remove the Station

Search

See Slacker Settings

Shut Down Slacker

One-Key Shortcuts for Slacker

- **N** = Skip to Next Song (with free Slacker you are limited to six skips per hour)

- **space** = Play / Pause Song

- **H** = Heart (you like the song playing, play more songs like it)

- **B** = Ban Song (you don't like the song, don't ever play it again)

Chapter 17: Snapping Pictures

Many BlackBerry smartphones sold today come with a built in camera—perfect for snapping a quick picture. Some BlackBerry smartphones issued by companies might have the camera disabled or removed for security reasons. Your camera and the photos you take can easily be shared with others via email, MMS messaging, or even uploaded to Facebook and other social media programs.

Using the Camera

Your BlackBerry includes a feature-rich camera. This gives you the option to snap a picture anywhere you are. You can then send the picture to friends and family, and share the moment.

Tips for Taking Great BlackBerry Pictures

Tip #1: Use Two Hands. Try to hold the BlackBerry with two hands to make it as stable as possible – shaky hands are one of the top reasons for poor pictures with smartphones.

Tip #2: Control the Flash. Make sure to turn on the flash when you need it. (We show you later how to do this). Sometimes the auto-flash sensor does not work if there is a very bright background. This is especially true when someone has the sun behind them, you should turn on the flash to make sure you see their faces without dark shadows.

Tip #3: Avoid the Zoom. Try to avoid zooming, instead try to move closer to the subject of the photo. The zoom is not a physical zoom, it is a software zoom so the image of a greatly zoomed in photo will look grainy or pixilated.

Tip #4: Scene Modes. Use the scene modes when required. We show you the various scene modes for the camera later in this chapter. For example, if you are out at the beach, then use the **Beach** scene mode. There is even a scene mode for taking pictures of text.

Tip #5: Work the delay. Sometimes, there is a half second or so delay between when you click the **Trackpad** to take the picture and it is actually taken. Make sure to hold the BlackBerry very still until you hear that the picture has been taken.

Tip #6: Maximize the Size. Use the camera options to set the picture resolution (number of pixels) to the maximum possible. This will give you the highest resolution images possible with your BlackBerry camera.

Camera Features and Buttons

You can get as involved as you want in your picture-taking with your BlackBerry. Every feature of your photo is configurable. Before we do that, however, let's get familiar with the main buttons and features.

Flash or No Flash

The BlackBerry Bold does have a Flash, while the BlackBerry Curve does not. So some of the language in this book about the flash will not apply to you if you do not own a BlackBerry Bold.

Starting the Camera

The camera can be started in one of two ways:

Option #1: The Right Side Convenience key

Unless you have re-programmed your Convenience key (see Chapter 7 for details), then pressing the **Convenience** key will start your camera—the one directly below the volume control buttons.

Push this button once, and the camera should start.

Option #2: The Camera Icon

Press the **Menu** key to see all your icons. Scroll to the **Camera** icon, and click.

Icons in the Camera Screen

Usually, when you open the **Camera** application, either the last picture you took is in the window or the camera is active. Underneath the picture window are five icons, which are described in Table 21-1.

Table 21-1: The Icons on the Camera Screen

Icon	Name	Description
	Last Picture Taken	Use this icon to view the last picture taken by the camera. You can then use this to scroll through pictures taken and upload to Facebook, Flickr, or another site if you have these apps installed (see Chapter 14 "Social Networking").
	Geotagging Options	You can use this icon to either **Show the Overlay** on the top of the view finder of your current GPS location. When this is on, each picture you take will be tagged with the GPS coordinates or you can **Turn Off** Geotagging.
	Take-a-Picture	Click this icon to take another picture. You can also press and hold the right convenience key to take a picture.
	Flash Mode	Click to cycle through the Flash settings – either **Automatic, On** (uses more battery) or **Off**.

> **NOTE:** If your BlackBerry lacks a flash, you will not see this icon. (e.g. BlackBerry Curve)

Scene Modes The BlackBerry has many presets for Scenes which will automatically adjust white balance and brightness depending on the scene. There are 11 preset modes, from **Auto**, to **Portrait**, to **Snow** to **Beach** and more.

You can also set a picture as a wallpaper image for your Home screen (like the desktop background image on your computer).

1. Open a picture.

2. Press the **Menu** key, select **Set as Wallpaper**, and click.

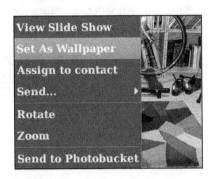

Sending Pictures with the Email Envelope Icon

Click the Last Picture Taken icon. Scroll through the pictures in the Camera Roll and click the **Envelope** icon, which brings up the email dialogue box. You can also press the Menu key and scroll through the same options.

Click one of the six options:

- **Send as Email** (attached to an email message as an image file)

- **Send as Text Message** (a multimedia message as the body of an email—learn all about MMS in Chapter 12

- **Send to Messenger Contact** (this option may not be available if you have not yet set up **BlackBerry Messenger**—see Chapter 13 for details)

You can also send your picture to your **Twitter**, as a **Group** message, or **Facebook** accounts by pressing the appropriate button.

NOTE: These additional options appear only if you have them installed on your device.

Adjusting Digital Zoom, Picture Review, Picture Size and Storage Location

The size of your pictures corresponds to the number of pixels or dots used to render the image. If you tend to transfer your BlackBerry pictures to your desktop for printing or emailing, you might want a bigger or smaller picture to work with. Notice that when you adjust the **Image size** setting for the pictures, the total number of pictures remaining will change.

1. From the Camera screen, press the **Menu** key and select **Options**.

2. You can disable **Digital Zoom** by un-checking the box next to it.

3. Adjust **Picture Review** – how much time you see a picture on the screen after you snap it..

4. Scroll down to the **Image Size** field and select the size of your picture: small, medium, or large.

5. At the bottom you can select to store your pictures on the **Media Card** (recommended) or **On Device**.

6. Press the **Menu** key and save your settings.

> **TIP:** If you email your pictures, then you will be able to send them faster if you set the **Picture Size** field to **Small**.

Geotagging Your Pictures

On your blackberry, you can either enable or disable geotagging. Geotagging means to assign of the current GPS (Global Positioning System) longitude and latitude location to each picture taken with your BlackBerry camera.

> **TIP:** You can learn how to get **Flickr** installed on your BlackBerry in Chapter 20.

Why would you want to enable geotagging?

Some online sites such as Flickr (photo sharing) and Google Earth (mapping) can put your geotagged photo on a map to show exactly where you took the picture (see Figure 17-1 for geotagged pictures on Flikr).

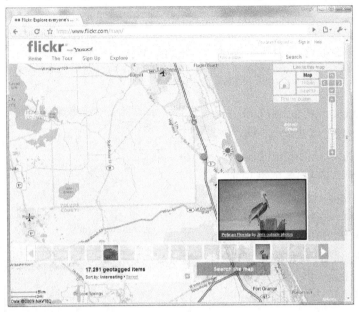

Figure 17-1. Viewing geotagged photos on Flickr

This is a map from www.flickr.com showing what geotagging your photos can accomplish. Essentially it will allow you to see exactly where you snapped your photos and help organize them.

Other programs you can purchase for your computer can organize all your photos by showing their location on a map (to find such software, do a web search for "geotag photo software (Mac or Windows)").

To turn geotagging on or off from the **Camera** screen, click the **Geotagging** icon

, second from left at the bottom.

Make sure your GPS is enabled on your BlackBerry—see Chapter 21.

Select **Hide Overlay** to get rid of the name of your location at the very top of the screen. In this image it says **Central Volusia, FL, USA**.

You know that geotagging is turned **on** if you see the red Geotagging symbol, in the

384

lower left of your Camera screen.

Changing the Scene Mode

Usually the automatic white balance works fairly well, however, there may be times when you want to manually control it.

The BlackBerry has a built in **Scene Mode** to make this process easy for you.

Click the **Scene Mode** icon (furthest to the right) and select form one of the built in eleven options.)

The **Scene Modes** work great. You can always just use the **Auto** setting, but a **Scene Mode** gives you more precise control of the exposure of the image.

The 12 available modes are described well on the BlackBerry itself and are: Auto, Face Detection, Portrait, Sports, Landscape, Party, Close-Up, Snow, Beach, Night and Text.

Using the Zoom

As with many cameras, the BlackBerry gives you the opportunity to zoom in or out of your subject. Your BlackBerry has a 4x digital zoom. Zooming on the BlackBerry could not be easier.

CAUTION: Zooming in will reduce the quality of your pictures and may make them look "grainy." We recommend walking closer to your subject, if possible, and avoid using the zoom.

There are a couple of ways to Zoom in and Zoom out:

Frame your picture and gently scroll up (Glide the Trackpad up.) The camera will zoom in on the subject.

Use the **Trackpad** to zoom. Scroll up with the trackpad to zoom in and scroll down to zoom out.

TIP: You can also zoom using your

Volume Up and **Down** keys.

NOTE: If you zoom seems to not be working, then make sure the setting in your Camera Options for Digital Zoom is checked. If it is correctly checked, then try soft resetting or hard resetting (Battery Pull). We show you how to do both in Chapter 23: "Troubleshooting."

Managing Picture Storage

Your BlackBerry comes with both internal media memory and an optional media card slot. If you find that you need to increase your storage capacity, you can purchase a high capacity (e.g. 16 GB or 32 GB) media card. For more information on inserting the media card, please see Chapter 1. See the following for help on storing pictures on the media card.

If you do not have a media card, then you will want to carefully manage the amount of your BlackBerry's main device memory that is used for pictures.

Viewing Pictures Stored in Memory

There are two primary ways to view stored pictures.

Option #1: Viewing from the Camera Program

1. Open the **Camera** application and press click on the View pictures icon in the lower left corner. (see Figure 17-2).

Figure 17-2. Viewing pictures from the Camera app

Option #2: Viewing from the Pictures App

1. Navigate to the **Media** icon and click.

2. Scroll to **Pictures** and click. Your initial options for pictures will be **Camera Pictures** or **Picture Library** (see Figure 17-3).

3. Click the appropriate folder and navigate to your pictures.

Figure 17-3. *Viewing pictures from the* **Pictures** *app in picture folders*

TIP: The bottom left icon is a View by Date icon that will, when clicked, list your pictures by month or year as opposed to by folder.

Viewing a Slide Show

1. Follow the previous steps and press the **Menu** key when you are in your picture directory.

2. Scroll to **View Slideshow** and click.

Scrolling Through Pictures

One very cool feature of your BlackBerry is that you can scroll through your pictures just by gliding the **Trackpad** left or right.

If you are looking at thumbnails (small images) of your pictures, then click on any picture to bring it into the full-screen mode.

Next, glide the **Trackpad** to the left or right to move through the pictures in that particular folder.

View Geotagged Pictures on a Map

If you have geotagged a picture, then you can press the **Menu** key and select **View on Map** to see where you took it. (Or at least where your BlackBerry thought you were when you took it.)

Adding Pictures to Contacts

As discussed previously, you can assign a picture as a caller ID for your contacts. Please check out our detailed explanation in Chapter 10.

Setting Convenience Keys

TIP: You can set the **Convenience** key from the Camera Options screen. (From the **Camera**, press the **Menu** key and select **Options** to see this screen.)

This will allow you to set the **Convenience** key to start your camera.

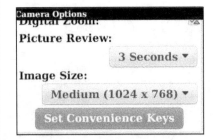

Transferring Pictures To or From Your BlackBerry

There are a few ways to remove pictures you have taken from your BlackBerry and transfer pictures taken elsewhere onto the BlackBerry.

Method 1: Send via email, multimedia messaging, or BlackBerry Messenger. You can email or send pictures immediately after you take them on your camera by clicking the **Envelope** icon. You may also send pictures when you are viewing them in your **Media** application. Click the **Menu** key and look for menu items related to sending pictures. See Figure 17-4 below.

Figure 17-4. Sending options for pictures

Method 2: Transfer using Bluetooth. If you want to transfer pictures to/from your computer (assuming it has Bluetooth capabilities), you can. We show you how to pair or connect Bluetooth devices in the "Bluetooth" section of Chapter 1.

Method 3: Transfer using your computer with special computer software.

Transferring pictures and other media to your computer is handled using the media section of your desktop software. For a Windows computer, see Chapter 3; for an Apple computer, see Chapter 5.

Method 4: Transfer using USB Drive mass storage mode. This assumes you have stored your pictures on a media card. (What's a media card? See Chapter 1)

The first time you connect your BlackBerry to your computer, you will probably see a **USB Drive** question. If you answer yes, then your media card looks just like another hard disk to your computer (just like a USB flash drive). Then you can drag and drop pictures to/from your BlackBerry and your computer. For more details, see Chapter 1.

Chapter 18:
Fun with Videos

We have already taught you how to get the most from music and pictures on your BlackBerry; however, your BlackBerry can handle even more media than what we have discussed so far. For example, your BlackBerry can also handle videos ranging from short videos you shoot on the BlackBerry to full-length movies.

Working with Videos on your BlackBerry

In addition to a camera, your BlackBerry also comes with a built-in video recorder that enables you to capture your world in full-motion video and sound when a simple picture will not work. Clicking the **Videos** icon lets you play all videos you record or transfer to your BlackBerry from your computer.

Some BlackBerry providers include a free 4, 8 or 16 GB media card with the devices they sell. All this extra storage and the strong video capabilities make the BlackBerry a very capable point-and-shoot video camera and video player.

Transferring Videos to Your BlackBerry

Check out Chapter 3 (Windows users) and Chapter 5 (Mac users) to learn how to transfer videos and other media (e.g., pictures and songs) to your media card.

Your Video Camera

One of the features of your BlackBerry is the inclusion of a video camera in addition to the still camera. The video camera is perfect for capturing parts of a business presentation or your child's soccer game. Like pictures, videos can be emailed or stored on your PC or Mac for later use.

Using the Video Camera

It's a simple matter to start the **Video Camera**; simply follow these steps to do so:

1. Scroll over to the **Media Home** screen and click on the **Video Camera** icon.

2. The BlackBerry should detect that you have a media card installed and ask you if you want to save your videos to the card. We recommend saying **Yes**.

3. Use the screen of the BlackBerry as your viewfinder to frame your picture.

4. When you are ready to record, scroll to and click the **Record** button . When you're finished recording, click the **Pause** button.

5. After pausing the recording, you will then see options at the bottom of the screen to **Continue Recording**, **Stop**, **Play**, **Send**, **Rename** or **Delete** the video.

6. Press the **Menu** button from within the **Video Camera** application after the video is recorded and choose one of the following options:

   ▪ Switch Application

   ▪ View Videos

   ▪ Media Home

- Options
- Camera
- Help
- Close

7. Adjust your video options by selecting **Options** from the menu.

8. In this screen, you can turn on or off the video light (if your BlackBerry has a camera flash). The default is off or unchecked, but you can check this to have a constant light from the camera's flash.

9. You can also adjust the resolution of the camera in the **Video Format** option, selecting either **Normal (640 x 480)** or to send as an **MMS Mode (176 x 144 pixels)**. The latter option delivers a lower quality image and a smaller file size.

10. Finally, the **Storage Folder** option lets you store your videos **On Media Card** or **On Device**. You should definitely choose the **On Media Card** option if you have a media card because this will give you more space.

Converting DVDs and Videos to Play on the BlackBerry

One cool thing about your BlackBerry is that you can use it is as a portable media player to help entertain your kids or yourself when you travel. If your car is equipped with Bluetooth, you can use this technology to send audio from your BlackBerry to your car stereo, so everyone can listen to the movie.

To convert a DVD, you need to follow these steps:

1. Copy the DVD onto your computer.

2. Use a video encoder program to transcode the video (convert it so it is viewable on your BlackBerry).

CAUTION: Please respect copyright laws! As people who make our living from intellectual property (e.g., BlackBerry books, videos, and so on), we strongly encourage you to respect the copyrights of any material you are attempting to copy to your BlackBerry.

For security and copyright reasons, some DVDs cannot be copied onto a device like the BlackBerry. Before you buy a video encoder or converter program, make sure that it supports the file formats that will play on your BlackBerry. Many of the user enthusiast forums such as www.pinstack.com, www.crackberry.com, or www.blackberryforums.com offer tutorials for video conversion. (We did not include details here because the process varies, based on which computer operating system you are running.)

Supported Video Formats on the BlackBerry

Video formats are fast-changing, and there are multiple versions of the BlackBerry operating system which support a variety of video formats. As of the time of the writing of this book, the following video formats were supported;

.mp4

.mov

.3gp

.3gp2

.avi

.asf

.wmv

To see if this changes, Simply do a search for "supported video formats BlackBerry Bold" or "BlackBerry Curve." This link worked at the time of writing and will get you to the web page which shows online manuals for each of the BlackBerry models:

```
http://docs.blackberry.com/en/smartphone_users/categories/?user
Type=1&category=BlackBerry+Smartphones
```

Viewing Videos on the BlackBerry

The BlackBerry contains a very sharp screen that is perfect for watching short videos. Another nice feature: The video player is as easy to use as the audio player.

Playing Videos

Playing a video is fairly straight forward:

1. Click on the **Video** icon in your **Media** folder.

2. From the video list screen, you can type a few letters to find the video you want to play. In this case, we typed **Calendar** to find the Made Simple Learning video tutorials related to BlackBerry Messenger.

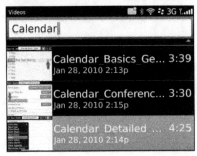

3. Click on any video you wish to play. Click on **Now Playing** to access the last video you were playing.

4. The **Video Player** screen looks very similar to the **Audio Player** screen – just scroll and then click the **Trackpad** to pause or play a video, using the volume controls on the side of the BlackBerry.

5. Click on the video you want to see with the **Trackpad** to make it start playing.

Showing or Hiding controls

You will notice that the controls disappear after a few seconds when you are playing a video. To get the controls back on the screen, click the **Trackpad** (see Figure 18-1).

Video still image from the Made Simple Learning BlackBerry video tutorials.

© 2011 Made Simple Learning.

Figure 18-1. *Scroll or click with the* **Trackpad** *to see video controls*

You can use the slider bar at the top of the controls to move to any other section of the video. Just click it and scroll left or right (see Figure 18-2).

Video still image from The Dark Knight Movie

© 2007 Warner Brothers and Legendary Pictures.

Figure 18-2. *Drag the slider to move the video location.*

At the top of the controls, you will also see two times. The time on the left is the amount of time already played, while the time on the right, a negative number, counts down how much time remains to be played in the video.

This list describes the four buttons along the bottom of the video player, from left to right:

- **Previous Track**: Takes you to the previous video in the list.

- **Play / Pause**: Pauses the video if it's playing and plays the video if it is paused.

- **Stop**: Stops the video and moves you back to the beginning of the video.

- **Next Track**: Takes you to the next video in the list.

The **Video Player** application includes a fairly extensive list of options you can choose from by clicking the **Menu** key. Specifically, pressing the **Menu** button brings up the following list of menu options for the application:

- **Switch Application:** Allows you to go to any other open application.

- **Video Size:** Choose between **Fit Screen**, **Full Screen** or **Actual size**.

- **Delete:** Deletes the current video.

- **Send to:** Sends to any installed photo sharing apps like Photobucket or Flikr.

- **Activate Handset:** Plays the audio of the video through your headset.

- **Media Home:** Go to the Media Home Screen.

- **Videos Home:** Go to the Video directory

- **Options:** Adjust the video options.

- **Help:** Displays contextual help with **Video Player** application.

- **Close:** Closes the application.

Chapter 19: Web Browser

A requirement for any smartphone today is that you need to be able to get online and browse the Web. While smartphone browsing the Web on your smartphone will never be a substitute for desktop browsing, you might be pleasantly surprised by surfing the Web on your BlackBerry.

BlackBerry 6, found on your BlackBerry, is the first web kit based browser for a BlackBerry. That means that pages load faster, zooming is quick and accurate and videos play in the browser.

In this chapter, we will show you how to get online, how to set your **Browser** bookmarks, how to manipulate your browsing history, and how to use some *hotkeys* to maneuver around the **browser** program quickly.

Web Browsing on Your BlackBerry

One of the amazing features of smartphones like the BlackBerry is that you can use them to browse the Web with ease and speed right from your handheld. Plus, an ever-increasing number of web sites are now supporting mobile browser formatting. These sites sense you are viewing the site from a small mobile browser, and they automatically reconfigure themselves for your BlackBerry so they can load quickly. The specialized mobile version of some sites load more quickly than when using their desktop browser equivalents!

Starting the Web Browser and the Start Page

Click on the **Browser** icon to start browsing.

You will usually be taken to the **Start Page** shown here where you see **Bookmarks, History** and can type a web address at the top.

Your wireless carrier may have made some changes, however and you may see your carrier's web page or something else.

Click on the **Pages** icon in the upper right corner to open or view more web pages.

TIP: You can simply type your web search right in the address bar without first going to your favorite search engine (Google, Yahoo, etc.)

Customizing your Startup Page

You can select three different views for your **Startup Page,** or the first page you see when you open your **Browser.**

From the **Browser,** press the **Menu** key and select **Options** to see this screen.

(If you exit the browser with the **Red Phone** key or jump out by multitasking with the **Menu** key, then you will see the last web page you were on when you left – not your Startup Page.)

Thumbnail View

List View

Home Page

Figure 19-1. *Customizing your Browser Startup page*

Using Tabs for Browsing

Tabbed browsing has long been available on desktop browsing to make it easier to jump between separate web pages – set as tabs. For the first time, tabbed browsing is now available on the BlackBerry.

Opening and Using Tabs

Click the **Tab** icon [2] next to the **Address** bar of the **Browser**. The number you see in the **Tab** icon (in this case "2") shows how many tabs are currently open.

Click the **Tab** icon and the open web tabs will be shown at the top of the web page. Just glide through the tabs to see the open pages.

To jump to one of the open tabs, just click it and the page will load.

Glide the Trackpad left or right to view more open screens.

Click on the red **X** under the tab to close it.

Click on any tab to open and view it.

Opening a New Tab

Glide with the **Trackpad** all the way to the end of the open tabs and click the **New Tab** icon (box with the plus sign in it) and click to load a new web page into a new tab. Choose from one of the items in your history or a bookmark or type in a new web site. Once the page is loaded, it will be set as a new tab in the browser.

Using Browser Keyboard Shortcuts

You can use various keys on your keyboard to perform common functions on your Browser. Some of the more useful ones are: **A** = Add Bookmark, **S** = Browser Options, **G** = Go To (Brings you to the Start Page where you can type a web address, view history and bookmarks), **R** = Refresh current page, **I** = Zoom In, **O** = Zoom Out.

To enable the keyboard shortcuts on the browser:

1. From a browser screen press the **Menu** key

2. Scroll to **Options** and click the **Trackpad**

3. Place a checkmark in the **Enable Keyboard Shortcuts** key

4. Press the **Escape** key and **Save** the changes.

TIP: See all the **Browser** keyboard shortcuts listed in Part 4 of this book.

Using the Browser Menu

Like most other applications on the BlackBerry, the heart of the **Browser** program lies in the capabilities you access from the program's **Menu** options. One push, one press, and/or one click can mean you are off to specific sites, bookmarked pages, recent pages, your internet history, and much more.

All the fun begins on the **Browser** program's **Start** page. The **Start** page view includes a **Web Address** box; a **Web Search** box (e.g., Google, Yahoo!, and so on); a **Bookmarks...** section that shows your bookmarks; and a **History...** section that shows, just as you'd expect, a list of recently visited pages (see Figure 19-1).

Figure 19-1. Type in a web address from the browser start page

To visit a Web site, you can Click on one of the links in **Bookmarks...** or **History...**; alternatively, you can type in a new URL, and then Click on it. (Remember: You use the **space** key for the "." in the address.)

Browser Menu Options

What follows is a list and short explanation of the **Menu** options that become visible when viewing a web page with the BlackBerry's native **Browser** program (see Figure 19-2). You can view these options by pressing the **Menu** key as you view a web page:

- **Switch Application:** Jumps or switches over to other applications, while leaving the current web page open.

- **Find on Page:** Searches for text on a web page.

- **Select:** Puts the Browser in Select mode to select text or pictures to copy to the clipboard.

- **Open Link in New Tab:** When the cursor is on a link to another page, you can open up a new tab with the new web page.

- **Add Link to Bookmarks:** Sets the new link as a bookmark in the web browser for future retrieval.

- **Send Link:** Enables you to send the web link to **Email**, **Text Message, PIN, Messenger Contact, Group Message, Social Feeds** or **Twitter**.

- **Copy Link:** Copies the web link to then paste into another app.

- **View Image:** Opens up a separate window with the web image highlighted.

- **Save Image:** Saves a web image to your **Pictures** folder.

- **Send Image Link:** Enables you to send the image link to **Email**, **Text Message**, **PIN**, **Messenger Contact**, **Group Message**, **Social Feeds** or **Twitter**.

- **Copy Image Link:** Copies the image link to then paste into another app.

- **Zoom:** Zooms you in on specific part of the page, so you can see that part of the page more clearly. You can zoom in several levels.

- **End Zoom:** Zooms you out, so you can see more of the page.

- **Refresh:** Updates the current web page.

- **Go To...:** Allows you to type in a specific web address.

- **Add to Bookmarks:** Sets the current page as a **Favorite** (i.e., a bookmark). For obvious reasons, this feature is extremely useful.

- **Add to Home Screen:** Creates an icon on the **Home** screen that will automatically take you to this web page in the future.

- **Send/Copy Page Address:** Very similar to **Send Link** described above, but with the address for the web page.

- **Page Properties:** Displays the properties for the current web page.

- **Tabs:** Shows you the open web tabs at the top of the screen. Just move between the tabs and click the page you wish to go to.

- **Bookmarks:** Lists all your bookmarks.

- **History:** Shows your entire web browsing history.

- **Downloads:** Displays your web downloads.

- **Options:** Sets the **Browser** program's **Configuration**, **Properties**, and **Cache** settings.

Figure 19-2. Reviewing *menu options in the native Browser program*

- **Help:** Shows text help for the **Browser** program. This is useful when you forget something, and need quick assistance.

- **Close:** Terminates the current instance of the Browser program and exits to the **Home** screen.

Using Your Address Bar

The first thing you will want to know how to do is get to your favorite web sites. In the case of one of this book's authors, that site is www.google.com. On your desktop computer, you simply type the web address or (URL) into your browser's **Address Bar** box. You will also see an **Address Bar** on the BlackBerry.

You can click the address bar to highlight it and just type in a new web address or, you can use the **Go To...** menu command to type in your web address. Follow these steps to do so:

Open the **Browser** program by clicking the **Browser** icon (see Figure 19-3).

Slide open your keyboard and start typing a web address or a web search string.

Figure 19-3. Using the Go To... Command from the menu.

> **TIP:** A fast way to get to the top of any web page (and be able to type a new web address or search) is to scroll the **Trackpad** to the very top of the screen and click. You will instantly see the address bar appear for you to click on and type in it.

The **Address Bar** comes up with the "http://www." part in place, waiting for you to type the rest of the address. Simply type in the web address of the site you wish to visit. Remember: pushing the space key will insert the dot "." automatically.

Or, just click and highlight the **Browser Bar** and then type in a new web address.

Press the **Enter** key when you are done. The **Browser** program will take you to the entered web page.

> **NOTE:** As you type in the web address, the BlackBerry will begin searching for matching web sites. If you see the site listed, just scroll to it and click the **Trackpad** to load it.

Once you have type in a few web addresses using the **Go To...** command, you will notice that they appear in a list below the web address bar the next time you select **Go To...** section. You can select any of these sites by scrolling down, and then clicking one (see Figure 19-4).

Figure 19-4. Frequently visited web sites in the Bookmarks... (if set) and History... sections

> **TIP:** You can save time by editing a bookmark. If you want to enter a web address that is similar to one that you have a bookmark for, you can highlight the previously entered address, press the **Menu** key, and then select the **Edit** option.

Using the Globe Shortcut Menu

Click on the **globe** next to the address bar to see a drop-down menu with quick links to:

Add to Bookmarks (add this page to bookmarks).

Add to Home Screen (add as an icon to your **Home** screen).

Send Page Address (email or otherwise send this web address).

Copy Page Address (copy this address to paste elsewhere).

Bookmarks (view your bookmarks list).

History (view your history).

Zoom In and Out of Web Pages

One of the great features of the new BlackBerry browser is the ability to Zoom in or out of a web page.

There primary way of zooming in and outis;

1. Press the **Menu** key and select Zoom – using the **Trackpad**, roll up or down to zoom in or out (see Figure 19-5).

Figure 19-5. *Zooming in and out of web pages.*

Copying or Sending a Web Page

The BlackBerry's native **Browser** program makes it easy to copy or send a page you might be viewing to someone else. Follow these steps to do so:

1. Press the **Menu** key while viewing a web page in the **Browser** program.

2. Scroll down to the **Send Page Address** option, and then Click on it.

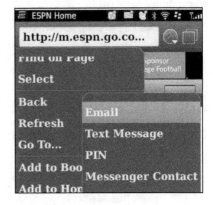

3. You will now see the option to send the page address via **Email**, **Text Message**, **PIN**, **Messenger Contact**, **Group Message**, **Social Feeds** or **Twitter**.

4. Select **Copy Address** to copy the web address to the clipboard; from here, you can easily paste the URL into any other app, email or memo.

5. Alternatively, click the **globe** next to the address bar and select **Send Page Address** or **Copy Page Address** to do the same thing.

Adding Bookmarks

One of the keys to a great web browsing experience on your BlackBerry is the liberal use of the **Bookmarks...** feature. Your BlackBerry comes with a couple of bookmarks already set. It is very easy to customize your bookmarks to include all your favorite sites for easy browsing.

> **TIP:** You can instantly find bookmarks by typing a few letters of a bookmark's name. You do this in exactly the same way you look up contacts in the **Address Book** program. Remembering this tip can save you a considerable amount of time!

Bookmark Naming Tips

One of the keys to a positive web browsing experience is to name add and name bookmarks in a way that makes them easy to find later. In the next section, we will cover how to set up an example bookmark that lets us look up our local weather instantly.

1. Open the **Browser** program and use the **Go To...** command (or the G keyboard shortcut) to input a favorite web page. In this example, we will type in www.accuweather.com.

2. Type in your ZIP code or city name to see your current weather (see Figure 19-6).

3. Once the page loads with your local weather, press the shortcut letter **A** on your keyboard to add a new bookmark. (If keyboard shortcuts are enabled.)

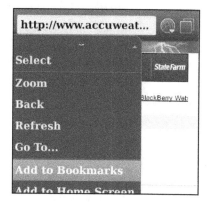

4. The full name of the web address is now displayed. In this case, you will probably see *AccuWeather Quick Look Weather for Marstons Mills, MA*. You may want to rename the URL (see the upcoming section on naming booksmarks).

Figure 19-6. Adding a bookmark for your local weather

5. In this case – in most cases, really – we recommend changing the bookmark's name to something short and unique.

> **NOTE:** If you were to bookmark four different weather forecasts, the default bookmark names would all show up as *AccuWeather*. This would be rather useless if your goal were to get straight to the ten-day forecast.

Be sure to keep the following tips and trick in mind as you edit and rename your bookmarks:

- **Keep all bookmark names short:** You will only see about the first 10-15 characters of the name in your list because the screen is small, so any characters beyond that won't be displayed.

- **Make all bookmark names similar, but unique**: If you were to add four bookmarks for the weather in New York or your area, you might adhere to this advice by naming them along these lines:

  - NY – Now
  - NY – 10 day
  - NY – 36 hour
  - NY – Hourly

This approach lets you instantly locate all your forecasts by typing the letters *NY* in your bookmark list. Only those bookmarks with the letters *NY* will be displayed.

Selecting Your Start Page

You might prefer to see your list of bookmarks rather than a **Home** page when you open the **Browser** program. The reason is probably obvious: this will allow you to use the **Find** feature in the bookmark list to instantly locate a bookmark, press it, and click it.

This approach speeds up the time it takes to get to favorite bookmarked web pages, whether you want to see the local weather or fire up your favorite search engine.

It might also be that your BlackBerry automatically opens up to your list of bookmarks, but you would prefer to see a particular **Home** page instead. If so, you can follow these instructions to change a given page your **Home** page:

1. Click on the **Browser** icon.

2. Press the **Menu** key and select **Options**.

3. Click on **Startup Page** and select one of the views: **Thumbnail View**, **List View**, or **Home Page**. Then type in a web address for the Home Page or click Use Current to use the web site you were just viewing (see Figure 19-7).

 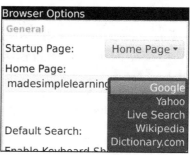

Figure 19-7. Exploring the *Browser Configuration options*

4. Scroll to **Default Search** and select the default search engine for your web browser.

5. under Web Content, we suggest keeping all the boxes checked for images loaded and pop-ups blocked.

Using Your Bookmarks

At this point, you are ready to begin using your bookmarks to simplify the process of browsing to your favorite sites on the Web. Follow these steps to do so:

1. Click on the **Browser** icon.

2. If you don't see your list of bookmarks automatically when you start the **Browser** program, press the **Menu** key, scroll down to **Bookmarks** option, and Click on it (see Figure 19-8).

Figure 19-8. Viewing your list of bookmarks

3. All of your bookmarks will be listed, including any default bookmarks that were put there automatically by your phone company.

You might want to Click on a particular folder to open all the bookmarks contained within or to see whether the bookmark you need is located within a given folder. To open a folder of bookmarks, Click on that folder to see its contents.

However, if you have a lot of bookmarks, then you should use the **Search:** feature and type a few letters that match the bookmark you want to find. For example, in Figure 19-9, typing the letters *go* will immediately find all bookmarks with *go* in the bookmark name (e.g., *Google*).

Once you get familiar with your bookmark names, you can type a few letters and find exactly what you need quickly and easily.

Searching with Google

Google also has a mobile version of its site that loads quickly and is quite useful on your BlackBerry.

To get there, just go to www.google.com in your BlackBerry's **Browser** program.

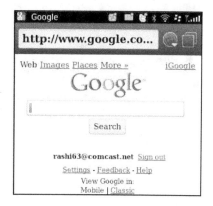

The BlackBerry's native Browser program includes a built-in **Search Address** box at the top of the **Start** page. You can type anything into the **Search Address** box and built-in search engine you configured above will start to search for matches (see Figure 19-9). Clicking the **Search Address** box and clicking the **Dropdown Arrow** icon to the right of the **Search Address** box will show you a list of availabe search engines.

Figure 19-9. Changing the Browser program's default search engine

We highly recommend creating an easy-to-use bookmark for this site and all your favorite web sites. Just as on your computer, you can type in your search string and hit the **Enter** key. This saves you the time it takes to scroll to, press, and click the **Search** button). If you want to find (and even call) pizza restaurants in a certain ZIP code or city, then you would enter in *pizza* and your ZIP code or city (see Figure 19-10).

Figure 19-10. Finding (and calling) a pizza place in a given location

Viewing a Google Search Location

It might be that you will want to determine the location of a place you find in a Google search on Google. For example, assume I want to figure out the location of the pizza place I found and called in the preceding example. In this case, I can click on the name of the restaurant from my search results.

Once I Click on the link to the pizza place, Google will display a map that shows the location of the pizza place. If I were to click on the **Get Directions** option, I could find a quick path from my current location to the restaurant – all from my BlackBerry!

Finding Places with Google Maps

After you start using **Google Maps** (shown in Chapter 21), you may not use the web-based Google search very much on your BlackBerry for finding directions and businesses.

Chapter 20: BlackBerry App World

App World is where you go to find thousands of great applications for your new BlackBerry. In this chapter we will show you where to find software for your BlackBerry and how to download and install both from the **App World** and from outside sources.

The App World Concept

Online application stores are all the rage in the world of smartphones these days. One of the great things about a BlackBerry is that you can find applications for it in lots of places – not just the sanctioned **App World**. The BlackBerry **App World** online store is certainly the easiest place to find software as it is all in one, well-organized location. App World also keeps track of your purchases and downloads so you can always re-install or even transfer the purchases to a new BlackBerry.

Downloading App World

You should have **BlackBerry App World** already pre-installed on your BlackBerry, however, if you cannot find it using the Search icon, then you'll need to download it.

1. Click on the **Browser** icon.

2. In the address bar of the browser, enter this address: **mobile.blackberry.com**.

3. Scroll up or down the page to locate **BlackBerry App World** and click the link.

4. Then click **Download Now** and click the **Download** button on the next page.

Starting App World for the First Time

The **App World** icon may be in your **Downloads** folder. If you want to move it to your **Home** screen, just follow the directions in Chapter 7.

Find the **App World** icon and click on it. The first time you run the **App World** program, you will have to scroll down a very long license agreement to click the **I Accept** button at the bottom.

BlackBerry ID, Credit Card, Direct Bill or PayPal Account

NOTE: Depending on your country and carrier, you may be offered different payment options for BlackBerry App World. In the US, you have options of being direct billed by the carrier (App World purchases are added to your phone bill), Credit Card (add a new credit card), or use a PayPal account. You may not see all of these options on your BlackBerry.

The first time you use **App World**, you will be asked to create a **BlackBerry ID**, which you will then link to your payment option.

If you have a PayPal account, all you need to do is input your PayPal user name and password when you purchase an app. If you do not have a PayPal account, go to www.paypal.com from your computer and follow the instructions to setup your account. Setting up a PayPal Personal account is an acceptable requirement for most users.

Downloading Themes

One of the cool parts about your BlackBerry is that you can find many applications that let you tailor the way it looks and behaves to suit your particular tastes. A BlackBerry "theme" changes the look and feel of all the screens, colors and fonts. Just click the **Categories** soft key as described below, and you can search for the **Theme** category. You can find detailed instructions for doing so in "Personalize Your BlackBerry" in Chapter 7.

Featured Programs

The opening screen of the **App World** program shows large icons for its featured items. Many of these items are free; others need to be purchased (you will learn more about this later in this chapter). Flick left or right through the featured programs to find one that interests you. To learn more about a program or to download it, just click it.

Soft Keys At Bottom

Along the bottom of the opening **App World** screen, you will see four small icons: **Categories**, **Top 25**, **Search**, and **My World** (see Figure 20-1). Each category gives you a different way to look for, download, or manage apps on your BlackBerry. Simply click any of these soft keys to go into that area.

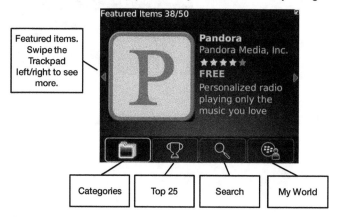

Figure 20-1. The layout of BlackBerry App World

Categories

As its name suggests, clicking the **Categories** icon shows you all the categories of applications available on the new BlackBerry App World site. The number of apps in any particular category is listed in parentheses next to the category name.

At the time of the writing, there were more than twenty categories, ranging from **Games** to **Sports** to **Finance** to various kinds of references and other items.

Clicking a category brings up more information about a particular application that may interest you.

Often, a category will have various sub categories listed once you click the category name, For example, in the Category of Games, there are at least ten sub-categories listed.

Once you click a category, the icons for the available programs will show on your screen. Flick up or down to see more apps in the list. You can read reviews or see screen shots for most applications before you decide to download them.

Top 25

As its name implies, clicking the **Top 25** icon will show you the most downloaded free applications from the **App World** site. As before, click any program to see screen shots, read reviews, or download the app to your BlackBerry.

Once you click on **Top 25**, the first list you will see will be Newest at the top.

Use the **Trackpad** and slide the screen from right to left to advance to the other **Top 25** screens. The categories under **Top 25** are; **Newest, Free Apps, Paid Apps, Top Themes** and **Recently Updated**.

Top 25 Paid Apps

Clicking the **Top** 25 and then sliding over to **Paid Apps** will show you the most downloaded applications from purchased from the App World site (prices start at $0.99). As you did previously, click any program to see screen shots, read reviews, or download an app to your BlackBerry.

Search App World

The **App World** program has a very good, built-in **Search** tool. Click the **Search** soft key at the bottom to go into search mode.

If you have an idea of what you might be looking for, but don't know its exact name, just type a word about the general subject into the **Search** bar. In this example, we want to find music applications that are currently available, so we enter *music* into the **Search** bar, which causes all available music-related apps to be displayed (see Figure 20-2).

Figure 20-2. Searching with the BlackBerry App World program

TIP: After you see your search results, you can sort the search results by clicking the **Sort** icon in the upper right corner of the screen (see Figure 20-3).

Figure 20-3. Sort Search results

Choose the sorting criteria; the choices are to sort by **Relevance**, **Newest**, **Rating**, **Price**, **Vendor** or **App Name**.

Downloading Apps

As the time of writing, the **BlackBerry App World** program accepts the PayPal payment system or credit card or carrier billing. (This may change in the future.)

As we mentioned above, the first time you start up **App World**, you need to create a **BlackBerry ID**, which is linked to your PayPal account.

Changing Payment Options

To set up or change your payment options, click the **My World** soft key and then press the **Menu** key and select **Payment Options** from the menu. Login with your **BlackBerry ID** (see Figures 20-4 and 20-5).

Figure 20-4. Logging in to your BlackBerry ID.

Figure 20-5. Choosing payment options for *BlackBerry App World.*

Downloading and Purchasing Apps

Scroll through the applications listed, as you did previously. When you find an app that you want to download, just click the **Download** button from the **Details** screen.

If the application is not a free download, the **Download** button will be replaced by a **Purchase** button. Click the **Purchase** button and input your BlackBerry ID information to buy the app.

NOTE: Your payment information will be stored to simplify making future purchases easier.

If this is your first time purchasing an app, you will need to log in or set up your BlackBerry ID and link it to a PayPal account, credit card or carrier billing account. PayPal can be tied to any major credit card or your bank account.

You will see a progress bar showing the progress of your application as it downloads, prepares to install, and then installs on your BlackBerry.

You may also be asked to grant the application **Trusted Application** status. We generally recommend saying **Yes** to this.

You can then choose to **Run** the application or select **OK** to go back to browsing for more apps.

Using the My World Area

All the apps that you purchase or download for free are listed in the **My World** area of the **App World** program.

Click on the **My World** icon (in the lower right-hand corner of the **App World** program) to see a complete list of your downloaded or purchased programs.

NOTE: If you restart your BlackBerry or do a battery pull, you will be logged out of your account, and you will be asked to re-enter your BlackBerry ID password.

Updating App World

Usually you will receive a message in your email inbox (**Messages**) on your BlackBerry letting you know an update is available for App World. It will look something like this image to the right.

When you click on it to open this notification, you should be taken right to the Upgrade screen in **App World** as shown here.

Click **Upgrade** and login using your **BlackBerry ID** to complete the process.

The My World Menu Commands

The menu associated with the **My World** area of the program has several commands associated with it. Follow these steps to access them:

1. Highlight any app in the **My World** area and press the **Menu** key.

2. From the menu that pops up, you can: **Switch Application**, **Show Application Storage Log in** or **Log Out** of your account, view **Account Information, Payment Options, Refresh List**, **View** the application highlighted, **Run** the selected program, **Review** the program, **Recommend** the program to someone else, **Archive** or **Delete** the program.

NOTE: If application updates are available, these will also be indicated in the **My World** context menu.

Archiving or Deleting Programs

After you start to download lots of new apps to your BlackBerry, you may decide that you do not want to use some of them or that you simply want to free up space for new apps.

To delete or uninstall an app, follow these steps from within the **My World** area of the **App World** program.

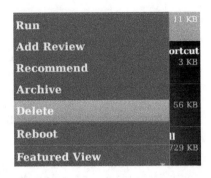

1. Highlight the app you wish to remove and press the **Menu** key.

2. Select **Archive** to temporarily remove the highlighted program from your BlackBerry. Select **Delete** to permanently remove the app. On the next screen, you will be asked to confirm your selection to remove the program.

3. Most programs will require you to reboot (reset) your BlackBerry to complete the uninstall process.

> **TIP:** If you are removing more than one application, select **Reboot Later** until you have selected and uninstalled all the apps. Then, when you're finished uninstalling apps, select **Reboot Now** to remove all the apps at once. Following this approach will save you a lot of time waiting for your BlackBerry to reboot!

Adding or Removing Apps

Your BlackBerry comes with most of the major apps you will ever need already installed. However, there are literally thousands of third-party apps available in virtually any category you can think of that can help you get the most out of your BlackBerry.

There are apps for productivity, reference, music, and fun – including lots of great games. One nice thing about the BlackBerry platform is that while there is an official **App World**, there are also lots of ways to find and download apps.

Downloading New Software Outside of App World

One of the cool things about your BlackBerry is that, just as on your computer, you can go onto the Web and find software to download. You can download everything from ringtones, to games, to content that is pushed out to your BlackBerry on a regular basis (using the same approach that you *probably* see with email on the BlackBerry – each phone company or carrier uses a slightly different approach).

CAUTION: Web sites change frequently. All of the web site images you see in this book are accurate at the time of writing. And while it's quite possible that a given page or site shown in this book will look exactly the same on your BlackBerry, it is also possible that the page or site will look completely different on your device. It is even possible that the site or page is no longer available. If a site is missing or looks completely different, we recommend searching for a link with approximately the same name.

Several news sites now allow you to put an icon on your **Home** screen that will automatically launch a given news site. For our purposes, let's say we wanted to put the icon for ABC News on our **Home** screen (see Figure 20-6). Follow these steps to do so:

1. Scroll down to the link for ABC News and select **Download** or **Get Web Signal** (depending on the site.)

*Figure 20-6. Downloading the **ABC News** app*

2. Click on the **Download** option to place the icon for *ABC* on your BlackBerry.

3. Once the program has successfully installed, you will see a screen that looks like the image to the right.

4. In the **Downloads** home screen, you should see the **ABC News** icon. Click on the icon to go directly to the mobile version of the *ABC* site.

Changing Your Default Downloads Location

By default, your BlackBerry saves the icon of all programs you download to the device's **Downloads** Home Screen. Follow these steps to change the default folder your BlackBerry saves new programs to.

1. Press the **Menu** key from your **Home** screen and select **Options**.

2. Next, click on the **Downloads Folder** button to change the download default location to a new location.

> **TIP:** Select **Home** if you want your new icons easily accessible!

Finding More Software

There are quite a few additional places where you can find software and services for your BlackBerry beyond **BlackBerry App World**.

Web Stores

You can find quite a few online stores that carry software for your Blackberry. You can usually purchase software directly from these stores. Here's a short list of online sites that sell software for the BlackBerry.

- www.crackberry.com
- www.shopcrackberry.com
- www.bberry.com
- www.eaccess.com
- www.handango.com
- www.mobihand.com

Reviews of Software, Services, and More

There are so many programs, services, and other items available for your BlackBerry that it can be difficult to know where to start or what is worth having. Fortunately, you can also find many web sites that provide reviews of all the software, services, ringtones, themes, wallpaper, accessories, and other items and services of interest for your BlackBerry. Some of the sites that provide these reviews include the following:

- www.crackberry.com
- www.bbhub.com
- www.berryreview.com
- www.blackberrycool.com
- www.blackberryforums.com
- www.boygeniusreport.com
- www.howardforums.com (The RIM-Research In Motion Section)
- www.pinstack.com
- www.RIMarkable.com
- www.blackberryrocks.com

Official BlackBerry Sites

In addition to the many web sites dedicated to providing and reviewing programs and services for the BlackBerry, you might also find it worthwhile to check out the official BlackBerry Solutions Catalog, which you can find online at: http://www.blackberrysolutionscatalog.com/

The software and services included in the Solutions Guide are tailored more for business users than individuals; however, you might find items of items on the site. Another official site is the "Built for BlackBerry" software site, which you can find at: http://appworld.blackberry.com/webstore/.

Removing Software

There will be times when you wish to remove a program from you BlackBerry, but you are not connected to your computer at the time. Fortunately, it is an easy and intuitive process to remove programs when using the BlackBerry itself.

You have a couple of ways to remove any software program installed on your BlackBerry, which you'll learn about in the next couple of sections. In addition to removing the software you add to the device, you can also remove some of the pre-installed apps that shipped with your BlackBerry.

Option 1: Deleting Apps using App World

Go into the **My World** section of **App World**, highlight or select the app you wish to delete, press the **Menu** key and select **Delete**.

Option 2: Deleting Apps from the Home Screen

We'll cover the easiest way to delete an app from your BlackBerry first. This approach relies on deleting the app directly from the **Home** screen. Follow these steps to do so:

1. Navigate to the app you want to delete, click and hold on it with the **Trackpad**.

2. Select **Delete** from the pop-up menu. (You could also select **Delete** from the menu).

3. Your BlackBerry will show a warning screen. Click on the **Delete** button to confirm that you want to delete the application.

NOTE: Not every program can be deleted.

Option 3: Deleting Apps from the Options Icon

You can also delete applications from the **Options** menu. Follow these steps to do so:

1. Click on the **Search** icon and type "Applications."

2. Click on the **Options** icon.

3. Click on **Application Management**.

4. Now type a few letters of the application you want to delete to find it. Or, you can scroll down the list of applications.

5. Click on the app you want to delete and click on the **Delete** key as shown.

6. Once you highlight the application you want to delete, you can Click on the **Menu** key and select **Delete** and confirm your choice.

7. Usually, the BlackBerry needs to restart or reboot to complete deleting the application. If so, Click on **OK** or **Yes** to finish the process of removing the application from your BlackBerry.

TIP: If you are removing a number of apps, wait to reboot until you delete them all.

Option 4: Deleting Apps with the Desktop Software

Check out Chapter 3 if you use a Windows computer or Chapter 5, if you are a Mac user to see how to add and remove apps via the BlackBerry Desktop Software.

Chapter 21: Traveling: Maps & More

Regardless of whether you intend to leave the country with your BlackBerry, there are a few travel-related things you should know how to do. For example, everyone with a BlackBerry can probably benefit from one of the many mapping applications for the BlackBerry that rely the device's built-in GPS (Global Positioning System). Such applications can help you find navigate to your destination with turn-by-turn directions, find nearby stores with services or products you might need, or even mark where you parked your rental car so you can find it when you're ready to leave.

If you to intend to travel to another country, however, there are some definite steps you should take before you, not least so you do not get surprised with a huge data or voice roaming phone bill. We'll cover these topics and many others related to traveling with a BlackBerry in this chapter.

International Travel: Things to Do Before You Go

Some BlackBerry smartphones are well equipped for international travel such as BlackBerrys with a SIM card that run on networks called "GSM" that are fairly common throughout the world. Connecting overseas with a GSM BlackBerry should be easier than phones without a SIM card.

In any case, we always recommend that you call your cell provider well in advance of a trip to see whether there is an **international** feature you can turn on in your BlackBerry.

Avoiding a Shockingly Large Bill

One thing you want to avoid when traveling is returning home to a shockingly large bill with high data or voice roaming charges. For example, we have heard of people who returned home after a trip abroad to find a phone bills over $500 in monthly data and voice roaming charges. You can avoid such a surprise by taking a few easy steps before and during your trip.

Before Your International Trip

There are a few simple steps you can take before you leave to ensure that your BlackBerry will always work – no matter where you might be in the world.

Call Your Phone Company

You should also contact the provider that supplies your phone service before you leave. When you call, you should check with your wireless carrier about any voice and data roaming charges you might incur when traveling. You can also try searching on your phone company's web site for this information, but usually you will have to call the company's Help Desk and specifically ask what the voice roaming and data roaming charges might apply for the country or countries you plan to visit. If you use email, SMS Text, MMS messaging, web browsing, and any other data services, you will also want to specifically ask about whether any of these services are charged separately when traveling abroad.

Some phone companies offer something that might be called an **International or Global Traveler** rate plan that you will need to activate before your trip. In some cases, you must activate such a plan to use your BlackBerry at all; in other cases, activating such a plan will allow you to save some money on the standard data and voice roaming charges. You should check out these plans in advance to see whether they can save you some money while you are on your trip, especially if you need to have access to data while you are away.

> **TIP:** If you decide to purchase an International Rate plan, then you should create a reminder calendar event for a day or two after you return reminding yourself to turn off this extra rate plan. The phone company will be happy to continue charging you the extra money until you contact them to turn off the plan.

Ask About Using a Foreign SIM Card

In some cases, your BlackBerry phone company won't offer special deals on international data roaming plans, or its rates will be unreasonably high. In these cases, you may want to ask your phone company to unlock your BlackBerry, so you can insert a SIM card you purchase in the country you're visiting. In many cases, inserting a local SIM card will eliminate or greatly reduce data and voice roaming charges. However, you should carefully check the cost of placing and receiving international calls on that foreign SIM card. Using a foreign SIM card may save you hundreds of dollars, but it's best to do some web research or try to talk to someone who has recently traveled to the same country for advice before settling on that approach.

Airplane Travel: Getting into Airplane Mode

Some airlines force you to completely power-down your electronic devices during take-off and landing, but then allow the use of "approved electronic devices" (read: you must turn off your BlackBerry's wireless radio) while in flight. This is easy to do – you simply click on the top of your **Home** screen to bring up the Manage Connections screen. Then click on **Turn All Connections Off.**

You know the radios are all off when you see the word **OFF** next to your radio in the upper right portion of the screen.

Click on **Restore Connections** to turn all connections back on, or, in some cases you can turn on **Wi-Fi** while in flight – to do that, click on **Wi-Fi** to selectively turn that radio on.

Things to Do When Abroad

Once you've completed the steps described so far to prepare for your trip, you will need to address some additional issues once you get to your destination. The next sections explain the things you need to keep in mind after you arrive at your destination.

Getting Your BlackBerry Ready

Once you arrive at your destination, you will need to do a couple of thing to make sure your BlackBerry is ready to use while you're traveling.

Step 1: Make Sure the Time Zone Is Correct

When you arrive, you will need to make sure your BlackBerry is displaying the correct time. Usually, your BlackBerry will auto-update your time zone when you arrive at a new destination. However, if it doesn't, you can manually adjust the time zone (see Chapter 7 for help with setting the time zone).

Step 2: Turn Off Data Roaming If It's Too Expensive

If you were unable to find out about data roaming charges from your local phone company, try to contact the phone company in the country in which you're traveling to find out about any data roaming or voice roaming charges.

The worst case: If you are worried about the data roaming charges, and you can do without your email and web browser while you're away, then you should disable data services for the duration of your trip. Follow these steps to do so:

1. Click on the top of your **Home** screen to bring up the **Manage Connections** screen.

2. Click on **Mobile Network Options** near the bottom.

3. Your **Data Services** will most likely say **On**, but there is a secondary tab for **While Roaming.** We recommend setting the switch to **Off** in the **While Roaming** field, so that you can continue to receive data in your **Home** network.

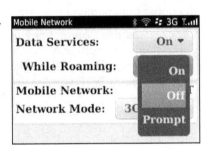

4. Press the **Escape** key; your new settings will be saved automatically.

Setting the **Data Services** value to **Off While Roaming** should help you avoid any potentially exorbitant data roaming charges. (You still need to worry about voice roaming charges, but at least you can control those by watching how much you talk on your phone).

The nice part about using the **Off While Roaming** setting: When you return to your **Home** network, all your data services (e.g., email, web browsing, and so forth) will work automatically.

> **NOTE:** If you want to use email, web browsing, GPS mapping and other services that require a data connection, you will have to set the While Roaming to On.

Step 3: Register with the Local Network

If you are having trouble connecting to the local wireless network, you may need to register your BlackBerry on the local network (see the steps shown in "Host Routing Table Register Now" section at the end of Chapter 12 for more information).

Step 4: Look for Free Wi-Fi Networks

In your hotel, international chain restaurants, coffee shops, some other types of restaurants and public libraries, you may find free Wi-Fi networks that will allow you to connect to the Internet from your BlackBerry. If you use Wi-Fi you will not be incurring any wireless data roaming charges.

Returning Home

As you did when you arrived at your travel destination, you will need to make a few changes to your BlackBerry's settings once you arrive back home before your device will work as expected.

Step 1: Check Your Time zone

As mentioned in the section on traveling abroad, your BlackBerry usually will auto-update your time zone when you arrive at a particular location. If the device does not auto-adjust after you return home, you can manually adjust your time zone (see Chapter 7 for help with setting the time zone).

Step 2: Reset Your Data Services

If you have turned the **Data Services** field to **Off**, then you will need to make sure to reset it to **On** or **Off When Roaming**, so you can receive data when you return home.

Step 3: Register Your BlackBerry on the Local Network

Depending on the actions you took while preparing for your trip or while traveling, you might need to re-register your BlackBerry on your local phone network (see the steps shown in "Host Routing Table Register Now" section at the end of Chapter 12 for more information).

Step 4: Turn Off Your Special International Plan

The final step is optional. If you have activated some sort of special international roaming rate plan with your BlackBerry phone company, and you do not need it any more, contact the company to turn it off to save yourself some money.

BlackBerry Maps, Google Maps, and Bluetooth GPS

In addition to the myriad ways your BlackBerry to help you manage your life, the device can also take you places – literally. With the aid of software that is either pre-loaded on the BlackBerry or easily downloaded from the Web, you can use your BlackBerry to find just about any location, business or point of attraction.

Enabling GPS on Your BlackBerry

You will need to turn on the GPS location (GPS is the longitude and latitude of your current location based on triangulation from orbiting satellites). GPS is on your BlackBerry is required to enable mapping software to track your precise location. You will also need to turn this feature on if you want to turn on the geotagging (see Chapter 17) feature for your camera. Follow these steps to do so:

1. Click on the **Search** icon from your **Home** screen and type "GPS" into the search bar.

2. Click on the **Options** icon and select **Location Settings**.

3. Make sure that the **Location ON** property is selected under **Location Services** as shown.

4. Leave **Location Data** and **Location Aiding** as **Enabled**.

5. Finally, press the **Menu** key and select **Save**.

Using BlackBerry Maps

Your BlackBerry usually ships with the **BlackBerry Maps** software, which is a very good application for determining your current location and tracking your progress through your GPS receiver.

> **NOTE**: Some carriers will install their own version of mapping software. If you do not have **BlackBerry Maps** installed, go to go to the mobile.blackberry.com web site from your BlackBerry and download the free **BlackBerry Maps** software.

Follow these steps above to enable GPS use with the **BlackBerry Maps** program.

Viewing a Contact's Map

Sometimes you may want to look up the location of one of the contacts in your device. For example, perhaps you want to meet near the contact's home, and you will use the address information in the contact's profile to look up where exactly the contact lives. Follow these steps to view a map for the contact (see Figure 21-1):

1. In the **Blackberry Maps** program, press the **Menu** key from the main **Map** screen.

2. Scroll down and select **Find an Address**.

Figure 21-1. Finding your location in the BlackBerry Maps program.

3. Just start typing a name or address. If the name is stored in your Contacts app, you will begin to see matches in the window below.

4. Scroll down to click on the name of a contact.

5. A map of that contact's location will appear on your screen.

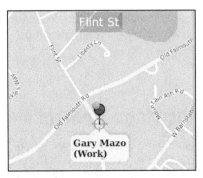

Getting Directions with BlackBerry Maps

After you map a location, it is easy to get directions to a particular location.

1. Click the **Directions** key in the middle of the bottom row .

2. If you need to adjust the **Start, End or Route Options** click on those buttons.

3. For **Start/End**, you can customize to select the address you just mapped, **Your Location, Select from map, Find Location**, or **From Favorites**.

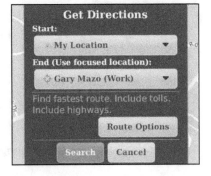

4. Click on **Route Options** to adjust the following: **Fastest, Shortest, Avoid highways,** or **Avoid tolls**.

5. After you click on **Search**, your route will be mapped and displayed in summary.

6. Click on **View Directions** to see the list of turn-by-turn directions.

7. Click on **View on Map** to see these directions on the map.

At the time of writing, the GPS will track you along the route, but it will not give you voice prompts or turn-by-turn voice directions.

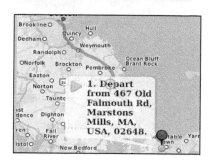

You can also press **Menu** key and then **Add as Favorite** to mark a location as a **Favorite** on your BlackBerry.

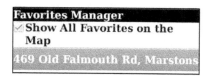

BlackBerry Maps Menu Commands

You can accomplish a great many tasks with the **BlackBerry Maps** application. You can get a sense of what it lets you do by pressing the **Menu** key, which brings up a screen with a ton of options you can choose from simply by scrolling, pressing, and clicking. Specifically, you can perform the following tasks from the screen displayed by pressing **BlackBerry Maps** program's **Menu** key:

- **Switch Application:** Jumps you to any other application while keeping the current application open.

- **My Location** – Zooms to your current location on the map.

- **Find Location:** Jumps you to an address you enter.

- **Zoom To Point:** Takes you from street level to the stratosphere (keyboard shortcut keys: **L** = Zoom In, **O** = Zoom Out).

- **Local Search:** Searches for restaurants, stores, or points of interest near your current location.

- **New Directions:** Lets you find directions using your location history or by typing in new addresses.

- **Get Link:** Connects you to a web site so you can find an address.

- **Get/View Directions:** Switches you to **Text** mode if you are in **Map** mode. Otherwise it brings up the **Get Directions** screen shown above.

- **Clear Map:** Erases the current map or route on the screen.

- **Add as Favorite:** Adds your current location as a Favorite for easy retrieval on the map.

- **Navigate to Here:** If the location on the map is not your Current Location, you can immediately get directions to that spot.

- **Display Details:** This will display the longitude and latitude of the selected location.

- **Send Location:** Forwards your map location via Email, Text Message, Group Message, Messenger Contact, PIN, Social Feeds or Twitter.

- **Send Directions:** Sends your directions via Text Message, Group Message, Messenger Contact, PIN, Social Feeds or Twitter (Only available if you are currently in **Direction** mode.)

- **Copy Location** – This will copy the location to the clipboard so you can paste it in another application.

- **Zoom to Point:** Shows the map detail around the currently selected point in your directions; this option is available only when viewing directions.

- **Favorites** – This will display those destinations set as **Favorites** in **BlackBerry Maps**.

- **Track up** or **North Up** – Changes the orientation of the tracking arrow in the app.

- **Options:** Changes **Global Map Options**. For example, this choice lets you disable the backlight timeout settings, change units from metric (kilometers) to imperial (miles), change the font and turn on **Address Recognition**.

- **About:** Shows information about the current provider of the mapping data and software.

- **Help:** Displays a contextual **Help** menu.

Google Maps

If you have ever used **Google Earth**, then you have seen the power of satellite technology in mapping and rendering terrain. **Google Maps Mobile** brings that same technology to handheld devices, including the BlackBerry.

With Google Maps, you can view 3-D rendered satellite shots of any address, anywhere in the world. To get started with this amazing application, you need to first download it onto your BlackBerry. Follow these steps to do so:

1. Click on the **Browser** icon from your **Application** menu.

2. Press the **Menu** key, scroll to the **Go To** command, and Click on it.

> **TIP:** Click on the letter G on your keyboard to execute the **Go To** command.

3. Enter this address to perform an *over the air* (OTA) download onto the BlackBerry: www.google.com/gmm.

4. Click on **Download Google Maps**, and the installation program will begin (see Figure 21-2).

Figure 21-2. Downloading the Google Maps program

5. Click on the **Download** button on the next screen.

6. Finally, you will see a screen indicating that the application was successfully installed. Select OK to close the window or Run to start Google Maps Mobile right away. Or, you can Click on the Google Maps icon on the BlackBerry, which should be in the Downloads folder. You might get prompted to reboot your device – if so, just Click on **Reboot**, and then try to run the program.

The first time you start up **Google Maps**, you will need to accept the terms and conditions for the program to continue.

Google Keyboard Shortcut Keys

Sure you can scroll around the map by gliding your finger over the **Trackpad**, but the true power of **Google Maps** can be unleashed with the keyboard shortcuts. To use these, just use your keyboard. Here is list of the available shortcut keys and what they do:

O	Zooms out.
2	Brings up the **Layers** menu.
I / 3	Zooms in.
5	Toggles between **Map/Satellite** view.
7	Show or hide **Traffic** status.
A / *	Shows the **Starred** items.
Q / #	Shows or hides lists (e.g. **Latitude** friends, directions list, etc.).
0	Shows **My Location**.

Google Map Commands

Google Maps is full of great features – most of which you can access right from the program's menu. A cool feature is **Street View**, which **Google Maps** tells you about at the first screen.

When you first start the program, it will try to determine your location based on the built-in GPS or the cell tower closest to your phone.

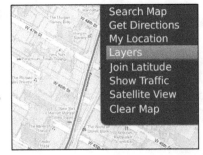

Google Maps Search - Locate Address or Business

It's easy to find an address or business with **Google Maps**. Follow these steps to do so:

1. Click on the **Google Maps** icon to start the application.

2. Press the **Menu** key and choose **Search Map**. Both suggested searches and recent searches will be shown below the **Search** button.

3. You can type just about anything in the search string: an address, type of business and ZIP code, business name and city/state, and so on. For example, if you wanted to find bike stores in Winter Park, Florida, you could enter *bike stores winter park fl* or *bike stores 32789* (assuming you know the ZIP code).

4. You may also hold the **Green Phone** key speak your search.

5. Finally, click the **Search** button or press the **Enter** key to begin the search.

6. Your search results may show a number of matching entries. Just scroll to locate an entry. To switch between List view and Map view, press the **List Toggle** shortcut # key. Click an entry to select it, and then click on the screen to see details for that entry (see Figure 21-3).

Figure 21-3. Search results in *Google Maps Mobile*

7. To see the new street view, Click on the **Street View** button which is the farthest to the right of the four buttons at the top (see Figure 21-4).

| View on map. | Get Directions | Call | Street View |

Figure 21-4. *Viewing map results with Street View*

> **NOTE:** If you look closely at Figure 21-4, you will notice that the address shown at the top of the street view image on the right and street address shown in the left image are different. This happens because the street view image database and main Google Maps databases are updated at different times. In this example, the bike shop has moved to a new address, but the street view image has not yet been updated.

Getting Directions

Obviously, one of the key reasons you might want to use Google Maps Mobile is because it can provide turn-by-turn directions for your BlackBerry that integrate nicely with the device's built-in GPS feature. Follow these steps to get directions on your BlackBerry:

1. Press the **Menu** key and select **Get Directions**.

2. Set your **Start Point**; the default will be **My Location.** and then

3. Set your **End Point**

4. Choose your **Travel by** (mode of transport).

5. Click on **Show Directions** to display turn-by-turn directions to your destination.

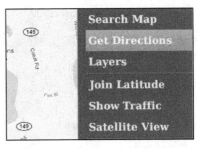

TIP: With the most current version of **Google Maps**, you can actually choose from **Car**, **Public Transit**, **Walking** and **Bicycle** as modes of transport for your directions. The **Bicycle** choice tries to route you on bike paths and bicycle-friendly roads.

Google Latitude

Another nice feature in **Google Maps** is **Google Latitude**, which enables people in your **Google Contacts** to see where you are in real time – you can also see them once you accept their invitations. Follow these steps to enable the **Google Latitude** feature:

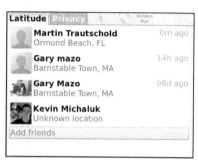

1. Press the **Menu** key and select **Join Latitude** to create or log in to your Google account.

2. Once you set this feature up, your location on the map is shared with whomever you choose.

3. From your **Friends** list, select **Add friends** to invite others to "share" their location with you. You will then be able to see your friends on the map.

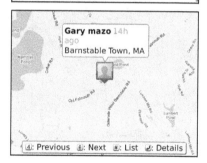

NOTE: While your kids may not like it, this is a great way to check in on them and see that they are where they are supposed to be. One of the authors used this feature to track his son soon after he got his driver's license.

Layers – Wikipedia and Transit Lines

Google Maps now includes a feature called **Layers**. Essentially, this feature will show you Wikipedia entries, traffic conditions, transit lines, or personal maps. The selected data will be overlaid on the current map.

In this example, we have used the **Layers** feature to show both **Wikipedia** entries and **Transit lines** in New York City (see Figure 21-5).

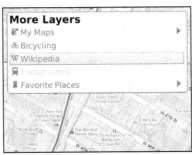

Figure 21-5. Using Layers in Google Maps Mobile

In the Wikipedia entries, I see that the Brooks Atkinson Theater is near to Times Square. I could click on it to view the Wikipedia entry and learn more about it. With the transit lines displayed, I can easily see the closest subway stop. (see Figure 21-6). I could even use the search feature with Transit selected to have Google Maps show me which subway line to take in order to get to the theater.

Figure 21-6. A street view of a Google Map layer

Viewing Current Traffic

Google Maps also includes another nice feature: you can view the current traffic in major metropolitan areas or on major highways (this feature does not work everywhere). Follow these steps to do so:

1. Map the location where you want to view traffic.

2. Press the **Menu** key and select **Show Traffic,** or use the keyboard shortcut key **Z or 7** (see Figure 21-7).

Green = 50+ mph.	
Yellow = 25 – 50 mph	
Red = Less than 25 mph	

Incident on SR-9 at E Cypress Creek Rd

Accident (click for details).

Construction (click for details).

Figure 21-7. Using the Show Traffic feature of Google Maps

Chapter 22: Other Applications

As if your BlackBerry doesn't do enough for you, RIM thoughtfully included even more utilities and programs to help you keep organized and manage your busy life. Most of these additional programs will be found in the **Applications** folder.

In this chapter, we will show you how to use your BlackBerry as a calculator and unit of measure converter, an alarm clock and timer, a voice-note recorder, a password keeper and a way to subscribe to and enjoy podcasts.

The Calculator – Tips and Unit Conversions

There are many times when having a calculator nearby is handy. I usually like to have my 15-year old "Math Genius" daughter nearby when I have a math problem to figure out, but sometimes she needs to go to school, and she isn't available to help. In such cases, I rely on the BlackBerry's built-in **Calculator** program:

1. To start the **Calculator** program, type "calc" in the **Universal Search** bar and click on the **Calculator** icon (see Figure 22-1).

Figure 22-1. Using the Calculator app on your BlackBerry

2. Type your equation as you would in any **Calculator** program.

3. One handy tool in the **Calculator** program is that it can convert between imperial and metric values. Just press the **Menu** key and scroll to the **From Metric** or **To Metric** options.

4. You can then choose which units you want to convert.

The Clock – Alarm, Stopwatch and Timer

The BlackBerry has long included a **Clock** program. However, it now includes some very cool new features and customization features that prove especially useful when the BlackBerry is on your bedside table (see Figure 22-2).

To start the **Clock** application, you can find and click the **Clock** icon; however, if you just want to set an alarm, it is easier just to click on the time in the top middle of your **Home** screen.

On some devices, the **Clock** icon might be located only in the menu, not a folder. By default, the **Clock** program displays an analog face – but that be changed.

*Figure 22-2. Setting an alarm on the **Clock** app.*

The first feature to look at is the **Alarm**. Follow these steps to bring up and manipulate the **Clock** program's **Alarm** settings:

1. Press the **Menu** button and click **Set Alarm**. The **Alarm** menu will appear in the center of the screen.

2. Click on the desired field and then scroll up or down in that highlighted field to change the option's value.

3. Highlight the right-most field and scroll to select **OFF, ON**, or **Weekdays** for the alarm setting.

4. Press the **Escape** key to save your changes.

The **Clock** application also includes **Stopwatch** and **Timer** features; you can start either feature by selecting it from the menu. Finally, you give the clock facelift, selecting the following faces from the Options menu: **Analog**, **Digital**, **Flip Clock**, or **LCD Digital** (see Figure 22-3).

Clock Options   Analog

Digital   Flip Clock

LCD Digital

Figure 22-3. Selecting various clock faces

TIP: If you do not want your clock to display every time you plug your BlackBerry to the charger, then change the setting for When Charging to Do Nothing in the Clock program's Clock Options screen.

Bedside Mode:

One of the nice new features of the **Clock** application is the **Bedside Mode** setting. Many of us keep our BlackBerry by the side of the bed – we now have the option of telling the BlackBerry not to flash, ring, or buzz in the middle of the night, which is accomplished by following a few simple steps:

Press the **Menu** key in the **Clock** application.

Scrolling down to **Options** and click, from which you can configure the **Bedside Mode** options.

You can find the specific **Bedside Mode** options towards the bottom of the **Options** menu. From here, you can disable the LED, the radio, and dim the screen when **Bedside Mode** is set.

To enter Bedside Mode, press the **Menu** key from the **Clock** app and scroll down to **Enter Bedside Mode** and click.

TIP: Bedside Mode is great for when you sleep so you won't be woken up by blinking lights, sounds or notifications.

Voice Notes Recorder

Another useful program in your **Media** folder is the **Voice Notes Recorder**. Say you need to dictate something you need to remember at a later time. Or, assume you would rather speak a note instead of composing an email. Your BlackBerry makes that very easy; simply navigate to the **Media** folder and select **Voice Notes Recorder** to launch the program.

This is a very simple program to use:

1. Launch the program, as just described.

2. Click on the **Record** button when you are ready to record your note.

3. Click on it again when you finish recording your note.

4. You will then see the following icons along the lower part of the program: **Continue recording**, **Stop**, **Play**, , **Rename**, , or **Delete** the Voice Note. Click on the appropriate icon to perform the desired action (see Figure 22-4).

Figure 22-4. Using the Vocie Notes Recorder app

Password Keeper

It can be very hard to manage passwords in today's web-oriented world, where you need to keep track of so many sites with different passwords and different password rules. Fortunately, your BlackBerry has a very effective and safe way for you to manage all your passwords: the **Password Keeper** program (see Figure 22-5).

Figure 22-5. Using the Password Keeper app to set a password

Using the Password Keeper app to set a password is easy:

1. Go to your **Applications** folder, navigate to the **Password Keeper** icon, and then click on it. The first thing you will need to do is set a program password for **Password Keeper** – pick something you will remember (see Figure 22-6)!

Figure 22-6. Using the Password Keeper app to set individual passwords

2. Once your password is set, you can add new passwords for just about anything or any web site. Press the **Menu** button and select **New** to add passwords, user names and web addresses that you want **Password Keeper** to help you remember.

Podcasts App

Podcasts

Social Feeds

This is the Podcast Icon you normally see on web sites that have RSS or podcast feeds available.

Podcasts icon on your BlackBerry where you can listen to audio, text and watch video and animated podcasts.

Social Feeds icon where you can read text only RSS feeds. Learn more about **Social Feeds** in Chapter 14.

Podcasts come in many flavors: text only (RSS feeds), audio (recordings), video and even animation (like a Dilbert cartoon). As you saw in the "Social Feeds" section of Chapter 14, you can subscribe to text-only RSS (Really Simple Syndication) feeds in your **Social Feeds** app.

Now on your BlackBerry, you can subscribe to and enjoy audio, video and animated podcasts using the **Podcasts** app.

Browse and Search for Podcasts

1. Click on the **Podcasts** icon which is usually found in your **Media** folder on your **Home** screen.

2. Click on **Explore Podcasts** to browse all available podcasts.

3. Glide left or right to view featured podcasts using the **Trackpad**.

4. Click on the **Top Episodes** (victory cup icon) in the lower left corner to view popular podcast episodes.

5. Click on the **Categories** (folder icon) to view all podcasts by category.

6. Use your keyboard to type a search string to find podcasts at the top of the screen. In this example, we have searched for all podcasts with the word "marketplace" in their name.

Subscribe and Unsubscribe

1. Once you see a podcast that interests you on the screen click on it to learn more.

2. Click on the **Subscribe** button to subscribe to this podcast.

3. After you subscribe to a podcast, the episodes will be downloaded to your BlackBerry. Large podcasts may be downloaded via Wi-Fi network connections.

4. To unsubscribe, press the **Menu** key and select **Unsubscribe**.

Enjoy Podcasts

To enjoy any podcast, from the main Podcast screen, click on the selected podcast series, then click on any episode that is not dimmed. (Dimmed episodes are ones that have not been downloaded to your BlackBerry).

TIP: To access dimmed podcasts, click on the dimmed episode, and select Download.

Podcast Options

In order to customize how your podcasts are sorted, you need to adjust your Podcast Options. Start the **Podcasts** app, press the **Menu** key and select **Options**. Then scroll down until you see the Podcasts Options section as shown to the right. You can change the sort to either **Newest to Oldest** or **Oldest to Newest**.

Chapter 23: Troubleshooting

Your BlackBerry is virtually a complete computer in the palm of your hand. However, sometimes it needs a little tweaking to keep it in top running order. This chapter provides some valuable tips and tricks you can use to fix problems and keep your BlackBerry running smoothly. This chapter particularly concentrates on walking you through how to resolve problems with sending emails or connecting to the internet. It describes several possible reasons for these issues, and provides tips for how you might work around the problems described.

Solving Connection Issues

Thanks to the engineers at RIM (Research In Motion) – the company that makes BlackBerry devices – traveling away from a wireless signal for a significant amount of time (a few hours) will prompt your BlackBerry to turn off its wireless radio automatically. This feature is intended to conserve the device's battery strength; the wireless radio that makes your BlackBerry so powerful also consumes a lot of power when it is trying to find a weak or non-existent wireless signal.

The nice thing about this feature: All you need to do to turn your wireless radio back on is to hit the **Menu** key and select the **Manage Connections** icon.

You can also click the top **Status Bar** to bring up the **Manage Connections** window.

Low Signal Strength

You may have already figured this out, but signal strength is usually stronger above ground and near the windows when you are inside a building. Signal strength is usually at its best outdoors and away from large buildings. We once worked in an office building that was on the edge of coverage, and we all had to leave our BlackBerry devices on the windowsill to get any coverage at all! We're not sure why, but sometimes turning your radio off and on will recover a stronger signal.

Managing Connections Manually (Airplane Mode)

Sometimes you might transition from a low signal to no signal at all. Many times the simple act of turning your wireless radio off and then back on again will restore your wireless connectivity. Follow these steps to manually turn your device off and then on again:

1. Go to your **Home** screen, and click the **Status Bar** at the top of the screen.

2. Click on **Turn all Connections Off**.

3. Click on **Turn All Connections On**.

4. Look for your wireless signal meter and one of the following uppercase phrases: **3G, 1X, 1XEV, EVDO, EDGE,** or **GPRS**. Check to see whether your email and internet connection are working.

Register with Host Routing Table

If you try all the steps we've outlined in the chapter so far, but you're still have trouble sending or receiving emails or experiencing other problems related to your wireless connection, you can try one more thing to solve the problem: registering with the Host Routing Table (see Figure 23-2). This technique lets you connect to your network provider's data connection, and it can sometimes help you resolve difficult-to-fix networking issues. Follow these steps to implement this technique:

1. From your **Home** screen, click on the **Search** icon and type "host." If **Universal Search** is enabled, just start typing.

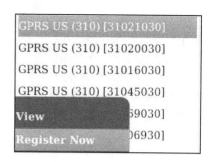

2. Click on the **Options** icon.

3. Click on **Host Routing Table**.

4. Press the **Menu** key and select **Register Now**.

On the **Host Routing Table** screen, you will see many entries related to your BlackBerry's carrier.

Managing Your Applications

Sometimes you want to view all your installed applications, check out how much of your resources (memory, CPU (processor) power, and disk space) each one is using and possibly remove apps that are causing trouble. You can do this all from the **Application Management** screens.

1. Type the word "application" in your **Search** window on your **Home** screen.

2. Click on **Application Management.**

3. The initial view shows you a list of everything installed on your BlackBerry.

4. You can view all required and optional apps installed by clicking on the top bar and selecting a filter.

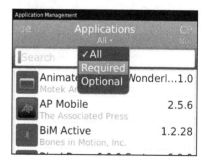

5. **CPU** - Glide the top bar to the left or right with the **Trackpad** to see more options **CPU** is amount of processor power used by each app. Click on the top bar to filer for specific time frames.

6. **Usage** – amount of time each application has been used on your BlackBerry. You can keep an eye on how long you have been playing games or working with your email (Messages).

7. **Memory** - Amount of memory used by each application when it is running. Again, you can click on the top bar to filter the time frame for the display.

8. **Application Storage** - Amount of space used to store the applications on your BlackBerry.

9. To view more details on any of the apps, click on them. You will be able to delete any optional apps and view specific resource usage if you scroll down the details screen (see Figure 23-1).

Figure 23-1. *Viewing the Application Details Screen from the Application Manager*

Diagnostic Help Me! Screen

Your BlackBerry's software includes a special **Diagnostic** "Help Me!" screen that shows you detailed information about your BlackBerry. You might need this information to talk with a Help Desk or technical support person. Follow these steps to access that screen:

1. Simultaneously press and hold three keys on your slide out keyboard: **Alt + Cap + H**.

2. At this point, you should see a **Help Me!** Status screen similar to the one shown here.

```
Help Me!
Platform:                   6.6.0.105
App Version:        6.0.0.418 (1676)
PIN:                         215ee81a
IMEI:                357360.03.011517.1
MAC:                   00:26:ff:e4:de:e8
Uptime:                    2444 secs
Signal Strength:             -70 dBm
Battery Level:                   85%
File Free:             38744372 Bytes
File Total:           192020480 Bytes
```

> **TIP:** To view your total call minutes and other call status information, from the **Phone** app, press the **Menu** key and select **Status** to see an abbreviated status of calls made.

Clearing the Event Log

Your BlackBerry tracks absolutely everything it does. You can use this fact to help with debugging and troubleshooting in what is called an **Event Log**. Periodically clearing this log helps your BlackBerry run smoother and faster. Follow these steps to clear the **Event Log**:

1. From your **Home** screen press and hold down the **Alt** key while typing **LGLG** on the keyboard to display the **Event Log.**

2. Press the **Menu** key and select **Clear Log** to erase all the log entries.

3. Confirm your selection on the next screen. Once the log is cleared, press the **Escape** key to return to your **Home** screen.

Saving Battery Life

Here's a tip that can both extend your BlackBerry's battery life and ensure that you receive the best signal possible. Specifically, you need to make sure your BlackBerry uses the optimal kind of network connection for the carrier you have your BlackBerry service with (see Figure 23-2). For example, if you're in the US, and you're using your BlackBerry on a GSM Network (such as AT&T), you will want to make sure that your device's Network Technology option is set to **3G & 2G**. This way, you will have faster coverage when available but still be covered if you roam outside of a 3G area.

1. Click on **Mobile Network Options** from the **Manage Connections** screen or click the **Status Bar** at the very top of the screen .

2. Make sure your **Data Services** are **On**, and then scroll down to **Network Mode**.

3. If you know you have good 3G coverage, you can set this to 3G & 2G. if you travel outside of the US, or if you are traveling through poor coverage and don't want to waste battery searching for 3G, just select 2G.

Figure 23-2. Choose the right network under Network Mode.

Resetting Your BlackBerry

There are two ways to reset or reboot your BlackBerry, a keyboard soft reset and a battery pull or hard reset.

Performing a Soft Reset

To soft reset your BlackBerry, slide out the keyboard and press and hold three keys (**ALT** + **CAP** + **DEL**) for about 15 seconds until you see the screen go black and the red LED light come on.

 = Soft reset

A successful soft (or hard) reset will show you the reboot screen shown to the right. As soon as the status bar on the bottom gets all the way to the right, your BlackBerry will come back on.

Performing a Hard Reset

Occasionally you will need to perform a *hard reset*; that is, you will need to remove and reinsert your battery.

Follow these steps to perform a hard reset:

1. Power down your device, if possible, by pressing and holding the power button (the **Red Phone** key).

2. Turn your BlackBerry over an slide the back cover downwards and off.

3. Gently pry out and remove the battery – look for the little indent in the upper right corner to stick in your finger nail.

4. Wait about 30 seconds, then replace the battery. Make sure you slide in the bottom of the battery first, then press down from the top.

5. Replace the battery door by aligning the tabs and then sliding the cover until it clicks into place.

6. Power-on your BlackBerry (it may come on automatically), then wait for the status bar to display. This part is similar to a soft reset.

7. Then your BlackBerry and radios should all come back on.

Let's assume you've tried all the techniques covered in this chapter so far, and your email and/or browser still aren't working. If you are using your BlackBerry with a BlackBerry Enterprise Server, please contact your organization's Help Desk or your wireless carrier's support number.

If your email and internet connection still aren't working, and you do not use your BlackBerry with a BlackBerry Enterprise Server, then proceed to the next section.

Sending Internet Service Books

At this point in the process, you might try sending your *service books*. BlackBerry service books are configuration files that determine how your BlackBerry will connect with the servers to enable certain features such as email and web browsing.

Without unique service books your BlackBerry will be limited in its functionality. For example, the web browser and each unique email address you have will have their own service book.

NOTE: This troubleshooting step will work for you only if you have set up at least one Internet Email Account on your BlackBerry.

Follow these steps to send your service books:

1. Click the **Setup** icon, which should be in the **All Home** screen.

2. Click on **Email Accounts**.

3. If you see this screen, click on **Internet Mail Account**.

4. Login to your Internet Email setup and click on **Continue**.

NOTE: If you have not yet logged in and created an account for your **BlackBerry Internet Service** with your carrier, you may now be asked to create such an account to log in for the first time.

5. Press the **Menu** key and select **Service Books.**

6. Finally, on this screen, click on **Send Service Books**.

7. If everything worked, then you will see a status window saying that the **Service Books** were successfully sent.

After sending the service books, you will see an **Activation Message** in your Messages email inbox for each one of your Internet email accounts set up or integrated with your BlackBerry. When opened, each message will look similar to the one shown to the right.

If the Problem Persists...

If you still cannot send email or connect to the internet, then we recommend visiting the **BlackBerry Knowledge Base** at http://www.blackberry.com/btsc. Or, you can post a question at one of the BlackBerry user forums such as www.crackberry.com, www.blackberryforums.com or www.pinstack.com.

Part 4:
Keyboard Shortcuts

You have learned the basics and can now navigate around your BlackBerry, but sometimes, you just want to get somewhere even more quickly. You may not use all the following information on a daily basis, but if you take the time to learn the keyboard shortcuts – you will save time doing thing things you do most often.

Throughout this book, we have shown you how to get the most out of your BlackBerry, where to find key information, and even suggested lots of tips and tricks to help along the way.

BlackBerry's built-in **shortcut hotkeys** will quickly start an app or perform a common function within an app at the single click of a button. For example, let's say you want to go to your **Messages** app – once your **Home** screen **Application Shortcuts** are enabled (see next few pages to learn how), just hit the letter **M**. No scrolling, searching, or fumbling. These shortcuts can be very useful.

Home Screen Hotkeys / Application Shortcuts

The Home Screen Hotkeys (**Application Shortcuts**) can help you start the most common apps on your BlackBerry with a single key click. You do sacrifice the immediate **Universal Search** by enabling these shortcuts, but you can decide – which do you use more – **Application Shortcuts** or **Universal Search**. If you turn on the **Application Shortcuts**, then all you need to do is click on the **Search** icon (magnifying glass) whenever you want to perform a search.

The Switch to Select Search or Shortcuts

By default, typing on the **Home** screen will start the **Universal Search**. To change this to **Application Shortcuts**, follow these steps:

1. Press the **Menu** key from the **Home** screen and select **Options**.

2. Change the **Launch by Typing** to **Application Shortcuts**.

3. Press the **Menu** key and **Save**.

Once you enable your **Home Screen Hotkeys**, you will be able to launch most of the built-in applications with just one letter. This is extremely useful when you have lots of programs and you don't exactly remember where the icons are located. Following are the list of one key shortcuts to start most of your major icons.

M	Messages (Email)	**H**	Help
L	Calendar	**K**	Keyboard Lock
C	Contact or **A** = Address Book	**O**	Options Icon
V	Saved Messages	**U**	Calculator
N	BlackBerry Messenger	**S**	Search Icon
T	Tasks	**D**	MemoPad
B	Web Browser	**P**	Phone (Call Logs)
W	WAP Browser		

NOTE: Don't press and hold any of these hotkeys, otherwise you will start Speed Dialing.

Email Messages Shortcuts

Not only are shortcut keys helpful to launch apps, they are also very useful from inside an app to take you to a specific menu command. The following are the hotkeys that can get you around your **Messages** email app.

> **NOTE:** There is nothing you need to do to activate the hotkeys in the **Mail** app, they just work from your keyboard.

T	Top of Inbox	**Space** key - Page Down		**C**	Compose new email
B	Bottom of Inbox	**ALT + Glide Trackpad** - Page Up/Down		**R**	Reply to selected message
U	Go to next newest Unread Message	ENTER - Open Item (or compose new message when on date row separator)		**L**	Reply All to selected message
				F	Forward selected
N	Next day	**E**	Find Delivery Error(s)	**K**	Search for next message in thread (Replies, Forward, etc.)
P	Previous day	**V**	Go to Saved Messages Folder		
ALT + U Toggle read / unread message		**Q**	(When highlighting email/name) Show/Hide Email Address	**S**	Search
			Or Friendly Name		
Shift + Glide Trackpad - Select messages		**ALT + O** – Filter for Outgoing Messages		**ALT + M** – Filter for MMS Multimedia Messages	
DEL Delete selected message(s)		**ALT + I** – Filter for Incoming Messages		**ALT + S** – Filter for SMS Text Messages	
CAUTION: If wireless email synchronization is on, this will also delete email from your inbox.					

Web Browser Shortcuts

Just like in your **Messages** app, you can quickly launch certain commands or jump to specific places in your **Browser** menu by using certain hotkeys, such as the ones in the following table.

> **NOTE:** These shortcuts will work while you are viewing a web page, if your cursor is in a field on a web page such as the Google search window, then typing these letters will simply type letters on the screen and not perform the shortcut functions listed here.

T Top of Web Page	**Enter** – Select (click-on) highlighted link	**I** Zoom into web page
B Bottom of Web Page	**Y** View history of web pages	**O** Zoom out of web page
Space key – Page Down		**F/V** Find text on the current web page
Shift + Space key – Page Up	**R** Refresh the current web page	**A** Add new bookmark
G Go to your Start page where you can type in a web address	**P** View the address for the page you are viewing with an option to copy or send the address (via email, PIN, or SMS).	**K** View your Bookmark List
H Go to your Home page (Set in **Browser** menu → Options → Home Page)		**S** View Browser Options
Escape key/**DEL** key Go back 1 page		
D View downloads		

> **NOTE:** These hotkeys do not work in your Bookmark List or **Start** page; only when you are actually viewing a web page. In the Bookmark List, typing letters will find your bookmarks that match the typed letters.

Calendar Shortcuts

You can turn on the **Calendar** shortcut keys listed in the following table on your BlackBerry using these steps:

1. Start your **Calendar**.

2. Press the **Menu** key.

3. Select **Options**.

4. Click on **Calendar and Display Actions** glide to **Enable Quick Entry** and change it to **No** by pressing the **Space** key.1

5. Save your **Options** settings.

D	Day View
W	Week View
M	Month View
A	Agenda View
N	Next day
P	Previous day
G	Go To Date
T	Jump to Today (Now)
C	Schedule new event (detail view)

Space key   Next Day (day view)

DEL   Delete selected event

Shift + glide Trackpad – select several hours – example if you wanted to quickly schedule a 3 hour meeting you would highlight the 3 hours and press **Enter**.

Enter – (in Day View – not on a scheduled event) Start Quick Scheduling

Enter – (in Day View – on a scheduled event) Opens it.

Quick Scheduling New Events in Day View:

Enter key -- Begin Quick Scheduling, then type the Subject of the appointment on the Day View screen.

> 4:00p Quick scheduling |
> 4:15p

ALT + Glide **Trackpad** up/down – Change **Start** time

> 4:30p Quick scheduling |
> 4:45p

Glide **Trackpad** up/down – Change **Ending** time

> 4:30p Quick scheduling |
> 5:30p

Enter or click **trackpad** – Save new event

> 4:30p Quick scheduling 🔔
> 5:00p
> 5:30p

Media Player Shortcuts

The shortcuts and tips below will help you enjoy media on your BlackBerry by performing many of the common functions with a single keystroke or special key combinations.

For BlackBerry Bold:

Use your **Mute** key on the top of your BlackBerry to play or pause any song or video.

Media / Mute Key
Pause/Play Music/Video or Mute Ringer/Call

Bold:
Top Edge

For BlackBerry Curve:

Use your **Next/Previous and Pause/Play/Mute** keys on the top of your BlackBerry to control a song or video.

Previous Track
Previous track (song, video, podcast, etc.)

Mute/Play/Pause
Pause/Play Music/Video or Mute Ringer/Call

Next Track
Next track on media.

Curve:
Top Edge

These keys work only inside the Media Player App	These keys work anytime (Whether inside the Media App or not)
N Next track/video **P** Previous track/video **Space key** Play / pause **Enter** key Selects highlighted button (same as clicking **Trackpad**) **DEL** Delete selected media item (song, video, and so forth, when in list or icon view)	Press and hold **Volume Up** key – Next track/video Press and hold **Volume Down** key – Previous track/video **Mute** Key on top – Play/pause **$/Speaker** key – Switch between speaker and handset/headset (including Bluetooth headset or Bluetooth audio speakers)
Jumping Out of the Media Player: Press and hold the **Menu** key to multitask or press the **Red Phone** key to jump back to the **Home** screen.	Jumping Back into the Media Player and currently playing song/video: Click on the **Menu** key and select **Now Playing**... from the top of the menu. Press and hold the **Menu** key, then select the **Media** icon from the pop-up.

Index

B

C

D

E

F

G

H

I

K

L

T

U

V

www.ingramcontent.com/pod-product-compliance
Lightning Source LLC
La Vergne TN
LVHW022258060326
832902LV00020B/3155